D1453061

Reform and Rebellion
in Afghanistan, 1919 - 1929

King Amanullah in *durbar* (court) regalia, about 1925.

REfORM and REBELLION in afGhanistan, 1919-1929

KING AMANULLAH'S FAILURE TO MODERNIZE A TRIBAL SOCIETY

Leon B. Poullada

CORNELL UNIVERSITY PRESS | ITHACA AND LONDON

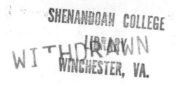

Cornell University Press gratefully acknowledges a grant from the Andrew J. Mellon Foundation that aided in bringing this book to publication.

First published 1973 by Cornell University Press.
Published in the United Kingdom by Cornell University Press Ltd.,
2–4 Brook Street, London W1Y 1AA.

International Standard Book Number 0-8014-0772-9
Library of Congress Catalog Card Number 72-12291

Printed in the United States of America by Vail-Ballou Press, Inc.

*Librarians: Library of Congress cataloging information
appears on the last page of the book.*

to the norris d. jacksons and
to their delightful daughter leila
and to los chicos in remembrance
of our afghan adventures

acknowledgments

Acknowledgments can never do justice to the many people who help make a book possible. How can an author weigh hours of patient but low-yielding contribution from one source against the flash of vision provided by another? In any case I want to express gratitude for all assistance received even though in some cases it must be in the form of collective thanks to many persons and institutions not mentioned by name.

My special thanks go first to the Joint Committee on the Near and Middle East of the Social Science Research Council and to the Fulbright-Hays Program of the United States Department of Health, Education and Welfare, both of which made this book possible by the grants which financed most of the research. I also thank Princeton University for the facilities and support it made available to me in the course of my research and writing.

Much inspiration, encouragement, and guidance came from Princeton University scholars, especially Manfred Halpern. Leon Carl Brown, Avram Udovitch, and Henry Bienen read the manuscript and offered many valuable suggestions. Morroe Berger, Harold Sprout, and Harry Eckstein provided, perhaps unwittingly, some very useful insights which I have incorporated into this book. A number of other scholars outside Princeton University contributed excellent suggestions for improving the manuscript. Chief among these were Louis Dupree of the American Universities Field Staff, Vartan Gregorian of the University of Texas, and Ludwig Adamec of the University of Arizona.

In Afghanistan two outstanding Afghan scholars, Dr. Abdul Ghafur Rawan Farhadi and Syed Qasim Rishtya, facilitated my work in innumerable ways and participated actively as informants, critics, and sources of information. Without their help my work in Afghanistan would have been much less productive. Two younger Afghan scholars, Faruq Farhang and M. A. Ansari, were most helpful in dealing with Persian legal terminology and with the intricacies of Afghan government administration. Mr. Ansari was an indefatigable researcher, tracker of lost or forgotten documents, and a fine translator. Professor Mohammed Ali of Kabul University was kind enough to serve as an informant and also to lend me several rare books. May Schinasi, a French scholar who lived in Afghanistan many years, was most generous in sharing with me her vast knowledge of written sources and of the labyrinthine family connections of the Afghan ruling elite.

I owe a special debt of gratitude to the staff of Cornell University Press for their expert guidance in moving this book to publication and in particular for the meticulous and enlightened editing which greatly improved the original manuscript.

Finally I thank Dr. S. Roy, of the National Archives of India, and Mr. Stanley Sutton, the former Keeper of the Archives of the India Office Library in London, for giving me access to their invaluable collections, especially those documents recently made available for scholarly examination which permitted me to present a re-evaluation of the fascinating period of King Amanullah's ill-starred reign.

Leon B. Poullada

Flagstaff, Arizona

contents

illustrations

tables

introduction

In recent years the authority structures and political processes which characterize tribally based societies have become increasingly important because of the wave of mid-century independence movements that brought to power a number of governments deeply influenced by tribal politics. Afghanistan, whose independent status is not recent and whose government has been tribally based for over two centuries, is a good living laboratory for the study of tribally based political development. In Afghanistan, tribes of varied ethnic and linguistic stock constitute the major portion of the population, and the political tensions resulting from this mixture make the country a subject of unusual interest to the political scientist.

Until the middle of the eighteenth century the territory that is now Afghanistan had been at various times a part or parts of many different empires—Persian, Greek, Mongol, Mughal, Indian, Turkic, and others. But with the formation of the Pushtun tribal confederation in 1747, led by Ahmad Shah of the Durrani tribe, Afghanistan began to acquire some form of independent identity. Since that time the royal family and the ruling elite of Afghanistan have been Pushtuns, with the very brief exception of the period of the Tajik ruler, Habibullah (Bacha-i-Saqao), who figures prominently in this book.

The study of Afghan politics, then, is intertwined with the nature and dynamics of tribal politics, and whatever lessons can be derived from such a study may perhaps add some substance to the shadow we all pursue—a systematic explanation of political behavior across barriers of space, time, culture, and social organization.

If the nature of its tribal society gives Afghanistan a certain importance for the study of politics, its geopolitical situation adds materially to this interest. Astride the principal passes from the Central Asian heartland to the rich lands of India and the Middle East, the area that is now Afghanistan has for millennia been subjected to external pressures and infusions of peoples and ideas which kept its internal politics in a state of perpetual ferment. Few regions in the world have had such a history of exposure to the currents of migration, invasion, and cultural penetration, and yet few people have shown such imperviousness to outside influences and such bitter stubbornness in preserving their own identity and culture. It can hardly be doubted that the intransigence and warlike qualities of the Pushtuns were largely responsible for the preservation of Afghan independence during the period when Western and Russian colonial expansion absorbed most of Afghanistan's neighbors. Afghanistan was thereby endowed with another unique feature, especially important to the study of modernization: it is one of the few nations of Asia that was not subjected to the traumatic and transforming influence of colonial administration.

From this dour, inward-looking, and indeed xenophobic political culture, it is remarkable that there should emerge one of the most talented, liberal, and dynamic modernizers of Asia, King Amanullah. This ruler was not content to be a passive witness to the growing power and development of more modern nations while Afghanistan was left in the backwaters of history. He actively conceived and initiated programs aimed at changing and indeed transforming Afghan society. For the student of modernization this experiment has special significance because it ended in a civil war that cost Amanullah his throne. So violent a clash tends to expose to scrutiny and highlight the underlying political forces of a society. And in spite of Amanullah's personal failure, he succeeded in laying the foundations for later, more successful efforts to modernize Afghanistan, including the one now in progress. His legislative and constitutional reforms of the early 1920's are the basis for the two later constitutions of 1931 and 1964, and most of the reforms initiated in his famous codes, or *Nizamnamah*, have later found expression in some form of legislation or practice.

This study attempts to dispel some of the mythology that has grown up about Amanullah's failure. One such myth has it that Amanullah's overthrow was caused by a widely supported popular rebellion against his social and religious reforms. Another is that the rebellion was secretly instigated by the British.

Of course, persistent myths are often symbolic embroideries of essential truths. It is true, for example, that many of Amanullah's social reforms, especially those dealing with the status of women and the eradication of corruption, were indeed resented by many Afghans. This does not mean, however, that the natural resistance to abandoning old and hallowed customs took the form of active rebellion by the majority of Afghan citizens against their king. The revolt, as we shall see, came from quite different quarters. Similarly, it is true that Amanullah and the British clashed on many points of policy and action. But it requires a leap into the void to conclude from this acknowledged fact that the British would assume the vast risks of clandestine operations to dethrone a king and plunge a country into chaos—a country, moreover, bordering on the Soviet Union, which was at that time actively hostile to the British and might easily have been tempted to move into such a political and military vacuum. In fact the secret official documents of the period fail to substantiate any such British intrigue. One should have no illusions, of course, that documented conclusions will lay myths to rest. Over the years legends acquire a life of their own which truth can at best weaken but not destroy.

I want to make clear what this work is and what it is not. It is an intensive and documented study of the dynamics of political development in Afghan tribal society at a particular period. It is not a history of the Amanullah period in the strict sense of the word, nor is it a biography of Amanullah. Likewise, it is not a comparative study of politics of tribal societies, and no attempt has been made to cover the growing literature in this field. Lastly, it is not a study on theory of modernization, and therefore no attempt has been made to examine the extensive and sometimes contradictory literature in this complex field. All these subjects no doubt constitute desirable areas for scholarly exploration. But we must do one thing at a time. My research provides the raw data, the empirical evidence, on which comparative studies and political theory can be built.

I have, of course, made liberal use of both historical and biographic materials, where they clarify, explain, illuminate, or add perspective to the political processes of the period. I have tried to shun historical minutiae and strictly chronological presentation and have resisted the temptation to include fascinating and dramatic material about Amanullah as an individual wherever this did not add materially to an understanding of the main currents and crosscurrents of political action.

I have relied extensively on official archival sources which only very recently became available to scholars and on oral-history techniques in the form of extensive in-depth interviews with several dozen informants who lived during, and participated actively in, the events of the Amanullah period. The methods and problems involved in these archival researches and interviews are explained more fully in the Bibliographic Essay at the end of this volume. In the footnotes my interviews with informants are identified only by place and year in deference to urgent requests for anonymity.

Anthropologists and sociologists often disagree among themselves as to when a social group constitutes a tribe. I have endeavored to avoid such controversies by using a simple definition which, in a book about tribal politics, satisfies the needs of political analysis. For this purpose, then, a tribe, in the context of

Afghan politics, is a social group with a largely shared common culture in which power, authority, and influence are based chiefly on kinship patterns. In pragmatic terms I have referred to groups in Afghanistan as "tribes" if they fit this definition and if, in addition, they have generally been identified as tribes in the literature of the area.

Transliteration is a subject over which scholars can and do wage interminable battles in musty journals. Few "sound" book reviews omit some glancing reference to improper transliteration (meaning usually a system different from the one preferred by the reviewer). Obviously exactitude and uniformity are needed in treatises on comparative linguistics and the like, which the present work is not. Esoteric diacritical marks often render simple words almost incomprehensible, and I believe most readers would agree. I have, therefore, used the simplest possible system: foreign words are written as they are most frequently spelled in the general literature of the area; only those words are italicized which do not appear in English form in Webster.

This book, then, should be of special interest to students of political modernization because its subject matter is the dramatic clash between a tradition-encrusted society, dominated by flinty and xenophobic codes of tribal politics, and an idealistic, uncompromising modernizer, whose ideas in many important respects preceded and overlapped those of better-known historical figures in neighboring countries, such as Ataturk of Turkey and Reza Shah of Iran. The period of Amanullah, whose revolutionary liberal political and social views shook his own country to its very foundations and astounded even Westerners, cries out for objective study and analysis. The storm which raged around the figure of this extraordinary modernizer and eventually engulfed him was compounded of a remarkable combination of internal tribal political dynamics and external geopolitical pressures.

Reform and Rebellion in Afghanistan, 1919-1929

chapter 1

the politics of
tribal power

In order to understand Amanullah's attempt to modernize Afghanistan, and his failure, we must understand something of this country's tribal politics and how they have influenced its history. Afghanistan's first steps toward nationhood were the result of a tribal confederation forged in 1747 by Ahmad Shah, a young leader of the Abdali (later called Durrani) tribe. In that year he was elected as a paramount chief by the chieftains of the subtribes and clans of the Abdali tribe. That election highlights one of the essential principles of political dynamics in Afghanistan, intratribal conflict.

The Abdali tribe is one of the largest and most important of the Pushtun tribes in Afghanistan. Since the election of Ahmad Shah in 1747 it has provided, with one exception (the brief reign of Bacha-i-Saqao), all the rulers of Afghanistan. This tribe, which we shall hereafter call by its present name of Durrani, was historically divided by rivalry between its principal subtribes, the Popolzai and the Barakzai. Ahmad Shah belonged to the Saddozai clan of the Popolzai Durrani. The Saddozai was a fairly weak and minor clan in the Durrani hierarchy. But Ahmad Shah had made a great name for himself as a warrior leading the Durrani mercenaries in the armies of the great Persian conqueror, Nadir Shah Afshar. When Nadir Shah was assassinated by his own mutinous soldiers while returning from one of his numerous raids on India, Ahmad Shah, after a vain attempt to defend him, escaped to Afghanistan with most of

Nadir Shah's treasure. He therefore had gold and a great reputation to recommend him when the elders of the Durrani chiefs were acting under the compulsion of fear of further Persian subjugation and a renascence of Ghilzai hegemony.[1] But the election was closely contested by the more powerful clans, specially the Barakzai. In the ensuing deadlock, Ahmad Shah's greatest asset was the fact that the powerful clans could agree on a member of a weak clan, who would lack a strong tribal base of his own and would have to court the good will of the chiefs of the more powerful elements.[2] Ahmad Shah proved himself not only a bold warrior but a consummate statesman. He kept the allegiance of the powerful chiefs by conferring on them military honors, positions of power, and preference in distribution of booty and by involving them closely in his extensive campaigns of conquest. On this basis of political compromise and accommodation with the powerful leaders of other clans, Ahmad Shah ruled and expanded his empire.[3]

Most chroniclers have called Ahmad Shah the founder of the Afghan nation. In Afghanistan he is always known as Ahmad Shah Baba, meaning "father of the nation." But it would be more correct to refer to him as a tribal unifier, the leader of a powerful tribal confederation which by conquest became an empire. Not only did he succeed in holding the Durrani together but also by his policies of balancing tribal animosities and his constant foreign campaigns he managed to channel tribal aggressiveness away from his own central authority toward exter-

---

[1] Harold Josif, "Political Stability on the Northwest Frontier of South Asia," mimeographed (Washington, D.C.: Department of State, Foreign Service Institute, August 1951), p. 35. See also L. Lockhart, *Nadir Shah* (London: Luzac, 1938).

[2] Ali Ahmad Kohzad, *Men and Events through Eighteenth and Nineteenth Century Afghanistan* (Kabul: Historical Society of Afghanistan, n.d.), p. 2. See also Ganda Singh, *Ahmad Shah Durrani: Father of Modern Afghanistan* (Bombay: Asia Publishing House, 1959).

[3] Ali Ahmad Kohzad, "Two Coronations," *Afghanistan* (Kabul), V, no. 3, 38–40.

nal enemies. He was considered to be a chief of chiefs and he earned high personal loyalty and respect for himself, but there is little in the structure or character of his rule or in subsequent developments to indicate that this *ramassement* of tribal power, held together by the charisma and magnetism of a bold leader, ever grew into a mature sense of nationhood in which the loyalty of the tribesmen was transferred from their own kinship groups to a central authority, much less to any concept of a state or even an ethnic "nation." [4] The period of Ahmad Shah's ascendancy seems much more the supreme example of the Pushtun maxim "The Afghans are at peace among themselves only when they are at war." Ahmad Shah was fortunate also in developing his power at a most favorable time in Afghan "foreign relations." Russia was quiescent; Persia was senescent; Mughal India was obsolescent. They were all fair game for tribal raiders organized on an imperial scale by a vigorous and dynamic chief.

Ahmad Shah's true genius lay in his unique ability to utilize favorable external political circumstances to reconcile long-smoldering intratribal conflicts. That this was essentially a personal achievement and not the triumph of nationalism is amply demonstrated by the fact that after his death the internal conflict between the Saddozai and the Barakzai flared up again in dynastic struggles which continued until the eventual transfer of the throne to Dost Mohammed in 1835. The throne thus passed within the Durrani tribe from Saddozai to Barakzai. Except for

[4] Throughout this work I have used the terms "Pushtu" (for the language) and "Pushtun" (for the people) in preference to the northern, hard dialect (Pukhtu, Pukhtun) or the Indianized version (Pathan). In this connection see H. W. Bellew, *Afghanistan and the Afghans* (London: Sampson Low, 1879), pp. 216–220.

The term "Afghan" was applied originally only to certain Pushtuns. Starting in Amanullah's time, the government of Afghanistan has tried to make the term apply to all citizens of Afghanistan, regardless of ethnic or linguistic origin. This campaign has not yet achieved complete success. During our residence in Kabul (1967–68) our *baghban* (gardener), a member of a minority tribal group, often spoke with bitter resentment about "those Afghans," referring to the Pushtun ruling elite.

a brief period during the First Afghan War in 1841 when the British by force of arms restored Shah Shuja, the Saddozai, and for the even briefer Bacha-i-Saqao interregnum in 1929, the Mohammedzai (descendants of Dost Mohammed) have ruled Afghanistan.

Dost Mohammed, the new Barakzai ruler, was severely hampered by the dynastic struggle between his own branch of the Durrani (the Barakzai) and the Saddozai branch, to which the former ruling house belonged. But the British did for him what he probably could not have accomplished even with his great ability—they united Afghanistan by invading it under the slimmest of pretenses, deposed Dost Mohammed, and restored the Saddozai Amir, Shah Shuja, who had been exiled in India. The First Afghan War (1838–1842), or "Auckland's Folly," as it was dubbed in honor of the Viceroy of India who initiated it, was a disaster both for the British and the Afghans. After initial military successes the British were annihilated in a famous winter retreat from Kabul. Of a force of some twelve thousand soldiers and camp followers fewer than two thousand survived.[5]

Afghanistan too suffered severe losses in men and property and, perhaps more significant for the long term, it developed a xenophobia and a determination to exclude foreign influences which persisted until the middle of the twentieth century and has not entirely disappeared even today. This isolation seriously retarded the modernization of Afghanistan. On the other hand, the war reinforced a sense of Afghan unity. Most of the tribes, even the fractious ones like the Ghilzai, rallied behind Dost Mohammed to repel the alien invader. It is true that when the British finally left and Dost Mohammed was restored to the throne he found the tribes in a much more powerful position vis-à-vis the central government than before. But at the same time the seed of an effective central authority which Ahmad Shah had

[5] Patrick A. Macrory, *The Fierce Pawns* (New York: Lippincott, 1966).

planted had survived as a tender plant which Dost Mohammed was able to cultivate.

Consolidate his kingdom he did, but again power accrued to the central government only to the extent that tribal rivalries could be exploited, balanced, and kept in check. Once again it was a tour de force of personality, acumen, wisdom, and cunning, relying more on the weaknesses of potential rivals than on the strength of an independent and institutionalized base of power residing in a central authority. On the death of the Dost the tribal chieftains regained their virtual autonomy, and by 1878 the throne had become a glamorous but empty bauble over which princelings constantly fought and scrambled.[6]

In 1878 the British, once again nervous over Russian advances into Central Asia, helped unite the Afghans by invading their country in the Second Afghan War. Initial British military successes again bogged down in such a political morass that the British, who had invaded Afghanistan to overthrow an allegedly pro-Russian amir, in the end were delighted to hand the country over to Abdur Rahman, an exiled grandson of Dost Mohammed, who had spent eleven years in Russia. Fortunately for the British, Abdur Rahman, "the Iron Amir," was first and foremost an Afghan, and, having won the throne in 1880, he did everything within his power to keep both Russia and Britain at arm's length. His importance for the purposes of our study lies in the fact that the central policy of this extremely able though cruel and cunning ruler was to weaken the power of the tribes and incidentally of the conservative mullahs (religious leaders), who were an important source of support for the tribal khans. The stories of his severities and the cunning ruses by which he controlled his recalcitrant countrymen are legion. He himself explains in his autobiography that under the guise of giving the tribal chiefs more power he "liberalized" his government by in-

[6] Arnold Fletcher, *Afghanistan: Highway of Conquest* (Ithaca: Cornell University Press, 1965), p. 126.

stituting a Royal Council with the most powerful chiefs as members. Of course he gave no power to the Council, but having all the chiefs in Kabul under his watchful eye insured they would not be off in the mountains plotting against the Amir.[7]

By devices of this sort and by sheer repression Abdur Rahman managed to keep the power of the tribes in check. He made a vital contribution to the modernization process when he went beyond merely keeping the tribes under control and proceeded to institutionalize the bureaucracy, the army, and the royal succession. In this way he hoped to avoid the dynastic struggles and the lack of continuity that had in the past weakened the central government and strengthened tribal power. Thus, Abdur Rahman laid down the policy which every Afghan sovereign, with the exception of Amanullah, tried to follow: gradual (or if need be, forceful) subjugation of recalcitrant tribes, deliberate extension of the civil power of the central government behind the shield of a strong loyal army, and strengthening the integrity and cohesiveness of the monarchy and the royal family. This policy is explicitly set forth in Abdur Rahman's political testament in his autobiography, a remarkable document which clearly demonstrates the clarity, vision, and wisdom that the Iron Amir brought to the art of governing a fragmented and unruly people.

How fragmented and how unruly the people of Afghanistan were, even as late as the reign of Abdur Rahman, can be judged from his own account of the incessant wars of pacification he

[7] Abdur Rahman, *The Life of Abdur Rahman*, ed. Mir Munshi (London: John Murray, 1900). This so-called autobiography was originally written in English presumably from material dictated by the Amir. It was not translated into Persian until 1904, after Abdur Rahman's death, so he had no opportunity to correct any errors. A few scholars have questioned the complete authenticity of the book but from internal and external evidence it would seem that its substance accords with the known views of the Amir. I was unable to ascertain whether Amanullah ever read this book. See also M. H. Kakar, *Afghanistan, A Study in Internal Political Development: 1880–1896* (Lahore: Punjab Education Press, 1971).

was compelled to wage in his efforts to impose his authority on the land. In his autobiography he identifies four major conflicts, which because of their scope and magnitude he calls "civil wars": (1) the rebellion of 1881 led by Mohammed Ayub and centered in Kandahar; this was essentially a dynastic war within the Durrani tribe; (2) the Ghilzai rebellion of 1886, which was in effect an intertribal war between the disaffected Ghilzai and the ruling Durrani; (3) the Turkestan rebellion of 1888 led by Mohammed Ishak, which was a secessionist movement of the Turkmen tribes led by a trusted kinsman of Abdur Rahman who had been appointed by him as governor of Turkestan; and (4) the Hazara revolt of 1891, which was a general uprising of the Hazara tribes against Pushtun tribal hegemony. In addition to these major conflicts Abdur Rahman refers to six less generalized revolts and a large number of local insurrections.[8]

Abdur Rahman also notes that he was compelled during his reign of twenty-one years to face two serious Russian attempts to penetrate and capture Afghan territory, at Shignan in 1882 and at Panjdeh in 1884. He prides himself on having achieved substantial pacification of Afghanistan by the time his son Habibullah inherited the throne, but the relative internal calm which prevailed during the latter's reign (1901–1919) can be viewed in retrospect as simply a respite during which the tribal forces of rebellion and disunity recovered from Abdur Rahman's stern repressive measures. These forces, as we shall see, broke out in even more virulent form during the reign of his grandson Amanullah.

One of Abdur Rahman's most notable achievements was his realistic policy of obtaining definitive boundaries for Afghanistan. In some cases this involved the renunciation of territory as a price for obtaining a prompt settlement. The Lumsden Commission in 1885 negotiated with Russia and fixed almost the en-

[8] Abdur Rahman, Vol. I, ch. 10, gives a graphic description of the disunited and parlous condition of Afghanistan and of the internal warfare waged by Abdur Rahman.

tire length of Afghanistan's Russian border. The Durand Agreement of 1893 settled most of the boundaries between Afghanistan and British India.

Abdur Rahman thus attempted to achieve two fundamental prerequisites for the political development of Afghanistan: he undertook the pacification of the tribes and he developed an equilibrium between the expansive Russian and British empires with Afghanistan to remain *terra intacta* between them. He thus assured for the developing nation-state a considerable measure of internal cohesion, external security, and territorial integrity.

Although the tasks undertaken by Abdur Rahman were formidable, and in spite of the assertion by historians that he successfully united and defended the country, it would seem that he himself had no illusions about the fragile quality of his accomplishment. He realized that internal security would be in constant jeopardy as long as the tribes represented separate centers of power. Only unity could form a strong nation-state:

The first and most important advice that I can give to my successors and people to make Afghanistan into a great kingdom is to impress upon their minds the value of unity; unity, and unity alone, can make it into a great power. . . . All my study of history brings me to one conclusion, namely, that the downfall of many kingdoms, especially those of believers in Mahomedanism [sic] in the East, has been caused by disunion and home quarrels.[9]

He also realized that external security depended upon a delicate balancing act, exploiting Russian and British rivalry to insure Afghanistan's territorial integrity:

On both sides of Afghanistan there are powerful neighbors, namely England and Russia. Though these neighbors are the cause of much anxiety to Afghanistan yet, as they are pulling against each other,

[9] Abdur Rahman was illiterate in his youth. Later he learned to read and write but his knowledge of world affairs and history was obtained by listening each evening for several hours to readers who read and translated to him.

they are no less an advantage and protection for Afghanistan than a danger. Indeed a great deal of the safety of the Afghan Government depends upon the fact that neither of these neighbors can bear to allow the other to annex an inch of Afghan territory.

The old Amir's testament then goes on to discuss in some detail economic policies to be followed by his heirs. He favors free trade in theory but protectionism in practice; he discusses the relative merits of highways and railroads, predicting that Afghanistan would some day enjoy a thriving tourist trade [10] and cautioning against giving too many concessions to foreigners; he adjures his heirs to "hold fast to their promises and avoid falsehood and breaking of faith, whether such promises are made to private individuals and merchants, or to Powers and Governments." Finally he voices his hopes that through good relations with Great Britain Afghanistan may one day be given an outlet to an ocean port. He summarizes his hopes and ambitions in a final paragraph:

I hope and pray that if I do not succeed in my lifetime in the great desire for making railways, introducing telegraphs and steamers, working the mines, opening banks, and issuing bank-notes, inviting travellers and capitalists from all parts of the world, and opening universities and other modern institutions in Afghanistan, my sons and successors will carry out these desires of my heart, and make Afghanistan what I desire it to become. *Amen!* [11]

It is especially worth noting, since all authorities agree that Abdur Rahman was skilled in the art of government and knew his country intimately, that the Iron Amir voiced no doubts about the feasibility of introducing radical social reforms such as women's education or about the Afghan people's capacity to ab-

[10] A prescient estimate considering that at that time Afghanistan was a "forbidden kingdom" and so remained for the next half century. But official figures for the year 1967 showed that over 37,000 tourists entered Afghanistan, and the 1971 estimate is over 100,000.

[11] The quotations given above from Abdur Rahman's "political testament" are from Vol. II, ch. 7, of his autobiography.

sorb large doses of social change provided the country could be united politically and the authority of the central government, backed by good intelligence and strong military power, could be preponderant. In other words he saw the problem (correctly, in my opinion) as one of nation-building and not one of resistance to social change. To those who later insisted that Amanullah's social reforms led to the uprising which cost him his throne in 1928 it must be pointed out that less than three decades earlier Abdur Rahman, who never got beyond the talking stage of social reforms, nevertheless was faced with ten serious internal rebellions, four of which were so extensive he classified them as "civil wars." Evidence from the writings of the Iron Amir, then, indicates that he would have disagreed profoundly with those who later propagated the myth that during the reign of Amanullah the Afghan people were not ready for change and resisted it to the point of rebelling against him and destroying his government. Such rebellions, judging from Abdur Rahman's own words, would not have seemed evidence of resistance to reforms but simply of lack of political unity in the country and of the resistance by tribal power and privilege against incursions by the central authority.

Abdur Rahman's son, Habibullah, succeeded to the throne in 1901 and his reign was an added tribute to the sagacity of Abdur Rahman, not only because Habibullah ascended the throne peacefully, a rare occurrence in Afghanistan up to that time, but also because of the cautious and steady pressure he exerted on the tribes, the amicable relations he maintained with both Russia and Britain, and the able manner in which he preserved Afghan neutrality during World War I. This latter policy, however, earned him the reputation of being pro-British and may have contributed to his mysterious assassination in 1919.

Habibullah became personally interested in Western technology. He was enamored of the "gadgetry" of modernization and indulged his hobbies by driving at breakneck speeds in imported automobiles and spending large sums on photographic equipment. He introduced the telephone and telegraph and employed an American engineer to build the first hydroelectric plant in Afghanistan.[12] He also founded the first school with a Western-type curriculum, Habibia College, and the first important newspaper in Afghanistan with excellent printing and photographic reproduction, the *Siraj-ul-Akhbar*.

For his various projects Habibullah brought in foreign technicians. Abdur Rahman had brought in foreigners, but the wily Amir had used them mostly to develop his pet project, an ordnance factory. Thus both Abdur Rahman and Habibullah had already made small chinks in the armor of isolation and xenophobia which Afghanistan had donned largely as a result of two British invasions. These modest efforts to modernize were deemed totally inadequate by the man who ascended the throne in 1919, Habibullah's third son, Amanullah.

Habibullah was assassinated on a hunting trip. Amanullah had been left in charge of Kabul and therefore in control of the garrison and the treasury. Although his two older brothers and his uncle had claims to the throne, Amanullah decided to seize power.[13] Habibullah had not imitated the wise example of his father and had failed to designate his successor. Afghan tribal custom does not recognize primogeniture as a matter of right, but it is customary for younger sons to defer to older ones or to the oldest living brother of the dead chief. Amanullah's action, then, in seizing power, while not "illegal" or even unusual in the Persianized Afghan court, did cause some of the more traditional chiefs to regard him as something of an usurper.

This lingering doubt about the legitimacy of his kingship made it easier for tribal leaders to foment the revolt against him

[12] Marjorie Jewett Bell, *An American Engineer in Afghanistan* (Minneapolis: University of Minnesota Press, 1948).

[13] Louis Dupree, "Mahmud Tarzi: Forgotten Nationalist," *American Universities Field Staff Reports*, South Asia series, VIII, no. 1 (January 1964).

and for the throne to pass to a collateral branch of the family. Moreover, Amanullah was a member of the so-called War party which had sympathized with the Central Powers and especially with Turkey in World War I and opposed Habibullah's neutral (or, as some claimed, pro-British) policies. A good many Afghans therefore suspected that Amanullah was in some way implicated in Habibullah's assassination. The fact that the true instigators or perpetrators of the murder were never discovered and that Amanullah hastily arranged for the execution of an apparent scapegoat added fuel to the fire.[14] In the view of some Afghans, then, Amanullah's ascension to the throne was tainted by overtones of usurpation and suspicions of patricide and regicide.

The story of Amanullah's attempt to modernize the country internally and at the same time to change its external affairs radically is told in subsequent chapters. It is enough to note now that in the end it was tribal separatism which defeated him and brought his elaborately constructed reform programs crashing down around him.

A consistent theme which runs through modern Afghan history is illustrated by the nation-building efforts of four of its outstanding rulers. This leitmotif is the ebb and flow of political power between the central government and the fiercely independent Pushtun tribes. Ahmad Shah Durrani (1747–1773) first achieved a degree of tribal consensus and is therefore considered by some to be the father of present-day Afghanistan; Dost Mohammed (1835–1863) founded the Mohammedzai dynasty, united the tribes against the British invasion, and increased the power and authority of the central government by skillful tribal diplomacy; Abdur Rahman (1880–1901) reduced tribal power by repression and cunning and by further institutionalizing the army, the civil bureaucracy, and the monarchy; and finally Amanullah (1919–1929) sought but failed

[14] Interview with informant, Kabul, 1967.

to create national unity by an extensive program of social, economic, and political reforms.

In order to inquire more fully into this historical tension between national authority and tribal power we must now look more deeply into the nature of the tribal political system.[15] Political dynamics in Afghanistan revolve around a number of basic conflict situations which are deeply rooted in Afghan tribal society. This was the case when Amanullah came to power in 1919 and is still true today in spite of greatly accelerated modernization in the past two decades. This does not mean that all Afgans are living in a pure tribal state. There are gradations ranging from pure nomadism to complete urban sedentarianism. But the social setting and value structure of the people whether living as tribesmen in the hills or as ministers in the court of Kabul are permeated by the customs, folklore, music, loyalties, and attitudes of the tribal point of view. This is true for the dominant Pushtun tribal stock as well as for other ethnic and linguistic groups such as the Tajiks, Turkmen, Uzbegs, Hazaras, and so on.

[15] For a variety of reasons the tribes in Afghanistan have not been adequately studied. Writings on the subject tend to fall into three categories: (1) anthropological and linguistic studies, (2) descriptive writings of travelers, officials, and the like, (3) studies of the tribes on what is now the Pakistani side of the Durand Line. It is difficult to obtain solid information from these sources on the political structure and dynamics of the Afghan tribes. The material in this book is based on a 1956 study by the staff of the American Embassy in Kabul in which the author collaborated, later personal observation and study, and on secondary sources. Rather than indulge in a surfeit of footnotes, I refer the reader who may be specially interested in details about the tribes to the following works, all of which may be found in the Bibliographic Essay: M. G. Aslanov, E. G. Gafferberg, N. A. Kisliakov, K. L. Zadykhina, and G. P. Vasilyeva, "Peoples of Afghanistan," translated by M. and G. Slobin in Grassmuck and Adamec, eds., 1969; Bacon, 1951 and 1958; Barth, 1959; Barton, 1939; Bellew, 1880; Bolton, 1907; Caroe, 1958; Darmesteter, 1888; Davies, 1932; Elphinstone, 1815; Ferdinand, 1959; Fletcher, 1965, ch. 2 and Appendix A; Fraser-Tytler, 1967, ch. 10; Gregorian, 1969, ch. 2; Klimburg, 1966; Pennell, 1927; Robertson, 1896; Schurmann, 1962; Spain, 1963; Thomas, 1925; Tuden, 1966.

1. King Amanullah
in northern tribal dress,
about 1923.

What then are these tribes, where are they located, how are they organized politically, and what is their relevance to the present study? Because of their overriding political importance, this study is primarily concerned with the Pushtun tribes, but some general idea of the size and location of the major tribal groupings is required. The total population of Afghanistan, estimated at eleven to thirteen million, is divided as follows in terms of tribal origins: [16]

[16] Estimates given are from the Royal Afghan Government, Ministry of Planning, unpublished studies. Although these estimates are relatively recent, there has probably not been a significant change (for the purposes of this study) since the reign of Amanullah.

Pushtuns	4–5 million
Tajiks	2–3 million
Uzbegs	1 million
Aimaks	.8 million
Hazaras	.7 million
Turkmen	.5 million
Other [17]	2.0 million
Total	11–13 million

The numerical predominance of the Pushtuns has been reinforced by Pushtun personal and cultural characteristics which have traditionally emphasized courage, vigor, and warlike prowess. These factors have tended to impart to Afghan society, as a whole, a distinctively Pushtun flavor, albeit seasoned with a measure of tolerance for other ethnic and linguistic groups. Also, approximately six million additional Pushtuns live across the Durand Line in a more or less autonomous tribal belt on territory over which formerly British India (and now Pakistan) have exercised various degrees of control. These trans–Durand Line Pushtuns are closely related by kinship and cultural ties to the Pushtuns on the Afghan side of the line and are for all intents and purposes the same people. They have played an important part in the tribal politics of Afghanistan, as we shall see, and are, therefore, an important factor in the internal political equation within Afghanistan.

Geographically there has been a considerable amount of dispersion of tribal groups throughout the country. In some cases this has been prompted by deliberate policy. Amir Abdur Rahman, for example, resettled a considerable number of Pushtuns in northern Afghanistan and in Nuristan in order to dilute the

---

[17] These include a number of smaller groupings, more or less tribal, such as the Nuristanis, Khirgiz, and Baluch. It also includes nontribal groups such as Sikhs, Hindus, Jews, Qizilbash, and Arabs. Since no official national census has as yet been completed and analyzed in Afghanistan, these figures are intelligent approximations.

power of both the settlers and those into whose area they were transplanted. It is nevertheless possible, in a rough way, to indicate certain areas as predominantly inhabited by certain tribal groups (see Map 2 in the Appendixes). The Pushtuns are mainly located in southeastern and eastern Afghanistan. As has been previously noted, they straddle the Durand Line and their principal urban centers in Afghanistan are Kandahar, Ghazni, Kabul, and Jalalabad. Pushtuns also dominate the area between Kabul and the Khyber Pass. It should be noted in passing that the Pushtuns are astride and completely dominate the major mountain passes between the great Central Asian plateau and the Indian plain, a fact of major geopolitical consequence which I shall later elaborate.

As noted on Map 2 in the Appendixes, the non-Pushtun tribal groups are widely dispersed throughout the central, northern, and western regions of Afghanistan. They speak a variety of Indo-Iranian and Turkic languages and are divided religiously among a Sunni majority and Shiah minorities. The social stratification of these tribal groups is shown in Table 1.

As might be expected, the principal levers of power rest firmly in the hands of Pushtuns. They constitute a preponderant portion of the elite, i.e., the royal family, top government officials, wealthiest merchants and landowners, and most influential chiefs and religious leaders. Pushtuns also prevail numerically and qualitatively in the intelligentsia, although in this somewhat amorphous group there are substantial Tajik and Qizilbash increments. The urban middle class, which is relatively small, as in most underdeveloped countries, consists almost equally of Pushtuns, Tajiks, and Uzbegs, but in terms of influence the Pushtuns are well in the lead because of the multitude of labyrinthine kinship ties with the elite and the intelligentsia. A substantial number of Turkmen can be found in this urban middle class group and even a sprinkling of more affluent Hazaras.

The lower classes, which include the bulk of the population in Afghanistan, can conveniently be divided into relatively small

Table 1. Social stratification of tribal and religious groups in Afghanistan

Social Class	Numbers *	Members	Tribal and Religious Affiliation
Elite	2–3,000	King, royal family and top government officials, wealthy merchants and businessmen, large landowners, tribal chiefs, top religious leaders and army officers.	Overwhelmingly Pushtun and Sunni. A few Tajiks, also Sunnis.
Intelligentsia	8–10,000	Higher ranks of government employees, professionals, teachers, some students, literati and artists, upper-level religious leaders, army and police officers.	Preponderantly Pushtun but substantial numbers of Tajik. A few Qizilbash (Shiah).
Urban middle class	2,000,000	Lower civil servants, shopkeepers, scribes, accountants, artisans, middle-level religious leaders, lower-level army and police officers.	Predominantly Tajik but many Uzbeg and Pushtun. Some Turkmen and a few Hazara (Shiah).
Lower classes Urban Proletariat	20,000	Factory and semi-skilled workers, mechanics, drivers, etc.	Mostly Tajik but with substantial numbers of Pushtun and a few Hazara (Shiah).
Service personnel	100,000	Enlisted men in armed forces, police and *gendarmerie*, small shopkeepers, servants, waiters, etc.	Mostly Pushtun and Tajik. Large numbers of Hazara. Some Turkmen.

Table 1. Social stratification of tribal and religious groups in Afghanistan
(*Continued*)

Social Class	Numbers *	Members	Tribal and Religious Affiliation
Rural Cultivators	8,000,000	Small landowners, ordinary tribesmen, mullahs, peasants, seminomads.	Mostly Pushtun with large numbers of Hazara, Uzbeg, and Turkmen.
Nomads	1,000,000	Pure nomads with no single fixed abode and no cultivation.	Almost all Pushtun with a few Turkmen.

Source: Leon B. Poullada, "Problems of Social Development in Afghanistan," *Journal of the Royal Central Asian Society*, XLIX, Part 1 (January 1962).

* All figures are estimates since no official national census has been taken. Local census figures for specific localities were examined in the Royal Afghan Government Ministry of Planning and in general supported the above distribution. See also, for example, [Richard Spencer], "A Demographic Study of the Village of Baghrami, Province of Kabul," mimeographed (Kabul: USOM Afghanistan Public Administration Service in cooperation with Columbia University, 1959). Confirmatory data are also contained in "Pilot Scheme for Collection of Employment Market Information in Kabul," mimeographed (Kabul: Royal Government of Afghanistan Ministry of Planning, February 1960). See also "Afghanistan's Young Elite," in W. Eberhard, *Settlement and Social Change in Asia* (Hong Kong: Hong Kong Press, 1967).

urban and relatively large rural sectors. The urban sector consists of a minuscule proletariat of factory and semiskilled workers plus a substantial number of service personnel such as small shopkeepers, servants, waiters, drivers, and so on. Included in this group would be military enlisted personnel and police. These urban lower classes are a fairly even mixture of Pushtuns, Tajiks, and Hazaras with a small element of Turkmen. Within this sector, however, Pushtuns tend to gravitate to those positions with a margin of power or influence, such as the police and the *gendarmerie*.

Finally the large rural sector of the population consists for the most part of cultivators, herders, and nomads. This would include small landowners, ordinary tribesmen, peasants, village dwellers, and the various types of nomads. Here the Pushtuns again are in a large majority although there are substantial Turkmen, Uzbeg, Hazara, and some Tajik elements. In one sense, therefore, the Pushtuns predominate at both the bottom and the top of the social hierarchy but, in the peculiar conditions prevailing in Afghanistan, this is true more in an economic than a social sense because the tribal Pushtun considers himself the inferior of no one and speaks to members of the elite on quite equal terms. It is more nearly correct, then, to view Afghan social stratification as a full cycle rather than as a pyramid.

It is also interesting to note religious affiliation within the various social strata. The Hazara are the only large Shiah group in the country and they are largely confined to the lower reaches of the social order. But the Qizilbash, descendants of an old elite military group, though also Shiah, have managed to secure a strong position in the intelligentsia.

The political history of the period starting with the emergence of Afghanistan as an inchoate nation-state in 1747 to the present has been decisively affected by tribal politics, and the dynamics of this tribal power can be analyzed in terms of five basic conflict situations: (1) interpersonal conflict within tribes; (2) intratribal group conflict, i.e., rivalry between subunits of the same tribe; (3) intertribal conflict between tribes of the same ethnic, religious, and linguistic backgrounds; (4) intertribal conflict between tribes of different ethnic, linguistic, or religious backgrounds; (5) conflict between a tribe or tribes in general and the central government authority. It will be rewarding to examine each of these conflict situations in turn. Again, for the purposes of this study our attention will be centered on, though not limited to, the Pushtun tribes.

Interpersonal conflict is deeply rooted in the value system, the political authority structure, and the physical environment of Pushtun tribal society. The question of the effect of geography and climate on the character of peoples is a controversial one among social scientists; I will confine myself to noting that in the Pushtun tribal areas from time immemorial certain features of character and social attitudes toward conflict have gone hand in hand with climatic and topographical features. To the ordinary mind this would suggest some connection.[18]

For the most part the tribes inhabit a land of extreme poverty. Not only is the land infertile and hostile to cultivation, but the topography of barren crags and steep isolated valleys tends to fracture social groups into tight suspicious communities. The terrain and the climate, which ranges from polar cold to desert heat, encourage the survival of only the most rugged individualists.

The fierce independence of the individual tribesman is reflected in the rather loose authority patterns of the tribe. Tribal leadership is not necessarily hereditary; factors such as reputation for learning, prowess in war, and wealth are important in the selection of chiefs. These maliks and khans wield influence rather than authority. Social control is not deeply affected by religious sanctions. Most tribesmen are devout Muslims though their religion is heavily encrusted with folk-Islam. But the influence of the mullah is largely based on his position as a man of superior knowledge, as an important landowner, and as a power broker and political intriguer in the constant conflicts which

[18] A discussion of the effect of climate and topography on the social organization of the Pushtun tribes is contained in Josif, pp. 5–10. See also Edward Stenz, *The Climate of Afghanistan* (New York: Polish Institute of Arts and Sciences in America, 1946), and J. Humlum, *La Geographie de l'Afghanistan* (Copenhagen: Gyldenal, 1959). See also W. K. Fraser-Tytler, *Afghanistan: A Study of Political Developments in Central and Southern Asia*, 3d ed. rev. (London: Oxford University Press, 1967), Part III, ch. 2, for an attempt to explain the history of the Afghanistan region in terms of physical environmental causes.

pervade this society. The tribesman is above all a political realist, and the subtleties of Shari'a (religious law) will seldom lead him to act against his immediate material interests.

In the tribe the ultimate instrument of social control is the jirgah or tribal assembly. The jirgah has been known to exist for many centuries and has become institutionalized by customary law. It is quasi-judicial and quasi-parliamentary in function. Parties to a dispute or proposers of a project, such as establishing a new mosque, may first take their problem to the malik or khan. This is in the nature of consultation though in certain cases the malik's advice may carry great weight because of his personal position in the tribe. If the matter is to be carried further a jirgah may be called. The composition of the jirgah may vary for different purposes. In general it must have representatives from all families who are involved or may be affected by the discussion. In major matters such as war and peace, major segments of the tribe must be represented. Decisions are not taken by a "vote" but rather by consensus. Full discussion is the rule and dissident opinions are heard with tolerance. In settling disputes the jirgah does not attempt to examine facts or determine rights and wrongs. In tribal conditions the facts are usually well known and the jirgah's function is to resolve conflict rather than impose punishment. Nevertheless a jirgah's "decision" is almost universally observed and defiance may result in burning of the defiant's house or in his ostracism, both sanctions being almost equivalent to capital punishment since they remove in the one case physical and in the other tribal protection from the offender. In its deliberations the jirgah may rely on *rawaj* or customary law as interpreted by the elders and/or on Shari'a as expounded by the mullah. This, it should be noted, gives the mullah another lever of power in the tribe.

Social control is also exercised within the tribe by powerful kinship ties and the elaborate code of honor known as Pushtunwali. In spite of his fierce individualism, the tribesman is surrounded, as it were, by concentric circles of protection and compulsion consisting of the nuclear family, the extended family, the clan, the subtribe, the tribe, and the major ethnic-linguistic group of tribes. Within these circles the individual tribesman exists in a constant love-hate relationship even with his closest kinsmen. It is not just coincidence that in Pushtu the word for cousin (*tarbur*) is closely related linguistically to the word for enemy. I asked a tribesman once why he was wearing his overcoat in the middle of a very hot summer day. His curt reply: "You don't know my brother!"

Within tribal society the individual is expected to adhere strictly to Pushtunwali. This unwritten law has many ramifications but its principal injunctions are (1) *badal* (revenge), (2) *melmastia* (hospitality), and (3) *nanawati* (asylum). [19] *Badal* is a form of self-help in avenging private wrongs which tribal society not only condones but requires. The result is the prevalent blood feud which affects not only immediate families but whole villages, and even tribes. Failure to take the prescribed measure of revenge brings dishonor (*sharm*) to all upon whom this obligation lies. This institution has brought entire tribal areas to a perpetual state of paranoic warfare. Houses in tribal villages are in effect fortified redoubts complete with watchtowers. Movements from one place to another by tribesmen are exercises in daring for some long-smoldering grievance may be lying in wait around each corner and boulder to be satisfied by blood. In this tense conflict situation all men carry weapons as soon as they are able to do so and learn to use them with lethal precision.

In spite of the ameliorative effects of hospitality and asylum and the conflict-resolving functions of the jirgah, the *badal* psychology of the blood feud pervades tribal society at all levels. According to a well-known Pushtu saying, all conflicts re-

---

[19] C. Colin Davies, *The Problem of the Northwest Frontier, 1890–1908* (Cambridge: The University Press, 1932), pp. 49 ff.; and James W. Spain, *The Pathan Borderland* (The Hague: Mouton, 1963), pp. 63 ff.

volve around *zar, zan,* and *zamin,* i.e., loot, love, and land.[20]

Poverty and a long history of raids on sedentary lowland communities and on peaceful commerce have given the Pushtun tribesman an extraordinary avidity for loot and gold. The prospects of loot will move him to political or warlike action more readily than principle or ideology. Organized governments, whether Mughal, Afghan, or British, learned through experience that the payment of bribes and blackmail (euphemistically labeled subsidies or subventions) was the touchstone of tribal diplomacy. The distribution of this gold, however, has been the cause of constant internal tribal conflict.

Land is often a generator of conflict. This would seem to flow logically from a number of interrelated causes. In the first place most tribal lands are infertile highland tracts. Water is very scarce and irrigation rights are a constant source of controversy. Imprecise systems of boundary markings and lack of land records add to the problem. Ownership of land is an essential element in the status of the individual tribesman.[21] *Badal* often transforms land disputes into blood feuds.

There are elements in Pushtun tribal society which aggravate the natural tendency for men to fight over women. Women are a valuable commodity not only as cheap labor but also as bargaining counters in the interminable battle for family honor and status. Most Pushtun tribesmen are monogamous though they can be polygamous if their wealth and circumstances permit. Daughters are frankly recognized as potential assets to forward the interests of the family through strategic marriage alliances.

[20] These basic conflict-producing factors are as prevalent today in Afghan society as in the past and are by no means confined to tribal areas but permeate the society even in sophisticated urban settings. This is made very explicit in articles by A. H. Waleh in the *Kabul Times,* July 20 and 27, 1968.

[21] Good discussions of land poverty and fragmentation and its consequences in the Pushtun tribal areas are found in Spain, pp. 80–84, and in Josif.

Their virtue must therefore be beyond question and any liberties taken by outsiders must be wiped away in blood. A marriage is arranged between family elders and the prospective groom is expected to pay a substantial bride price. Betrothals are often made during childhood and any attempt on either side to violate the contract even under changed circumstances often results in bitter family quarrels calling for *badal*. Needless to say infidelity by a woman demands blood, both hers and her lover's. Ordinary tribeswomen do not observe purdah, nor do they wear the veil, since they generally work out of doors with the men. Wives and daughters of tribesmen of higher status such as those of maliks or wealthy men often do observe purdah. Divorce by the man is possible and theoretically simple as prescribed in Shari'a but in Pushtun tribal society this is likely to be considered *sharm* by the bride's family and result in *badal*. The possibilities for quarrels, misunderstandings, and desperate feuds in such a system can well be imagined.[22]

Complex political, economic, and social factors, then, combine to create a high level of interpersonal conflict in Pushtun tribal society. Among these numerous factors we have singled out lax authority patterns and loose social control, both secular and religious, powerful kinship love-hate relationships, economic deprivation coupled with historical rapacity, and interwoven with all of these the revenge motif of the tribal honor code which often transforms private quarrels into public blood feuds. Because of the prevalence of Pushtun tribal values throughout Afghan society, the high level of interpersonal conflict has permeated the Afghan political system, has tended to perpetuate national disunity, and at times has escalated the family blood feud to national levels of rebellion and regicide.[23]

[22] Donald Wilber, *Afghanistan: Its People, Its Society, Its Culture* (New Haven: Human Relations Area Files Press, 1962); see chapters 6, 7, and 9 for discussions of the role of women in Afghan society.

[23] The most notorious example in recent times was the blood feud which developed between the Musahiban family led by King Nadir

The second type of conflict situation that affects the political system of Afghanistan is intratribal, that is, involving rivalry between subunits of the same tribe. Although bound by kinship ties, most Afghan tribes are far from united internally. The Ghilzai tribe, for example, is one of the largest, most warlike and potentially one of the most powerful tribes in Afghanistan, but its proverbial disunity has kept it from achieving the national prominence of which it is capable. Its most powerful subdivision, the Suleiman Khel, for example, is distrusted and feared by other sections of the tribe. In addition there is hostility between the large nomadic sections and the more sedentary groups of the same tribe. Because of their disunity the Ghilzai have often been reduced to the role of political scavengers, at times fighting on both sides of dynastic struggles and at others using the threat of intervention to obtain loot and advantage for themselves. Similarly, as we have noted, the rivalry between the Barakzai and Saddozai branches of the great Durrani tribe led to

---

(1929–1933) and the prominent Charkhi family led by Ghulam Nabi. The two families were political rivals but their differences escalated when Nadir, in a conciliatory gesture, offered to marry one of his young nephews to one of the Charkhi daughters and was snubbed. Rivalry was then transmuted to enmity and after Nadir ascended the throne he accused Ghulam Nabi of fomenting rebellion and had him summarily executed. In *badal* Nadir's brother, Mohammed Aziz Khan, was assassinated in Berlin by an Afghan student allegedly incited by Ghulam Siddiq (Nabi's brother). In addition, an attempt was made in Kabul to assassinate Prime Minister Hashem Khan, another of King Nadir's brothers. In retaliation all male Charkhis over fourteen years of age in Afghanistan were ordered executed. A few months later, on the anniversary of Ghulam Nabi's execution, a student who was a Charkhi family retainer assassinated King Nadir at a school function. Nadir's death so soon after the revolution which brought him to the throne was a serious blow to Afghan national recovery. Thus the entire nation suffered because of tribal *badal* between two top families. Several versions of this feud have been recorded by, among others, Fraser-Tytler, Spain, Fletcher, and E. Caspani and E. Cagnacci, *Afghanistan: Crocevia dell' Asia* (Milan: Antonio Vallardi, 1951). I carefully checked the above account in Kabul in 1968 with informants who had first-hand knowledge of the events.

2. King Amanullah
in Pushtun tribal dress,
about 1923.

the election of Ahmad Shah as supreme chief in 1747 and was
later responsible for long and bitter dynastic quarrels over the
throne in Kabul.

The third fundamental tribal conflict situation which has cast
its pall on Afghan political development is *inter*tribal antagonism between tribes of the same ethnic stock. This has been
most marked among the Pushtun tribes themselves even though

(or perhaps because) one of them, the Durrani, has provided the rulers of the country for more than two centuries.

While conflict between Pushtun tribes both large and small has been more the rule than the exception in Afghanistan, the most powerful rival Pushtun tribes involved in Afghan history have been the Ghilzai and the Durrani. As we have seen, the Ghilzai have never taken well to "civilization" or settled ways. They have remained to a large extent nomadic, aloof, and war-like. They had a brief moment of unity, glory, and foreign con-quest in the eighteenth century under Mir Wais and his son, Mahmud Shah. As the national hegemony of the Durrani tribe increased, the Ghilzai retreated more deeply into tribal isolation, hostile to any Durrani dynasty and now and again openly chal-lenging its rule as in the great Ghilzai rebellion against Amir Abdur Rahman in 1886. In situations of national stress the Ghil-zai-Durrani conflict became crucial. As we shall see in subse-quent chapters it was Ghilzai power, thrown in decisively at the last moment, that dealt Amanullah the *coup de grâce* in 1929.

A fourth type of conflict situation which has affected political modernization in Afghanistan has been intertribal antagonism between tribes of different ethnic, linguistic, or religious back-grounds. Politically, the most important of these conflicts is, of course, the antagonism between the Pushtuns and the non-Push-tuns. This has been accentuated by the fact that for two centu-ries Pushtuns have held political power in the country as well as by inhibitions on intermarriage and social mobility. Ever since Ahmad Shah possessed himself of the Afghan kingdom the non-Pushtuns have resented Pushtun domination. They have resisted Pushtun hegemony, sometimes bitterly and by force of arms, sometimes by trying to ignore Pushtun governors and adminis-trators, but mostly by displaying a repugnance or apathy to-ward national objectives which they have rightly or wrongly felt are intended for the benefit of the ruling Pushtun classes. Armed revolts and insurrections among the Hazaras, the Uzbegs, and even the Tajiks have taken place.[24] To many non-Pushtun tribes the very term denoting national citizenship, "Afghan," has been synonymous with "Pushtun." This sense of tribal alienation has struck at the very roots of all efforts to build a united nation-state.[25]

The fifth conflict is the overarching one between any central government that seeks to impose its authority and the centrifugal forces of a tribal society whose way of life demands untrammeled freedom from external restraints. The Pushtun tribes in particular have always been known as among the most fiercely independent in the world. We have noted that for the individual tribesman significant political relationships are filtered through the concentric rings of kinship and tribal rights and responsibilities. Only marginally, and then only for utilitarian purposes or to the extent that the interests of the central government happen to coincide with those of subnational tribal groups, is there any congruence between the political culture of the tribesman and the demands of the nation-state.

Historically, then, the Pushtun tribes, secure within their mountain bastions centered on the Suleiman range and the Safed Koh, have successfully resisted all attempts to subdue them by Greeks, Persians, Kushans, Mongols, Mughals, Sikhs, British, and other Afghans. Most conquerors of the subcontinent were content to bypass these tribes, wherever necessary paying transit tribute and submitting to their raids and lootings. Only Britain, with its inbred sense of the need to impose law and order on subject peoples, felt sufficiently outraged by the persistence of Pushtun rapacity and brigandage to maintain a consistent campaign of pacification. This went on for more than one

---

[24] Note the many tribal rebellions by non-Pushtuns during the reign of Abdur Rahman mentioned earlier in this chapter. In a later chapter we will see that the attack led by Bacha-i-Saqao against Amanullah was deeply rooted in Tajik resentment of Pushtun domination.

[25] See John C. Griffiths, *Afghanistan* (London: Pall Mall Press, 1967), pp. 65–74, for a present-day evaluation of conflict between Pushtuns and non-Pushtuns with its contemporary political implications.

hundred years of the history of British India and as W. K. Fraser-Tytler says, "The British did not solve the problem of the tribes, and when in August 1947 they handed over control of India's north-western defences to the untried Government of Pakistan, they handed over likewise a fluid, difficult situation, fraught with much danger to the future of India." [26]

This resistance to integration within a "civilized" community on the part of the Pushtuns was vexing to the various empires that flourished in the vicinity but did not affect their essential character or purpose; they were able in most instances to ignore the Pushtun island of disaffection by taking steps to contain it from overflowing into the settled areas. In this regard the frontier policy of the Mughal Emperor, Babur, did not differ radically from that of the Sikh Maharajah, Ranjit Singh, or the British Viceroy, Lord Curzon. But for Afghanistan, as it began to take its first tottering steps toward forming a nation, tribal reluctance to accept integration into the national fabric became a crucial problem. This was all the more true since the new rulers of the embryonic Afghan state were themselves Pushtuns not far removed from the realities of tribal life.

The struggle for power between the central government and the tribes has been heightened by a number of interrelated factors, some favoring the tribes, others the central authority. On the whole, geography and social organization favored the tribes: their isolated position in mountainous terrain, their warlike culture in which every man and boy is an armed and seasoned warrior, their loose authority structure which makes it difficult to pacify them by winning over the chiefs and causes them to repudiate the mystique of kingship. We have already noted that to most tribesmen central authority, since its founding by Ahmad Shah, has been little more than an emanation of a tribal confederation and the amir merely a paramount chief, a *primus inter pares* (with the stress on the *pares* rather than on the *primus*). Thus the concepts of legitimacy and of religiously sanc-

[26] Fraser-Tytler, p. 270.

tioned royalty have developed slowly and only in relatively recent times.[27]

Geopolitics and perennial dynastic wars also helped the tribes defy the central government. Afghanistan's strategic position in Central Asia between the expanding Russian and British empires invited foreign intervention in domestic quarrels. This often meant supporting one tribal faction against another. Contenders for the throne actively sought tribal alliances to support their cause and rulers tried to counteract foreign interference by raising the tribes as a "prickly hedge" against external influence. This placed a high blackmail value on the temporary allegiance of the tribes and confirmed them in their rapacious and separatist tendencies. The buffer-state principle spared Afghanistan from prolonged colonial occupation and rule but this lack of a powerful central administration also enhanced the position of the tribes as alternative sources of political power.

Other factors, however, favored the central government. Tribal disunity was certainly one of these. Dr. Pennell, who spent many years with Pushtun tribes, quotes the Afghan proverb to the effect that "the Afghans of the frontier are never at peace except when they are at war," and goes on to say:

These tribal jealousies and petty wars are inherent among the Afghans and greatly diminish their formidableness as foes. If you ask them about it they will acknowledge this defect in their character, and tell you how one of their ancestors displeased the Almighty, who to punish him wove the strands of discord in the web of their nature from that time onwards. . . . For when some enemy threatens their independence, then for the time being, are their feuds and

[27] In Amanullah's case it will be remembered that his royal position was further weakened by questions regarding possible usurpation and suspicions of patricide and regicide. It is also interesting to note that the concepts of a legitimate line of succession and of religiously endowed royalty have now been explicitly written into the 1964 Constitution. See Louis Dupree, "Constitutional Development and Cultural Change— The 1964 Afghan Constitution," *American Universities Field Staff Reports*, South Asia series, IX, nos. 1–4 (1964).

jealousies thrown aside and they fight shoulder to shoulder to resume them again when the common danger is averted. Even when they are all desirous of joining in some *jihad*, they remain suspicious of each other, and are apt to fail one another at the critical moment; or else one tribe will wait to see how it fares with those already in it before unsheathing their own swords.[28]

That this discord and disunity in Pushtun society is not of recent vintage is testified to by no less a man than the idol of all Pushtuns, the great warrior, patriot, and poet, Khushal Khan Khattak, who early in the seventeenth century wrote:

> Ah God! Grant them but concord, sweet refrain,
> And old Khushal will rise a youth again![29]

Sir Henry Rawlinson, a leading authority on Afghanistan in his day, wrote in 1875: "[Afghanistan] never has had and never can have the cohesion and consistency of a regular monarchical government. The nation consists of a mere collection of tribes of unequal power and with divergent habits, which are held together more or less closely according to the personal character of the chief who rules them." [30] The eminent contemporary Afghan historian Rishtya has indicated how tribal disunity rather than Sikh military power led to Afghanistan's irreparable loss of the Peshawar area and to the forced renunciation by Dost Mohammed in 1855 of all legitimate Afghan claims in the northwest frontier and the Punjab.[31]

Another factor favoring the accretion of power to the central

[28] Theodore L. Pennell, *Among the Wild Tribes of the Afghan Frontier* (London: Seeley, 1927), p. 60.

[29] Quoted in Sir Olaf Caroe, *The Pathans* (London: St. Martin's Press, 1958), p. 306.

[30] Henry Rawlinson, *England and Russia in the East* (London: John Murray, 1875).

[31] Syed Qasim Rishtya, *A History of Afghanistan in the 19th Century* (Kabul: Education Press, 1949), pp. 68–80. This loss of territory rankled in the Afghan breast and in more recent times fueled the Pushtunistan dispute which has poisoned Afghan-Pakistan relations and has been instrumental in enhancing Soviet influence in Afghanistan.

government has been the periodic rule of strong amirs. Such an amir could expand central power if he commanded a strong base within his own tribe and were an expert in tribal diplomacy. By skillful use of military strength, gold, and tribal influence he could play on the disunity of the tribes and suck power from them. When such an amir sat on the throne the tribes tended to be quiescent and brooded in their own hills. A strong central ruler usually could command better finances, communications, and weapons than the tribes, thus further enhancing the power of the throne.[32]

Under strong amirs like Ahmad Shah, Dost Mohammed, and Abdur Rahman, who were adept at maximizing sources of government strength and at exploiting tribal weaknesses, central authority advanced and tribal power receded. On the other hand, whenever weak or inept amirs occupied the throne, tribal power expanded, brigandage increased, dynastic quarrels flourished, and the writ of the central government did not run throughout the land.

Historically the conflict between the central government and the tribes manifested itself in a state of dynamic tension, favoring now one side, now the other, always seeking a precarious balance of power. But periodically the balance was destroyed, either by outside causes such as foreign interference of by an attempt by one of the antagonists to push its power too far into the domain of the other. Then there would be violent confrontation ranging from local disturbances to civil war. To a large extent the very existence of the central government depended on maintaining this delicate balance with tribal power. Thus the tribes in Afghanistan have rightly been termed "king-makers and breakers."

---

[32] This was not always the case. For a period in the late nineteenth century the tribes were able to obtain, through profitable gun-running operations, large shipments of the new breech-loading rifle. This added greatly to the firepower of the tribes and threatened to upset the balance of power in their favor. See Josif, p. 51.

The oscillations of power between the tribes and the central government are discernible in historical syndromes. Whenever the tribes perceived weakness or vacillation in the central government the level of conflict and defiance would rise in predictable stages. First would come delinquency in payment of taxes, followed by discreet probes against isolated government outposts. If these succeeded, a more serious raid on some small population center would follow. This usually resulted in the capture of arms and booty. If this met little or no opposition, other tribal groups, inflamed at the prospect of capturing arms and loot, began to join the rebels. If the central government was still not able to retaliate and punish, more dissatisfaction spread among the tribes, usually accompanied at this stage by political propaganda disguised in religious garb. At this point, too, a charismatic tribal leader might emerge, an Abdul Karim, a Mullah-i-Lang, or a Bacha-i-Saqao. If the challenge to the central government authority was allowed to reach this stage, the country was in for serious trouble.

On the other hand, history gives us many examples of the opposite trend—i.e., the incursion of government power into the tribal domain. Here the syndrome takes the form of creeping administration spearheaded by small military outposts and by an attempt to support these scouts with logistical devices such as roads, telegraphs, and the like. Behind the tribal administrator usually came the school teacher and the tax collector. The former was viewed by the tribesman as a threat to his value system, the latter as a menace to his economic freedom. The promised prospects of economic development and a better life did not ring true to the tribesman on at least two counts. He shrewdly realized that in this world everything has its price. Economic benefits would probably be absorbed by the tax collector or by corrupt officials, while on the other hand the authority patterns of his tribal society which he understands and cherishes would become disrupted and eventually destroyed. The fact that the allegedly beneficent moves of the central government were usually supported by military force reinforced the tribesman's paranoiac conviction that no good was intended toward him, else why the need for force or threat of force?

Thus the relative power of the tribes and the central government shifted as the contestants utilized, more or less skillfully, the sources of strength available to each. The interaction of these two centers of power, seeking to encroach on each other's domain, resulted at times in a precarious temporary balance which in turn fell into disarray and plunged the country into internal strife until a new balance was found.[33] It is against this complex political backdrop of history and tribal conflict that King Amanullah's dramatic attempt to modernize Afghanistan was played.

---

[33] This in essence is what occurred in Amanullah's attempt to modernize Afghanistan even though neither he nor his supporters, critics, and chroniclers seemed to understand the dynamics of the aborted experiment.

chapter II

the molding of
a modernizer

The analysis of the politics of tribal power contained in the previous chapter provides the background for an understanding of Amanullah's program of modernization. Such a program, however, was not conceived in a vacuum. In many respects it was a reflection of the man who sat on the throne of Afghanistan during this critical period of the nation's development. We must, therefore, know something about the influences that molded this man.

King Amanullah was born in 1892 and grew up during a period when the Islamic world was in ferment. Muslim reformers such as Mohammed 'Abduh, Jamal-ud-Din al Afghani, and Syed Ahmed Khan had preached a gospel of Muslim renascence from North Africa to India. The Young Turks had openly broken with tradition in that most arcane sanctuary of Islamic orthodoxy, the Ottoman Empire. These currents of modernism had to some extent bypassed Afghanistan. Abdur Rahman had been too busy subduing tribal and religious separatists to trouble himself too much with ideas which for Afghanistan seemed premature. Indeed he did not hesitate to exile even powerful families who appeared too advanced for his crude but effective notions of law and order. Four leading families, in particular, played dominant roles in King Amanullah's attempt and failure to modernize Afghanistan: Amanullah's own royal family, the Musahiban family headed by Nadir Khan, the Charkhi family led by Ghulam Nabi, and the Tarzi family whose head was Mahmud

Beg. The exile by the Amir Abdur Rahman of two of these families, the Tarzis and the Musahibans, proved fateful for Afghanistan. The Tarzis went to Syria in what was then part of the Ottoman Empire. The Musahibans went to India and lived under British influence and protection.

Abdur Rahman's son and heir, Habibullah, permitted both these families to return and gave them positions of honor and influence. Mahmud Beg Tarzi had married a Syrian lady of Daghistani extraction and moved to Istanbul during his years of exile. When Tarzi returned to Kabul, Amanullah was still a young, untried, but ambitious princeling. Tarzi had a profound influence on him. In a different way the Musahiban family also had a profound effect on Amanullah's life—Nadir Khan succeeded him to the throne.

But long before the Tarzis or the Musahibans came on the scene, Amanullah had already felt many pressures shaping his personality and future course of action. Without doubt the most potent of these in his early life was the overpowering character and ambition of his mother, the Ulya Hazrat, the "first queen" in the court of Amanullah's father, Habibullah. The power situation in Habibullah's court, especially on the distaff side, was complex and confusing. Habibullah, in addition to having the four royal queens authorized by Muslim law, had contracted numerous "dynastic" marriages with a large number of tribal women (both Pushtun and non-Pushtun) who, with their sons, occupied a somewhat inferior position in the court. The Ulya Hazrat came from a top-drawer Pushtun family of a powerful Barakzai clan, the Loynabs. Her father was Loynab Sher Dil Khan and her brother was Loynab Khushdil.[1] In her mind there

---

[1] "Who's Who in Afghanistan," enclosure to Despatch no. 22, 28 February 1931, from British Legation, Kabul, to Foreign Office, London, Archives of the India Office Library, London (hereafter abbreviated IOL). The "Dil" clan was originally known as the Kandahar Sardars who were brothers of Amir Dost Mohammed, the first Barakzai king. "Loynab" was a title roughly equivalent to governor general of a province.

3. A rare and perhaps unique photo of the Amir Habibullah (Amanullah's father) taken with his wives at a time when strict purdah was in force in Afghanistan and women were seen only veiled. The photo was probably taken about 1905.

was no question that her only son, Amanullah, was entitled to succeed to the throne. True, Habibullah had two older sons, but Inayatullah's mother was a non-Pushtun and Hayatullah's mother was a *surati*.[2] In the Ulya Hazrat's eyes this, plus Amanullah's superior energy and ability, gave him the inside track in the race to the throne. As may be seen in Table 2, the only real competitors in sight were Habibullah's brother, Nasrullah, and Amanullah's younger half-brother, Asadullah, who was the son of another royal queen, the Ulya Janab. Asadullah presented a threat because the Ulya Janab was the sister of Nadir Khan, of

[2] Interview with informant, Kabul, 1968. It is difficult to convey in terms of our culture the exact status of a *surati*. The term is often translated as "concubine" but this implies a pejorative relationship which did not exist. The *surati* was considered in every sense a legal wife and her children were neither illegitimate nor automatically barred from the throne. They were entitled to royal titles and to inherit. Nevertheless, socially they did not rank on an equal basis with the "royal" queens and their offspring. Perhaps the concept of a morganatic wife most closely approximates the status of the *surati*.

Table 2. Partial genealogy showing origins of claimants to succeed Amir Habibullah

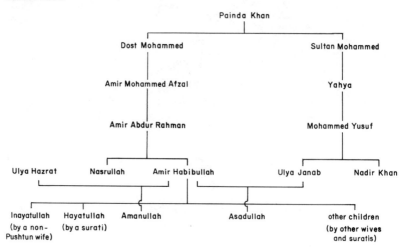

the influential Musahiban family, and her credentials were therefore as valid as those of the Ulya Hazrat.[3]

In any case, the Ulya Hazrat set out to exert all her considerable skill, intelligence, and influence to prepare Amanullah for the throne. According to Ali Ahmad, the Ulya Hazrat put Amanullah, while still a boy, through a rigorous course of training in the arts of political intrigue and government.[4] To this effect the indomitable lady, who was later to be described by Major Fraser in her moment of defeat and exile as "this interesting old eagle," [5] summoned her most experienced kinsmen to

---

[3] Interview with informant, Kabul, 1967. Later it will be seen that this early rivalry between the Amanullah family and the Musahiban family ripened into the equivalent of a typical Pushtun feud which deprived Amanullah of the loyal services of Nadir Khan when they would have been most useful to him.

[4] Ali Ahmad, "The Fall of Amanullah," manuscript, translated by R. N. G. Scott, IOL, LPS/10 P53/1285/1929, Parts 1 and 2.

[5] Confidential Letter from Major W. A. K. Fraser to Secretary of State for India, dated 20 July 1929, IOL, LPS/10/1232 P50/1929. Major Fraser was the escort on board the ship which carried Amanullah and his party into exile from Bombay to Europe. See the obituary of Ma-

act as Amanullah's tutors. From his subsequent career it would appear that Amanullah was not an apt pupil and learned little of the wiles and ruses of tribal political warfare. It seems he did, however, absorb both from the Ulya Hazrat and from her kinsmen a deep and abiding Anglophobia based on family tribal experiences in two wars fought against British invasion, on both of which occasions the Barakzai, though having fought with the utmost courage, had been roundly defeated and chastised by British arms.

Not much more is known with certainty about Amanullah's boyhood. He is said to have been fond of outdoor sports, especially hunting, but in later life he played tennis often and vigorously to the discomfiture of his more effete courtiers whom he often dragooned into unaccustomed exertions on the courts. His formal education seems to have been acquired in the military school which Habibullah had set up for young Afghan aristocrats and which, from all reports, left much to be desired in quality. A number of my informants told me that he was for several years a voracious reader, but this practice was apparently largely abandoned after his kingly duties claimed his time. Nearly all of the informants who knew him testify to his keen and alert intelligence and his inquiring mind. He was a good listener and asked penetrating questions, especially about the world outside of Afghanistan. He was intensely interested in religious questions and often engaged mullahs in lengthy conversations in which he refused to accept pat answers and insisted on rational explanations, which the mullahs often found it impossible to provide. At the early age of fifteen he confided to one of his aides that he was deeply ashamed of the backwardness of his country and manifested great frustration that Afghanistan had been denied the greatness it deserved. He ascribed this low condition to the ignorance of the Afghan people and the deliberate imperialist policies of Britain.[6] Both these convictions seem to

jor-General William Archibald Kenneth Fraser (known as Wak Fraser) in the *Royal Central Asian Journal*, LVI, Part II (June 1969).

[6] Interview with informant, Kabul, 1968.

have remained with him in later life and to have conditioned his subsequent actions when he came to power.

The unhappy experience of his first two marriages may have shaped his later attitude toward women's rights and marriage customs. He apparently married first when he was sixteen. A good deal of mystery surrounds this marriage. I could find no one who remembered the name of the girl. The marriage lasted only a few days and ended in divorce. He was married again at eighteen to a girl of noble lineage named Shahzada Khanum, who died on giving birth to their only son, Hidayatullah. Both these marriages were arranged for him by the Ulya Hazrat and must have been unhappy experiences for a young man. He contracted his third marriage when he was twenty-one, this time with a bride of his choice, the lovely and talented Soraya Tarzi, daughter of the returned exile Mahmud Beg Tarzi. At about the same time his older half-brother Inayatullah married Soraya Tarzi's sister.

We come now to the period of Amanullah's association with Mahmud Tarzi.[7] This remarkable man who had lived in exile most of his adult life and drunk deeply in the fountains of the Young Turks was a worldly, early twentieth-century liberal in the older and more dignified sense of the term. He had a bitter dislike for colonialism in general and for Britain in particular. He was a brilliant writer, a fine conversationalist, fluent in Pushtu, Persian, Arabic, Turkish, Urdu, and French. He had a commanding presence which inspired respect and affection. When Tarzi was permitted by the Amir Habibullah to return from exile, his charm and personality soon captured the good will of the Amir, who permitted him to publish the liberal

---

[7] The sketch of Mahmud Tarzi is based on the following sources: Wilber, pp. 20 ff.; Fletcher, pp. 180 ff.; Dupree, "Mahmud Tarzi: Forgotten Nationalist." Sorab Katrak, *Through Amanullah's Afghanistan* (Karachi: D. N. Patel, 1929), pp. iv and v; Vartan Gregorian, "Mahmud Tarzi and Saraj-ol-Akhbar," *Middle East Journal*, XXI (1967), 345–368; and on interviews with informants in Kabul, 1967–68.

newspaper *Siraj-ul-Akhbar*. Tarzi developed this journal into a powerful instrument to propagate his two great themes: "Muslims must modernize or perish" and "Colonialism and imperialism must go."

Vartan Gregorian has given us an excellent and comprehensive résumé of the importance and contents of the *Siraj-ul-Akhbar*.[8] Without doubt this journal (for it cannot properly be considered a newspaper), which appeared every two weeks between the years 1911 and 1918, provided the most powerful single impetus to Afghan modernization. Amanullah read it faithfully and avidly during his most formative years, and his marriage to Tarzi's daughter gave him ample opportunity to discuss the ideas and programs set forth in the journal within the privacy of his own family.

The ideological content of *Siraj-ul-Akhbar* centered on the message that Afghanistan, along with most of the Muslim world, was in a state of political, social, and moral decline. This was principally due to ignorance, especially ignorance of modern institutions and scientific knowledge, which in turn created disharmony, disunity, and misunderstandings among Muslims. The fault lay not with Islam, if properly understood, but with the Muslims and what they had made of Islam. The remedies for this low estate were self-evident: education, knowledge of modern ways and techniques, and the adoption of scientific discoveries. Modern knowledge was of universal applicability and need not be identified with non-Muslims or Western civilizations. It belonged to all humanity for the asking and taking. The columns of the *Siraj-ul-Akhbar* urged that this dynamic fusion of modernism with the true spirit of Islam should be fueled by the fires of nationalism. Islam itself propounds the concept of

[8] Gregorian, pp. 345–368. This article contains many specific references to articles in the *Siraj-ul-Akhbar* as well as to other writings by Mahmud Tarzi. Rather than repeat here numerous citations most of which duplicate those gleaned in my own research into now rare copies of the *Siraj-ul-Akhbar*, the reader is referred to Gregorian's article.

the fatherland (*watan*) within the broader Muslim community (*umma*). Therefore to "love one's country was to love one's religion and vice versa." [9] Islamic nationalism was the ideology that could cement the ethnic, linguistic, religious, and political separatism of a country like Afghanistan and insure loyalty to a legitimate and progressive government.

This dynamic linking of Islam, modernization, and nationalism had for its ultimate purpose the combination of revivified and powerful Muslim and Asian nations into Pan-Islamic and Pan-Asian confederations capable at last of facing the European juggernaut of imperialism and colonialism which threatened to extinguish their freedom and independence. Needless to say this gospel of hope found sympathetic listeners throughout the Muslim world and in the remotest corners of Asia. For example, it was avidly read and quoted by the Jadists, an influential group of reformers in the Muslim areas of Soviet Central Asia. It was often cited in the indigenous press in India and in many countries of the Muslim Middle East and North Africa.[10] Within Afghanistan itself its influence was, of course, limited to the intelligentsia and the ruling classes.

Over the years *Siraj-ul-Akhbar* pontificated and advised on all manner of subjects pertinent to Afghan modernization: equality of women, early marriages, polygamy, compulsory education, modern curricula, the existence of germs and the need for cleanliness, the need for railways, the establishment of proper pharmacies, telephones, telegraphs, roads, industrial machinery, and the like. This modernizing fare was liberally sprinkled with "think pieces" on political and religious subjects, prepared by Tarzi and by a number of contributors, who hammered away at the main themes: nationalism, reformed

[9] *Ibid.*, p. 360.

[10] May Schinasi, a French scholar, is preparing a detailed study of the influence of *Siraj-ul-Akhbar* in areas outside Afghanistan. See, for example, her article "Sir Âdj Al-Akhbâr: L'Opinion Afghan et la Russie," *Cahiers du Monde Russe et Soviétique*, XII (1971), 467–479.

Islam, modernization, Pan-Islam, Pan-Asianism, anti-imperialism. Inevitably, because of British world power and the large number of Muslims under British rule, Britain's policies came in for a large share of condemnation. This earned both the *Siraj-ul-Akhbar* and Tarzi personally an unfavorable reputation in British government circles, a reputation which his subsequent career as Amanullah's foreign minister substantially enhanced.[11] So long as Amir Habibullah reigned, he kept a tight rein on Tarzi's advocacy of modernization, his attacks on the orthodox Islamic divines, and his fulminations against the British. Indeed, even before Habibullah's death in 1919 Tarzi had fallen into disfavor and *Siraj-ul-Akhbar* had ceased publication. With Amanullah's ascension to the throne, *Siraj-ul-Akhbar* was succeeded by *Aman-i-Afghan*, a journal edited at first by Abdul Hadi Dawi, one of Tarzi's early collaborators. As a literary product *Aman-i-Afghan* was inferior to *Siraj-ul-Akhbar*. It also reflected much more closely the official government view, serving to a considerable extent as a propaganda organ. It did, however, print much more news, both favorable and unfavorable to the government, right up to the day before Amanullah abdicated and had to flee from Kabul. During most of its life under various editors it maintained a steady anti-British line and was finally banned by the British authorities in India.[12]

Siraj-ul-Akhbar during its years of publication was the voice of the "Young Afghan party." This was not a political party in

[11] Percy Sykes, *A History of Afghanistan*, 2 vols. (London: Macmillan, 1940), II, 264 ff. Sykes points out that the *Siraj-ul-Akhbar* was consistently anti-British, reflecting Tarzi's nationalist and pro-Turkish bias. He also makes the point that this had a powerful influence on Amanullah.

[12] Report by Criminal Investigation Department (CID) on *Aman-i-Afghan*, National Archives of India, New Delhi (hereafter abbreviated NAI), Home and Political Department, Secret Deposit no. 21, July 1916; no. 31, October 1916; and no. 53, November 1916. The effects of *Aman-i-Afghan*'s anti-British tirades will be discussed in more detail in the subsequent chapter on Anglo-Afghan relations.

the modern sense but a group of young nobles and intellectuals who rallied round Tarzi's banner. It included such diverse personalities as Abdul Hadi Dawi and Abdul Ghani, and of course it counted Amanullah, the promising young prince with liberal ideas, as one of its leading lights. At first the Young Afghans operated openly, meeting to discuss their ideas and aspirations. The coming of World War I changed all that. Amir Habibullah's decision to remain neutral (or, as many Afghans claimed, pro-British) drove most of the Young Afghans underground and into the company of their natural enemies the traditionalists, the conservatives, and the religious orthodox leaders. The principal reason for this was Turkey's entrance into the war on the side of the Central Powers with Britain as its principal enemy. As the official seat of the Caliphate, Turkey commanded the loyalty of most Muslim religious leaders who therefore became anti-British for religious reasons, whereas the Young Afghans were anti-British for nationalist reasons. The situation was aggravated by the arrival in Kabul on September 26, 1915, of the joint German-Turkish mission headed by Niedermeyer and Kazim Bey.[13] The activities of this mission, whose goal was to induce Afghanistan to attack India and thus create a major diversion of British strength, polarized the Afghan power structure into two factions. One was the so-called War party which included Young Afghans like Tarzi, Amanullah, Dawi, and Ghani, as well as more conservative anti-British and pro-Turkish elements such as Nasrullah (the Amir's brother), Nadir Khan, and most of the ulema. The faction more favorably inclined to the British, or at least to neutrality, included such men as Kuddus Khan (the Chief Minister), Inayatullah (Amanullah's half-brother) and—secretly, of course—the Amir himself.[14]

[13] For a complete account of the political storms raised in Afghanistan as a result of the activities of the German-Turkish mission, see Ludwig W. Adamec, *Afghanistan, 1900–1923: A Diplomatic History* (Berkeley: University of California Press, 1967).

[14] NAI, Foreign Secretary Notes, no. 245, 1916. Habibullah is reported to have secretly told the British agent in Kabul (an Indian Muslim) to

As the war progressed the friction between the two factions became more and more pronounced. At one point the Young Afghans wrote an unsigned letter to Habibullah urging him to break with Britain and also to institute reforms. To show his displeasure over this kind of pressure the Amir accused Abdul Ghani of plotting against his life and sent him to prison.[15]

A complete break between Habibullah and the Young Afghans occurred in 1918 when an attempt was made on Habibullah's life while he was driving through the Shor Bazaar. The assailant was a student of Habibia College where the Young Afghans had great influence with the developing intelligentsia. Habibia was the first school of higher learning in Afghanistan to offer a secular and foreign-oriented curriculum. Shortly after this incident many of the Young Afghans were jailed or fell into official disfavor. These included Tarzi and, to some extent, Amanullah. Early the following year Habibullah was assassinated and neither the real assassin nor the instigators (if any) were ever publicly revealed. Under these circumstances it was natural that a certain amount of suspicion should fall on the Young Afghans and hence on Amanullah. Other prime suspects as instigators were the Ulya Hazrat (for reasons of harem politics) and Nasrullah (for anti-British reasons). According to one informant interviewed in Kabul in 1968 the assassin was Shuja-ud-Daula, who later rose to high office in the Amanullah government.

Habibullah's premature liquidation did present Amanullah with the opportunity to seize the throne. He had remained in

---

inform the British government that Habibullah would have to make some anti-British pronouncements and gestures in order to pacify religious and pro-Turkish sentiments but that the British should judge not by what he said or did but by the results, which would be the preservation of Afghan neutrality in accordance with British wishes.

[15] Abdul Ghani, *A Review of the Political Situation in Central Asia* (Lahore: n.p., 1921), ch. 3. Ghani remained in prison without trial for several years. He was released when Amanullah came to the throne in 1919 and in 1921 was elevated to the newly formed Legislative Council.

Kabul when Habibullah went on the hunting expedition from which he never returned. Amanullah, in control of the capital, was thus in a key position to assert his claims. In this he was supported by his mother's influence. Tarzi and the Young Afghans were behind him and this included many supporters of the War party whose sympathies and religious sentiments favored Turkey against England. He also had the unanimous support of the fledgling intelligentsia because of his known liberal and "modern" views. Most important, he won the support of the army by promising them a raise in pay and the prospects of war with England in order to achieve complete independence from British tutelage in foreign affairs.[16]

It will be noted that one of the persistent influences in Amanullah's early life was the anti-British sentiments to which he was exposed—first from his mother, later from Tarzi and the Pan-Islamic anticolonial propaganda of the *Siraj-ul-Akhbar*, and finally from his political companions in the War party. Amanullah's anti-British feelings continued to grow and flourish during his entire reign. As we shall note in a later chapter, serious policy differences with Britain and unfortunate personality clashes tended to reinforce the mutual antipathy between the Amanullah regime and the British government, especially the Government of India.

Both sentiment and policy thus impelled Amanullah to try to unite the country which was still reeling from the shock of Habibullah's mysterious death and Amanullah's seizure of the throne. He did so by launching a "holy war" of independence against the British. Britain had sought to protect itself from the threat of Russian intrigues in Afghanistan by a provision in the

---

[16] *Ibid.*, ch. 4. See also Ikbal Ali Shah, *The Tragedy of Amanullah* (London: Alexander Ousley, 1933). The promise to raise the army's pay was confirmed by three informants interviewed in Kabul, 1967 and 1968. They all agreed that Amanullah fulfilled his promise. They disagreed, however, as to whether he later rescinded the raise. It seems that the matter was not clear-cut because of other amenities and reforms regarding terms of service which involved less cash pay. This question is discussed more fully in Chapter V.

1879 Treaty of Gandamak and again by a written commitment from Amir Abdur Rahman in 1880, which gave the British the right to conduct Afghanistan's foreign affairs. Amanullah and most Afghans felt this to be a dishonor to their national independence and sovereignty. The third Anglo-Afghan war, launched by Amanullah in 1919, ended in military stalemate, but at the peace negotiations in Rawalpindi that same year Afghanistan was given the right to control its own foreign affairs. Amanullah thus emerged from the conflict as the champion of Afghan freedom and Afghans look upon this war as their "War of Independence."

Amanullah emerged from the war against the British with enormous prestige, not only as a nationalist fighter who had successfully twisted the British lion's tail, but as one who had done so in the name of jihad or holy war, thus raising the pride of Muslims everywhere. For a time he rode high on this current of Pan-Islamic "nationalism." He enjoyed the support of religious leaders not only in Afghanistan but also in other Islamic countries and was even mentioned as a possible successor to the deposed Turkish caliph.[17] Any aspirations which Amanullah may have had to become a leader of the Pan-Islamic movement collapsed, however, before the rude realities of the Khilafat movement which brought thousands of emigrating Indian Muslims into Afghanistan and left them stranded there, and before the complications in Afghan-Soviet relations which resulted from Amanullah's help to the Basmachi leaders, Ibrahim Beg and Enver Pasha.[18]

---

[17] According to two informants interviewed in Kabul in 1968, feelers were made in 1919 and 1920, through Foreign Minister Tarzi, by religious leaders in several Islamic countries suggesting Amanullah's succession to the caliphate. Amanullah was reported to have been highly pleased but felt the proposal was somewhat premature.

[18] Fletcher, pp. 201 ff. The Khilafat party was started shortly after World War I by Indian Muslims who, offended by British treatment of defeated Turkey which they interpreted as an attempt to destroy the spiritual leadership of the sultan (caliph or khalif) over all Muslims, launched a mass movement to migrate from India to Muslim countries.

Amanullah's anti-British sentiments, fed by early influences and the bitter feelings generated during the Third Afghan War, were considerably reinforced in the course of his reign by continual friction over British policy in the tribal areas under British control and by the poor personal relations between Amanullah and the British envoy to his court, Sir Francis Humphrys, who was in Kabul from 1922 until Amanullah's exile in 1929. The total lack of sympathy between the two men was, without doubt, influential in the progressive alienation between their governments. The reports and recommendations by Sir Francis to his government reflect a consistent and bitter antipathy for Amanullah and his policies. Amanullah and his ministers, on their part, often went out of their way to bait the British and their representative at the court of Kabul.[19]

Another important influence on Amanullah as a modernizer was his travel abroad. Until 1927 Amanullah had never been outside Afghanistan. Then in 1927–28 King Amanullah and Queen Soraya made a highly successful tour of the Middle East, the Continent, England, and Russia. The wonders of the West of the "roaring twenties" made Amanullah more resolved than ever to modernize his country at forced draft. His stay in Turkey with Ataturk and in Persia with Reza Shah convinced him that modern ways could be introduced at a rapid pace.[20] There-

---

Most of them went to Afghanistan. The Afghan government, unable to absorb such a large influx, had to limit their entry and eventually expelled some. The Basmachi revolt grew out of resistance by Muslims to Soviet Bolshevik control of regions in Soviet Central Asia just north of Afghanistan.

[19] The Amanullah-Humphrys "feud" is fully documented in Chapter XI. The serious international repercussions that resulted from this hostility are also recorded there.

[20] Fuller accounts of Amanullah's "Grand Tour" may be found in F. Taillardat, "Le Voyage du Roi Amanullah," *L'Asie Française*, February 1928, and "La fin du voyage du Roi Amanullah," *L'Asie Française*, September–October 1928. There are also good résumés of the trip in Gregorian, pp. 256–258; Fletcher, pp. 213–215; Fraser-Tytler, pp. 207–210.

4. King Amanullah and Queen Soraya during their trip to Europe in 1928.

fore on his return to Afghanistan in 1928 the tempo of his modernization program was accelerated. But later that year the entire edifice collapsed in the wake of a major tribal revolt which cost Amanullah his throne.

Such, then, were some of the varied influences behind the ideas which were later to influence Amanullah's extensive modernization program. But before proceeding to an examination of the reforms themselves we must try to learn something about Amanullah's character. For although this is not an attempt at political biography and although I do not subscribe entirely to the "great man" view of history, it must be admitted that in the special context of the Afghan tribal situation the personality of the leader is often important and sometimes even crucial.

What manner of man was this young king who set about to modernize a tribal society? In spite of the many records and the personal recollections of many who knew him, Amanullah remains something of a mystery. Everyone agrees that he was intelligent, intense, and full of vibrant energy. He undoubtedly had the gift of creativity and passionately believed in change. Ideas for improving his country bubbled out of his head and the line between thought and action seems to have been exceedingly thin.

Writing in 1921, Abdul Ghani describes him as follows:

A young man of nearly thirty, of medium height, handsome, well-built, of fair complexion, dark hair and eyes and strong healthy physique. . . . He is very amiable and polite in manners and never becomes nervous. He has a good deal of humor, is moderate in food and simple in dress. He works very hard—from eight in the morning till midnight he is generally hard at work with only about three hours as intervals for dinner, prayers and a ride or motor drive. He has broad social and political views and always declares in court and in public that he should be considered one of the people. He is proud of being an Afghan and prefers clothes of native manufacture to foreign imported materials. Within the Council he is very democratic and he once said "Supposing your majority voted for adoption of the Bolshevik system of government, I would be the first to offer my services to work even as a Bolshevik for what according to your belief might determine the welfare of Afghanistan." [21]

This rather extreme form of expression was one of Amanullah's traits and was often misunderstood. His penchant for democratic gestures no doubt won him some popularity but probably cost him a good deal of respect among tribal Afghans who were accustomed to be ruled by fear. Bagehot has sagely ob-

[21] Ghani, p. 143.

served that "The mystery should not be removed from royalty." In Afghanistan legitimacy is at best a fragile concept. Most Afghan amirs of the past had been creatures of mystery, aloof, untouchable, to be feared like ogres whose powers are unknown. Amanullah democratized his personality. He was accessible to his people, visible, his weaknesses exposed. He was not feared and he apparently deluded himself into believing that he was loved.

His gestures of personal democracy were many, but they were intermixed with gestures of personal arrogance and displays of arbitrary power. For example, he wore native materials by preference but his Turkish aide, Tewfik Bey, relates how Amanullah would sneak up on his courtiers with large shears and cut up their clothes if they were made from foreign cloth. He personally taught literacy courses in a small mosque and often roamed the bazaars unaccompanied, like Harun-al-Rashid, and some old shopkeepers still remember him with nostalgia. Yet on his royal tour to Europe he insisted on the strictest protocol and on its first leg in Bombay disrupted all the elaborate arrangements made for him, much to the chagrin and resentment of his British hosts, because he disagreed with the seating arrangement at the state banquet. He often insisted that he was no better than any other Afghan citizen and that the government must be one of laws and not of man. Yet Maurice Pernot notes that when Amanullah was shocked by the dirty mud buildings in Kabul he simply ordered the police to tear them down as well as the mud walls surrounding private gardens. At the same time he built beautiful royal gardens in the mountain resort of Paghman and threw them open to the public at large. He once rewarded an outstanding student in a school he was visiting by handing over to him the arrest warrant that had been issued against the boy's father for participating in a revolt against the government.[22]

[22] Lowell Thomas, *Beyond Khyber Pass* (New York: Century, 1925), p. 206; Rosanne Klass, *Land of the High Flags* (New York: Random

It is no wonder that a man capable of such paradoxical idio-
syncrasies produced many conflicting opinions of his character.
In 1924 Lowell Thomas found him

a jovial, vital, aggressive personality. He wore clumsy top-boots
made in his own factory. His native-made Norfolk coat of checked
cloth buttoned up to his throat, a garment as unpretentious as any
in a Bowery bargain emporium. A closely cropped mustache ran the
length of his rather loose mouth. His dark brown eyes protruded
under his heavily arched brows; they were quick, quizzical eyes
with a considerable knowledge of human nature and showed enjoy-
ment of the good things of life. . . . My impression of him is that he
has not been through the fires of hardship like his grandfather
[Abdur Rahman].[23]

It is an interesting reflection on human nature that the assessments of Amanullah's character made while he was still king
tend to be much more favorable than those which followed his
deposition. For example, Pernot wrote after his interview with
Amanullah in 1925:

In those three-quarters of an hour I learned more about the situation
in Afghanistan than during the entire course of my inquiry. In listening to Amanullah speak I have perceived the essential fact. A
sovereign, young, intelligent, encouraged by his first successes, has
resolved to insure the political and economic fortunes of his country. He sees large and wants to go fast. . . . I have visited in Kabul

---

House, 1964), pp. 195, 197; Secret Report by Major E. T. R. Wickham,
July 17, 1929, IOL, LPS/10/1232 P4656/1927 (Major Wickham was special escort for the Amanullah party during the Indian portion of the
royal trip itinerary. He was later detailed to escort Amanullah through
India on the king's way to exile in Europe. Wickham's analysis of
Amanullah's personality reproduced at the end of this chapter was
probably colored by his unpleasant experiences with him on the occasion when Amanullah, as a royal guest of the British government, had
the upper hand); Maurice Pernot, *En Asie Musulmane* (Paris: Hachette,
1927). The last incident was confirmed in a personal interview in Kabul
in 1968 with an informant who had been the student in question.

[23] Thomas, pp. 214–215.

a college, a museum, a large factory, a printing press. In the midst of a vast desert plain I have seen rising an entirely new city. And whenever I asked to whom the Afghan people owed these signs of power or these instruments of progress, the answer was always the same—always they named Amir Amanullah.[24]

Yet just one year after Amanullah's downfall, one of his own kinsmen described him in a confidential briefing to a British officer in India as "rash and headstrong and I should add a fool. He was impervious to reason and remonstrances and dug his own grave." [25]

A somewhat more temperate assessment was made by one of Amanullah's brothers-in-law, writing in 1961:

King Amanullah was a patriotic nationalist. He was a supporter of the freedom movements of the East, which made him very popular among the nationalists of India, the Arab world, and Turkey, but caused at the same time the reaction of the more powerful conservative colonial circles against him. Those circles were looking also with apprehension at Russo-Afghan relations. Amanullah in his early thirties was a sincere man, but emotional, inexperienced in the intricacies of European diplomacy and impatient in his plans to modernize an isolated and armed people, unconsciously subject to foreign provocation and incitements by selfish, ambitious and fanatical elements of the nation. His position became more vulnerable, having around him adventurous men, who were isolating him from his loyal and more experienced servants. His new colleagues were not able to assist the king in drawing up a sound economic plan, promoting the standard of living, and securing the stability of the royal schemes of progress.[26]

[24] Pernot, pp. 37–38.
[25] Sardar Gul Mohammed Khan (formerly Amanullah's envoy in India), "Secret Memorandum of Conversation," IOL, LPS/10/1292, 1929.
[26] Najibullah Khan, "Afghanistan in Historical Perspective," in *Current Problems in Afghanistan* (Princeton: Princeton University Conference, 1961), pp. 1–14. Najibullah was a seasoned professional diplomat at the time he wrote these lines.

But apparently back in 1921 Amanullah's abilities and projects looked far more promising. Joseph Castagne wrote at that time:

Amanullah is an energetic man—very patriotic and thirsty for the liberty of his people. The second son [sic] of Habibullah, he is 30 years of age and endowed with great spiritual force. He is courageous and far-seeing. At this moment he is engaged in the great work of uniting all Muslims.[27]

British confidential reports and official correspondence of the period seem to have been uniformly unfavorable to Amanullah as a man and as a ruler. Of course, as we shall see later, there were sharp policy differences between Afghanistan and Britain, but the opinions expressed often went beyond official friction and were much more *ad hominem*. W. K. Fraser-Tytler, who served in the British legation in Kabul at that period and later became a historian, describes Amanullah as follows:

His Majesty the Amir Amanullah Khan was a difficult and baffling personality. He possessed much of the charm and affability which is characteristic of the descendants of Painda Khan. . . . He was a patriot inspired with devotion to his country, hard-working and zealous to promote her interests and to establish the position of Afghanistan among the free nations of the world. For a man who had never been out of Afghanistan until he embarked on his world tour in December 1927 he was well, if superficially, informed on world affairs.

A key to his character may perhaps be found in his curious stammering, staccato manner of speech and in his lack of chin indicating an abrupt, impulsive, and at the same time a weak character. Weak that is to say in his inability to choose good advisers . . . impulsive in that he was governed not by any reason or understanding of the requirements of his country but by sudden decisions based on imperfect knowledge. . . . To these fatal weaknesses must be added an absurd conceit and arrogance of disposition.[28]

[27] "Notes sur la Politique Extérieure de l'Afghanistan depuis 1919," *Revue du Monde Musulman*, December 1921, 23.
[28] Fraser-Tytler, p. 200–201.

In the privacy of official correspondence British officials were often even less charitable, characterizing Amanullah as rash, unprincipled, and even cowardly. This last charge came from the British view that Amanullah had fled from Kabul when it was under siege by the bandit Bacha-i-Saqao and abdicated the throne in favor of his half-brother Inayatullah. Again in his attempt to recapture Kabul, Amanullah, according to the British, turned and fled the country at the first sign of opposition around Ghazni. Major Fraser refers scathingly to the fact that other Afghan members of Amanullah's party considered Amanullah's behavior cowardly and that even his mother, the fierce old Ulya Hazrat, "if I have correctly interpreted the looks she casts upon him, had little admiration for his courage." This charge of cowardice under fire is a recurring theme in the reports of Sir Francis Humphrys, British minister in Kabul, to his home government. George MacMunn, who is perhaps the only British historian sympathetic to Amanullah, is clearly puzzled by Amanullah's character. He admires Amanullah's dreams of progress but is disappointed by what he regards as lack of force and virile leadership. MacMunn is, of course, a great admirer of Abdur Rahman and he implies that if Amanullah had had the drive and ruthlessness of his grandfather, he could have made Afghanistan into a great country.[29]

On the other hand, there are many apparently authentic accounts by people who knew Amanullah well which indicate that his physical courage was above question. He often walked around the bazaars unprotected and unguarded—a practice which, considering the small number of Afghan amirs who died of old age, was bold to the point of heroism. He circulated with complete nonchalance among wild tribesmen, many of whom

[29] Confidential letter from Major W. A. K. Fraser, cited above; for Humphrys' opinions see, for example, his Secret Telegram No. 71 of Jan. 29, 1929, IOL, LPS/10/53, 1929, Part 3; George MacMunn, *Afghanistan from Darius to Amanullah* (London: G. Bell and Sons, 1929), pp. 283 ff.

he knew were hostile to his ideas, although it is true that here the Pushtunwali code of hospitality probably protected him. Several attempts were made on his life. On one such occasion he was driving at night from Paghman to Kabul, which he often did at high speed, when an assailant shot at him (and missed) from behind some bushes lining the highway. He had no way of knowing whether one man or twenty were attacking him. Nevertheless he stopped the car and gave chase, caught the assailant, and took him to the nearest police post.[30] This was hardly the act of a physical coward.

Amanullah explained his flight from Kabul and from Ghazni in a press statement issued from Bombay on his way to exile in Italy. He stated that he had abdicated and left Kabul because he believed at that moment that the rebellion was aimed personally at him and that his cession of the throne to Inayatullah would bring peace. Similarly he abandoned the enterprise at Ghazni when he was treacherously attacked by the Ghilzai tribes and betrayed by some of his officials.[31] These explanations are plausible and in keeping with Amanullah's known personal courage and his distaste for plunging the country he loved into a bloody civil war. This version of his abdication is also confirmed by an eyewitness to the discussions between Amanullah and Inayatullah at this critical period.[32]

Two other important character traits affected political events: Amanullah's reported arrogance and his susceptibility to flattery. Many observers have commented on his complete self-assurance and his conviction of being right, often in the face of indisputable evidence to the contrary. That this self-confidence at times appeared as cockiness and bravado has been noted even

[30] This incident was related to me in very similar terms by four separate informants during interviews in Kabul, 1967–68.

[31] This press statement has been reproduced in slightly differing versions in Jean Melia, *Visages Royaux d'Orient* (Paris: Bibliothèque Charpentier, 1930), pp. 60–61, and in the secret report dated July 17, 1929, by Major E. T. R. Wickham, cited above.

[32] Interview with informant, Kabul, 1967.

by sympathetic reporters. Thus the only American diplomat to interview him remarked that Amanullah seemed far too sure of himself and quite unaware of the opposition he was arousing even among his close associates.[33] This same trait led Amanullah to lecture Sir Henry Dobbs on the duties and responsibilities of the British Empire toward subject peoples on the occasion of signing the treaty of "friendship" with Great Britain in Kabul in 1921.[34] Amanullah's air of didactic hauteur also helped to sour his crucial conversations with Sir Austen Chamberlain in London during his royal visit to England in 1928.[35] But here again the complexity of the man shines through, for time and time again he showed humility in his willingness, for example, to sit and talk with any man about his problems no matter how poor or simple the suppliant might be. One can only deduce from the evidence that he tended to carry a chip on his shoulder toward anyone he felt was patronizing him or displaying disrespect toward him as a sovereign or toward his country.

There seems to be little doubt that Amanullah was easily flattered. The evidence of observers both friendly and unfriendly points to the fact that at the beginning of his reign Amanullah had around him a number of trusted and seasoned advisers such as Mahmud Tarzi and Nadir Khan and his brothers. Gradually

[33] Conversation in May 1969 with the Hon. Cornelius Van H. Engert who went on an official mission from Tehran to Amanullah's court in 1924. See also Engert's *A Report on Afghanistan*, U.S. Department of State, Division of Publications, Series C. no. 53, Afghanistan, no. 1, 1924.

[34] Reported in *Aman-i-Afghan*, II, no. 23, 1–11, and also in *L'Afghanistan Nouveau*, an undated, illustrated Afghan government booklet which extols Afghan progress under Amanullah. Internal evidence suggests that it was probably published in late 1924 or early 1925. Because of irregularity of publication and calendar changes during Amanullah's reign, references to Aman-i-Afghan are not uniform. In each case the maximum amount of information available has been included.

[35] Confidential Memorandum of Conversation between King Amanullah and the Secretary of State, March 21, 1928, IOL, LPS/10/1203 P135/1927.

5. Mahmud Tarzi, intellectual and ideological mentor of King Amanullah. He became Amanullah's father-in-law and his minister of foreign affairs when Amanullah ascended the throne.

the sycophants gained ascendancy, and in the end flattering "yes men" like Mohammed Wali Khan, Mahmud Sami, and Ghulam Siddiq insulated Amanullah from political realities. This susceptibility to flattery was a complementary trait to his self-assurance. On the other hand only a self-assured ruler would set himself the task of modernizing an entire tribal society. This is the very stuff of which charismatic leaders are compounded. He became convinced he was always right, which made it easy for those who fed his ego to gain ascendancy over him. This, in turn, drove away the advisers he needed, men who understood political realities and would not compromise their integrity. The courtiers were men of inferior talents and by all accounts venal and disloyal into the bargain. With such friends Amanullah hardly needed any enemies to insure his downfall.[36]

One more vital aspect of Amanullah's character must be considered with relation to the modernization program and that was his personal attitude toward religion. Perhaps the most effective piece of propaganda used against him was the accusation that he was a kafir, an unbeliever, and anti-Muslim. To a man who at one time commanded support from the ulema as a possible successor to the Turkish caliph this indictment must have seemed at least ironic, but the charges were widely believed. Amanullah was in fact a pious Muslim. He believed in the substance of his religion but had little regard for its outward forms. He lectured the Egyptians during his trip abroad on what he described as their nonsensical belief that Islam prescribed certain forms of dress. Well armed with historical material he often asserted that such cultural encrustations as the veiling of women had nothing to do with true Islam. Needless to say, these views about Islam led him to undertake many of his reforms and in most cases did not endear him to his more orthodox and conservative coreligionists. He was, nevertheless, according to those who knew him intimately, a deeply religious man.[37]

[36] Louis Dupree, *Afghanistan* (*Princeton: Princeton University Press, 1973*). Dupree perceptively indicates that Amanullah's catering to dishonest sycophants alienated the powerful chiefs on whom Amanullah had to rely in his relations with the tribes.

[37] There was general agreement on this point among informants who knew Amanullah. The only exceptions were one informant who in several ways displayed considerable bias against Amanullah and three others who disclaimed adequate knowledge on this point.

A rather penetrating, though perhaps somewhat biased, description of Amanullah's personality was recorded by Sir Henry Dobbs, who went to Kabul in 1921 to negotiate a treaty between Great Britain and Afghanistan.

His Majesty Amir Amanullah Khan is himself probably the most interesting and complex character in his dominions. His manners are popular, jocular and easy to such a degree that even in his public appearances he sometimes lays himself open to a charge of want of proper dignity. In private he loves to indulge in sheer horseplay, changing hats with his courtiers, throwing bits of bread at them or sprinkling them with soda-water, and making most intimate and daring jokes about their wives, families and personal appearance. He eschews all ceremony except in the most formal durbars, dislikes elaborate uniforms and affects a spartan simplicity in his clothes, usually not even wearing a shirt beneath his rough military jacket. Collars, ties and cuffs, which were *de rigueur* in his father's time, are now forbidden at his Court. The costly trappings and furniture installed by his father in the various palaces and royal houses are however, still maintained, so that except in the matter of clothes his surroundings are very luxurious. When transacting business he is extremely polite and gentle in manner to his Ministers and courtiers and bears himself among them merely as *primus inter pares*, encouraging them to argue with him freely and appearing to trust to his superior agility of mind for the gaining of his ends.

Nevertheless, and despite the studied familiarity of his behaviour, those surrounding him show a flattery almost amounting to servility which seemed to me far more pronounced and deep-seated than what I had observed in the Court of his father. It was evident that all stood in terror of the iron hand within the velvet glove; and the constant shifting of precedence in durbar, the occasional disappearance of prominent personages and the obvious and universal pressure of the spy-system bore witness to the veiled working of a powerful and capricious tyranny. With the common people he is, I believe, decidedly popular. For though they complain a good deal of his close fistedness . . . and of his attempted regimentation of their lives, they admire the energy with which he enquires into their complaints. It is hard to prophesy the developments in the Amir's character. He might end either as a Caligula or as a Trajan. His temperament is highly strung and he suffers cruelly at times from neuralgia. He has a tremendous appetite for work, and, except on the Friday holiday, he is constantly employed from eight o'clock in the morning until midnight, or, allowing for meals, for about fourteen hours a day. A great part of this time he spends in visiting his various Ministries and supervising their work. For the rest of the day he sits in his office giving orders by telephone. On Fridays he usually takes violent exercise, either walking and playing tennis when at the hill capital of Paghman, or riding and shooting when at Kabul. He is a good shot and hard rider and drives his own motorcar with skill and some recklessness. When talking and especially when making speeches, of which he is fond, he gesticulates freely, more like an Italian than an Afghan. This is doubtless one of the indications of his neurotic temperament. In his family relations he is very affectionate. We constantly saw him driving his motor-car alone with his pretty little daughters and several times, when I was alone with him at private conferences, he allowed them to come into his office room and interrupt our talk with their prattle. He has only one wife and no concubines, having pensioned off the only one whom he formerly kept, the mother of his elder son.[38]

Dobbs then goes on at some length to say that the Amir is full of contradictions. He is dedicated to saving money yet spends lavishly on public buildings, parks, fountains, and the like; he has great physical courage but is terrified of germs (there was a cholera epidemic in Kabul while Dobbs was there); he alternates between "moods of patent dissimulation and engaging frankness" (he confessed to Dobbs that he had been anti-British since his boyhood); he seems to invite dissent and different points of view but is very sensitive to contradiction; he expresses views bordering on agnosticism but is scrupulous in his religious observances. In sum, Dobbs found him a complex and somewhat mystifying individual.

Maurice Fouchet, the first French minister to the court of

[38] Secret Report on the Kabul Mission by Sir H. R. C. Dobbs to the Vice-Roy of India, dated January 9, 1922, IOL, LPS/10 809/1919.

Kabul, collaborated closely with Amanullah in founding the considerable French cultural and educational program in the years 1922 to 1924. Fouchet, then, knew Amanullah at the summit of his power and his description of the Amir is something of a panegyric. Writing in 1924 he tells us:

The present Amir, with astonishing political sense for a man of his age, is directing all his efforts towards his audacious goals. . . . The young Afghan king, drsssed in a general's uniform, greeted me in a completely European manner surrounded by his high officials in a palace reserved for solemn occasions. Of good height, he has large black eyes and light complexion. An air of complete authority, tempered by a certain reserve in his eyes imposed by a natural prudence, radiates from this new chief of state. . . . The monarchy has preserved its ancient character by choosing always the best, the strongest, and it is not surprising therefore that Amanullah produces an impression of combined vigor and masterfulness. This impression is augmented by the evidence that he possesses an intuitive and profound political sense capable of handling the most difficult situations in relations with both England and Russia, situations which require complete *sang froid*, courage and self control. . . . His unique will, though not yet ripened by age, has sufficed also to accomplish this marvel [obtaining for Afghanistan recognition of the major European powers] and though the Amir has never left the country of his birth and was not expected to ascend to the throne, his superiority as a man can only be attested to, it cannot be explained. . . . Each day he works long hours in a different ministry and he attends personally to the smallest details of administration. The daily effort of the master is the only bond which unites the various parts of a state as yet unformed and which maintains a vague cohesion between the different departments of government. The normal regime for Afghanistan is anarchy and the genius of Amanullah must somehow impose the rule of his will on the tribes which are the effective masters of most of the country.[39]

[39] This last statement is probably the most perceptive ever made in Afghanistan by a newly arrived envoy. It correctly analyzes the problem as being the lack of national cohesion and pinpoints the tribes and their separatist powers as the principal obstacle to Amanullah's moderni-

Major E. T. R. Wickham had known Amanullah when the major served in the British Legation in Kabul in 1926, a time when Amanullah was still in control of the situation in Afghanistan but cracks in his administration were becoming evident. In 1929, after the revolution, when Amanullah passed through India en route to exile in Italy, Major Wickham was detailed to escort him to Bombay and see him on board ship. Major Wickham, then, knew Amanullah at the start of his period of decline and in his hour of despair and defeat. He paints for us a somber and tragic figure of the King:

The personality of the ex-King has been analysed by others far better qualified to do so than I and I am only concerned with what I saw and heard of him in his hour of trial and subsequent disaster. Though possessed of a courage which enabled him to enter unprotected a vast crowd of wild tribesmen any one of whom might have been bribed to knife him, to undertake long journeys by motor car through inhospitable tracts sometimes with no escort whatever, and to press his preposterous schemes of reform on a people as warlike as they were unwilling to accept them, there is no doubt that as a leader in the field he proved to be completely lacking in the essential qualities of courage and decision. One saw him in India as a pricked windbag, shrinking from the public gaze endeavouring by shameless cadging from the Government of India and by the preparation of perjured affidavits to supplement his savings from the wreck. He was a pathetic figure for with few exceptions, his Sardars turned against him like wolves against a worn out leader and he is sufficiently sensitive to have felt acutely the contrast between his recent sojourn in Bombay, when he had taken advantage of our courtesy to conduct himself with such ill judged arrogance, and his return to that city as a refugee. The hospitality and consideration extended to him by the Government of India on this latter occasion

---

zation efforts. Maurice Fouchet, *Notes sur l'Afghanistan* (Paris: Maisonneuve Frères, 1931), pp. 164 ff. This is my translation from the French. Fouchet died in 1924 on board ship returning to France on leave. His notes were edited and published posthumously by J. Hackin, who was then head of the French archeological mission in Afghanistan.

would seem to have made him realize his own smallness, for one evening when we were alone he suddenly blurted out "the Government of India have put me to shame."

More than one of his Sardars told me that he had been false to everyone, that he was deeply imbued with the idea that diplomacy, whether external or internal, was synonymous with deceit and that he carried his policy of deception and of setting his Sardars one against the other to such lengths that no one could repose the smallest confidence in him. My own impression certainly confirms this opinion.[40]

These assessments are probably not as contradictory as they may at first glance appear. Amanullah was a gifted person with many contradictory facets to his character. He could one moment be the gifted orator swaying thousands with his spellbinding magnetism and the next be the retiring introvert who would spend every free moment in solitary walks and silent prayers.[41] He could be both the brilliant and bold innovator and the bumbling advocate of abrasive change. He could be the humble servant of his people, setting a shining example of democracy and egalitarianism, and at the same time the petty autocrat taking the law into his own hands. He could be the sagacious statesman and the dilettante diplomat, the courageous leader and the frightened refugee. In short, he was a complicated human being who voluntarily assumed the responsibilities of reshaping his country externally and internally simultaneously—a task so enormous under the circumstances and in the light of what we know now about the problems of modernization that we must be chary of making rash over-all judgments of this remarkable man. The usual comparisons with Abdur Rahman miss the point. This was no Ivan the Terrible

[40] Major Wickham's scathing assessment of Amanullah is an appendix to his secret report of July 17, 1929, above.

[41] Various informants interviewed in Kabul during 1967–68 mentioned Amanullah's oratorical powers. His speeches, though flowery and even bombastic to Western ears, had dramatic impact on poetically minded Afghans. These same informants also testified to Amanullah's shy and retiring nature in private life.

attacking a feudal system with fire and sword. This was more a Peter the Great trying to introduce light and reason into a darkened and inward-looking society. Perhaps the enlightenment could not be achieved until the pacification had proceeded further than Abdur Rahman had carried it.

But apparently Amanullah could be neither an overt nor a covert tyrant. What he tried to be unsuccessfully was a "democratic tyrant." He was a democrat by conviction but constantly found himself forced to assume arbitrary powers in order to get anything done. The final judgment of Amanullah's character must be deferred until a definitive biography is produced.[42] In the meantime we can only note that, to a considerable extent, the influences on Amanullah's early life, his anti-British conditioning, and his controversial personal character all had a direct bearing on the content and the ultimate failure of the modernization program which he launched with such high hopes and good intentions.

[42] Rhea Talley Stewart, *Fire in Afghanistan 1914–1929* (New York: Doubleday, 1973). This recent book only partially fills the need for a definitive biography. Although journalistic and anecdotal in nature, it does provide a number of interesting biographical details on Amanullah.

chapter III

the amanullah reforms:
stages and social dimensions

Amanullah launched his modernization program at a time
when international factors and domestic conditions were both
favorable and unfavorable to his plans. Both external and internal situations deteriorated and adversely affected his programs as
they unfolded. In 1919, following World War I, many ideas of
change were circulating in the Muslim world. Amanullah's
personal prestige was very high with his own people as a result
of his diplomatic victory in the aftermath of the Third Afghan
War. Amanullah's popularity, however, proved to be fragile
and evanescent. His philosophy of government was to rely on
the political affection and loyalty of his subjects rather than on
force to achieve his ends. The political loyalty that he undoubtedly commanded at the commencement of his reign was based
on his reputation as an anti-British nationalist and his strong
Pan-Islamic leanings. But after he achieved independence,
when he was faced with the responsibilities of power, his need
to maintain at least nominally friendly relations with both his
powerful neighbors, Britain and the USSR, forced him to assume a milder tone on both nationalistic and Pan-Islamic problems. For example, Britain, having at last made its peace with
Turkey, and having to some extent recovered from the ravages
of World War I and the attacks of Indian nationalists, launched
a "modified forward policy" into the Pushtun tribal areas on its
side of the Durand Line.[1] Amanullah's hands were to a large ex-

[1] Fraser-Tytler, p. 203.

tent tied by the treaty he had signed with Britain in 1921 and he could only give vent to his frustration by resorting to clumsy intrigues in the tribal areas, which caused his credit as a nationalist to evaporate. Similarly his efforts in Central Asia to help Enver Pasha and the cause of his Islamic brethren there came to naught when Soviet forces overwhelmed the Basmachi Muslim nationalists.[2]

Externally the first few years of Amanullah's reign saw some remarkable changes in the position and power of the countries whose influence on Afghanistan had to be taken into account. Russia, which at the beginning of Amanullah's reign seemed about to disintegrate as a result of the White counterrevolution supported by her erstwhile allies and the revolt of the Muslims of Central Asia, had nevertheless managed to survive, maintain her territorial integrity, and begin the long uphill struggle which was to make her eventually into a superpower. The Turks, who had been reeling under the attacks of the Greeks supported by the Allies, had in the end succeeded in driving them out of Asia Minor and had founded in 1923 the Turkish Republic under Ataturk. The following year the Turks abolished the Caliphate. This undermined the position of the Indian Muslims and their Khilafat party. It also strengthened British power in India and incidentally shattered Amanullah's Pan-Islamic aspirations. Britain's position in India had been further strengthened by the failure of the Non-Cooperation Movement and her prestige as a paramount power had been restored in Mesopotamia and to a large extent in Persia. Although at first Amanullah had staged a diplomatic coup by obtaining recognition for Afghanistan from the principal powers of Europe, his prestige as a statesman in foreign affairs suffered a severe setback when a Soviet-inspired revolt in Bokhara resulted in the deposition of the amir and the eventual incorporation of Bokhara into the Soviet Union. Amanullah attempted to recoup this setback by

[2] A fuller account of events in Soviet Central Asia which affected Amanullah's position is given in Chapter X.

sending General Nadir Khan to the north to help the Muslim Basmachi revolt then led by Enver Pasha, but Soviet military successes and the death of Enver ended his dream of playing a leading role in the affairs of Muslim Central Asia.[3] As Amanullah's extensive reform programs unfolded, he found himself progressively facing growing pressures from both the Soviets and the British, pressures which constrained his role as an Islamic and Asian nationalist leader and which thereby reduced the fund of political credit at home he so badly needed to support the modernization efforts.

His internal political problems were more acute though less obvious. Chapter I alludes to the divisive and fractious quality of the tribal society with which he had to deal. At this point in Afghan history this tribal society had, to some extent, recovered from the centralizing and pacifying restrictions imposed by the Amir Abdur Rahman. It was now ready to resume its more normal state, that of a confederation of highly autonomous tribal units which more closely resembled the small domains, baronies, counties, and duchies of Europe during the period of Henry II and Eleanor of Aquitaine than the organization of a modern nation-state. And as in the days of the Plantagenets, Afghanistan in the second decade of the twentieth century was crisscrossed with complicated patterns of intrigue and political maneuver.

Such, then, was the political climate in which Amanullah launched one of the most far-reaching and daring modernization programs ever to be attempted in Asia. It is important to note, however, that this program consisted of three successive stages. This fact has been overlooked by many critics of the Amanullah reforms. Unless the stage in which a particular program occurred is identified and understood, the program is taken out of context and its purposes are easily misunderstood. This has been especially true of last-stage programs, most of which were proj-

---

[3] Sykes, Vol. II, ch. 54. See also Said Alim Khan, *La Voix de la Boukharie Oprimée* (Paris: Maisonneuve Frères, 1929), and Joseph Castagne, *Les Basmatchis* (Paris: E. Leroux, 1925).

ects on paper or hopes for the future, but have often been reported as though they happened in fact. Some writers have even
ascribed Amanullah's deposition to projects of this kind which
were never even put into operation.[4]

Although there was considerable overlap, Amanullah's reforms can be divided into three successive stages. The first,
roughly covering the period from 1919 to 1923, was characterized by its emphasis on the formulation of a legal, judicial, and
administrative framework of government. The revolt of the
Mangal tribes in Khost in 1923-24 created a transition period
between Stage I and Stage II. In this second stage few new reforms were undertaken. Earlier reforms were continued but at a
greatly decelerated pace. Stage III commenced after Amanullah's return from his European trip in July 1928. What he had
seen abroad brought him home more ashamed than ever of the
backwardness of Afghanistan and he resolved to move the modernization program forward at a revolutionary pace. This stage
lasted, of course, only a little over six months because by January 1929 Amanullah had been forced to abdicate and leave
Kabul.

Most of the reforms of this third period, therefore, never got
beyond the proposal stage. The new program was outlined by
Amanullah to a Loya Jirgah, or Great Tribal Assembly, convoked specially in August 1928 and was repeated in more detail
in a series of lectures delivered by Amanullah over a four-day
period in October of that year.[5] Less than three months later he

---

[4] Into this category should go such works as Ikbal Ali Shah's and Roland Wild, *Amanullah, Ex-King of Afghanistan* (London: Hurst and
Blackett, 1932).

[5] Secret Telegram from the British Minister in Kabul to the Secretary
of State for Foreign Affairs in London, no. 123, September 3, 1928; Secret Despatch from the British Minister in Kabul to the Secretary of
State for Foreign Affairs, London, no. 107, October 31, 1928; Appendix
to the Intelligence Bureau Diary, North West Frontier Province, no. 21
for the period ending October 19, 1928. All three documents are in IOL,
LPS/285 for 1929.

was deposed. Clearly not much could have happened during this last stage. Yet most of the misrepresentations, propaganda, tales, myths, and legends about the reforms refer to items proposed in this last stage and almost entirely ignore the much more solid work already accomplished in the earlier stages.

The following list of Amanullah's reforms will serve the triple purpose of demonstrating the broad and comprehensive scope of the modernization program, of providing a brief explanation of the nature and purpose of the program, and of identifying the stage during which each reform was introduced.[6]

COMPREHENSIVE CLASSIFICATION OF AMANULLAH'S REFORMS

I. Social Reforms

A. Reforms principally concerned with customs and mores

1. Western dress was required at court functions, in the areas around the summer capital at Paghman, and in certain parts of Kabul. This was a third-stage reform and only partially implemented. So also was the prohibition against wearing the *kulah* (cap or turban) and the *karakuli* (Persian lamb or karakul hat). (LAST STAGE)

2. Wearing of the veil by women was officially discouraged as early as the first stage. It was never prohibited by law. Government officials were under pressure to unveil their women, or at least have them wear the modified Syrian yashmak rather than the complete face and body covering of the *chadri* or *burqa*. The movement to unveil was pushed hard only in 1928. (LAST STAGE)

3. Purdah, the seclusion of women, was also officially discouraged but never prohibited by law or decree.[7] (LAST STAGE)

---

[6] This list was compiled from a wide range of sources including personal interviews, documents, newspapers, and books. The taxonomy (social, political, and so on) is only for purposes of convenience and method.

[7] Purdah and the veil are often confused. Purdah (literally, "a curtain") is a customary institution whereby women are segregated from males who are not close relatives. "The veil" is the practice of covering women's faces or even their entire bodies when in public or in the presence of males who are not close relatives. Though the two practices

4. Women's rights were granted as early in the first stage as 1922 when one of the codes (Nizamnamah) gave women freedom of choice in marriage. During the middle stage women were encouraged to organize a woman's association. (ALL STAGES)

5. Polygamy was never officially prohibited. The campaign against it was proposed in 1928. (LAST STAGE)

6. Slavery was abolished in 1921 by decree and by the 1923 Constitution. (FIRST STAGE)

7. Begir (forced labor or *corvée*) was abolished in 1922. (FIRST STAGE)

8. Extravagant expenses for weddings, funerals, and other ceremonies were regulated by law in 1922–23. (FIRST STAGE)

9. Regulation of student life was proposed in 1928. Students were not to marry, were to wear uniforms, and were to salute each other in whatever foreign language their school taught. (LAST STAGE)

10. Minimum age for marriage was proposed by Amanullah in 1928 (twenty-two for boys and eighteen for girls) but was rejected by the Loya Jirgah. (LAST STAGE)

11. Social welfare projects that were put into effect or proposed:

   a. A few orphans' homes were in operation. (FIRST STAGE)

   b. Two general hospitals were in operation by the mid-1920's. A large expansion was proposed in 1929. (MIDDLE AND LAST STAGES)

   c. One maternity hospital was in operation in the mid-1920's. (MIDDLE STAGE)

   d. The Red Crescent Society was organized in 1928 and Afghanistan joined the International Society in the same year. (LAST STAGE)

   e. Midwife training was proposed in 1928. (LAST STAGE)

   f. Mobile hospitals were proposed in 1928. (LAST STAGE)

   g. A pure water supply for Kabul was provided from Paghman. (LAST STAGE)

---

often go together it is quite possible to have purdah without the veil, or the veil without purdah. Amanullah actively campaigned against veiling but declared that purdah should be a matter of personal and family choice. See, for example, the article in *Aman-i-Afghan*, October 10, 1928, where the voluntary aspects of purdah are explained.

B. Reforms principally concerned with education

1. Secular curricula were introduced in 1920 by Indian educators and strengthened by French educators after 1923. (ALL STAGES)

2. Vocational training was proposed in 1928. (LAST STAGE)

3. Compulsory primary education was first proposed in 1924 and a stronger commitment to this goal was announced in 1928. (MIDDLE AND LAST STAGES)

4. Coeducation for students aged 6 to 11 was proposed in 1928. (LAST STAGE)

5. A medical school was proposed in 1928. (LAST STAGE)

6. A home economics school for women (Maktab-i-Razia) was proposed in 1928. (LAST STAGE)

7. A Turkish school to supplement the English-, German-, and French-language "colleges" was proposed in 1928. (LAST STAGE)

8. Adult classes, principally in literacy but also in civic and religious subjects, were introduced in 1920. Amanullah himself taught some at one time. Some compulsory attendance was required of government servants. The program continued during all of Amanullah's reign. (ALL STAGES)

9. Schools for clerks and accountants (Maktab-i-Usul-i-Daftari) were in operation by the mid-1920's. (MIDDLE STAGE)

10. In 1928 Roman lettering and Arabic numerals were required in doctors' prescriptions and Arabic numerals were to be used in all government accounts, but this change was just under way when the revolution came. (LAST STAGE)

11. A school for governors was part of the early effort to reorganize provincial administration. Students included not only prospective governors but also lower-ranking administrators. (MIDDLE STAGE)

12. Foreign-language schools where the medium of instruction was French (Amaniyah, later called Istqlal), German (Nejat), and a school staffed by British Indians (Ghazi) were established in the mid- and late 1920's. (MIDDLE AND LAST STAGES)

13. A teachers' college (Dar-ul-Mo'lamein) was established in 1927. (MIDDLE STAGE)

14. Itinerant teachers were recruited in the mid-1920's to accompany the nomads. This was a small, experimental program. (MIDDLE STAGE)

15. The Pushtun Academy (Pushtun Tolana) was founded in the mid-1920's. (MIDDLE STAGE)

16. The Police Academy was founded in 1924. (MIDDLE STAGE)

17. Provincial colleges (high schools) similar to Amaniyah and Nejat were proposed in 1928. (LAST STAGE)

18. Girls' education was stressed during the entire period. Two girls' schools were sponsored in Kabul by Queen Soraya and her mother. In 1928 it was proposed to expand this program in Kabul and extend it to the provinces. In addition 28 girls were sent to Turkey in 1928 for secondary studies. (ALL STAGES)

19. Education abroad was provided in 1923 when a group of boys from leading families were sent to France. In 1928 it was proposed to send a large number of boys to work in European factories as apprentices and some boys to Persia to learn carpet-weaving. (FIRST AND LAST STAGES)

C. Reforms principally concerned with cultural matters

1. An art school to teach drawing, music, sculpture, and carpet-weaving was proposed in 1928. (LAST STAGE)

2. Films and plays were introduced into Afghanistan in the late 1920's. An opera house was constructed in Paghman in this same period. (LAST STAGE)

3. The press saw considerable expansion during the entire period of Amanullah's reign. In addition to the semiofficial *Aman-i-Afghan*, a number of small journals appeared, many of them house organs of government ministries or departments, such as *Haqiqat* published by the Ministry of War. Several newspapers were also published in the provinces. (ALL STAGES)

4. Calendar reform was introduced in 1922 with the adoption of the *shamsi* (solar) calendar. (FIRST STAGE)

5. Archeology received a strong impetus with the signing in 1923 of an agreement with France establishing the Delegation Archeologique Française en Afghanistan (DAFA). This was the beginning of serious and continuous archeological research in Afghanistan. (FIRST STAGE)

6. The establishment of a museum was incident to the archeological agreement with France. (FIRST STAGE)

7. The proposal to establish public libraries was made in 1928. Funds were to be raised by an assessment of 5 rupees from each student. This program, too, was a victim of the revolution. (LAST STAGE)

II. Political Reforms

A. General governmental reforms

1. Afghanistan's first constitution was promulgated in 1923. (FIRST STAGE)

2. The basic organization of the state was defined in a special law in 1923. (FIRST STAGE)

3. A reorganization of the central government setting up ministries (at first called "commissariats" in imitation of the USSR) was undertaken in 1919 soon after Amanullah took power. (FIRST STAGE)

4. A reorganization of provincial and local administration was undertaken in 1923 and regulated by a special law. (FIRST STAGE)

5. Civil rights were granted to all Afghan nationals, first by decree in 1920 and later in the 1923 Constitution. (FIRST STAGE)

6. An organized political party was proposed in 1928, to be called the Party of Independence and Reform. It never came into being. (LAST STAGE)

7. A national identification system was established by law requiring universal registration and issuance of identity cards. (FIRST STAGE)

B. Legislative reforms

1. A Legislative Council (Mahfal-i-Qanun) was established in 1919. (FIRST STAGE)

2. State and provincial councils, partly appointive and partly elective, were provided for in the 1923 Constitution. (FIRST STAGE)

3. A High Assembly (a kind of Loya Jirgah) was to meet once each year to review government operations. This was provided in the 1923 Constitution. (FIRST STAGE)

4. The State Council undertook an extensive legislative program incorporated into special codes (Nizamnamah). The original drafts were prepared in the ministries with the help of legal experts

(mostly Turkish) and submitted to the King and State Council for approval and promulgation. This program went on from 1921 to 1926. (FIRST AND MIDDLE STAGES)

5. A bicameral legislature was proposed in 1928. The lower house was to be fully elective by general suffrage. The upper house was to be partly elective and partly appointive. (LAST STAGE)

C. Judicial reforms

1. A separate and independent judiciary was established for the first time in Afghanistan under Article 50 of the 1923 Constitution. (FIRST STAGE)

2. A system of courts ranging from trial courts to appellate tribunals was organized under a General Law on Courts (Nizamnamah-ye-Mohakam) in 1923. (FIRST STAGE)

3. Secular codes for penal, civil, and commercial cases were legislated for enforcement by the courts as provided in Article 24 of the 1923 Constitution. (FIRST STAGE)

4. Shari'a was preserved as the basis for the secular codes and as residuary doctrine where the codes were silent. The influence of Shari'a was more prominent after the Khost revolt in 1924. (MIDDLE STAGE)

5. Blood money awarded by the courts in criminal cases was to be prohibited according to a proposal made in 1928. (LAST STAGE)

D. Executive reforms

1. Foreign relations were established with a number of European and Asian nations for the first time and a concerted effort to develop political and commercial ties with a broad spectrum of countries was undertaken. This was a radical departure from previous Afghan policy. (ALL STAGES)

2. Anticorruption campaigns were initiated by Amanullah and at times pushed very vigorously, particularly when he first came to power and toward the end of his reign. (FIRST AND LAST STAGES)

3. Abolition of stipends, subsidies, and privileges for tribal chiefs, courtiers, hangers-on, and distant members of the royal family was put into effect early in Amanullah's reign. (FIRST STAGE)

4. Abolition of titles, special ranks, and strict protocol was pro-

posed by Amanullah in 1928. In 1923 decorations and other honors had been strictly limited. (FIRST AND LAST STAGES)

5. Pensions for civil servants were instituted by law in 1923. Previously they were granted as favors by the amir. A more elaborate retirement and pension scheme, calling for contributions by the employees, was proposed in 1928. (FIRST AND LAST STAGES)

6. The national flag was changed in 1928 with symbolism intended to reflect nationalist and Islamic ideals. (LAST STAGE)

E. Military reforms

1. The draft system was changed after the 1924 Khost rebellion from one of local selection (*hasht nafari*) to a universal lottery system (*pishk*). In 1928 it was proposed to extend the period of service from two to three years. (MIDDLE AND LAST STAGES)

2. Reduction in size and pay of the army commenced in 1920 and continued until 1928. Fringe benefits, however, were substituted for cash and an extensive training program was initiated in 1922. (ALL STAGES)

3. The Military Academy was reorganized and strengthened with foreign (mostly Turkish) instructors in 1921. (FIRST STAGE)

4. A model battalions program was started under Turkish instructors in 1922. (FIRST STAGE)

5. Disbanding of veteran units and replacing them with younger recruits started in 1921. The older units drew pay at the rate of 20 rupees per month, the younger units drew only 14 rupees and later this was reduced to 5 rupees per month. (ALL STAGES)

6. The Afghan Air Force was first organized in 1921 with Russian planes and pilots. Afghan officers were trained first in Russia and later in France, Italy, and Turkey. (ALL STAGES)

7. Afghan cadet training abroad was started in 1928. Amanullah had obtained agreement from Britain to a proposal to send Afghan cadets to Sandhurst and others went to France, Italy, and Turkey. (LAST STAGE)

8. A school for noncommissioned officers was proposed in 1928. (LAST STAGE)

9. A military club was proposed in 1928. (LAST STAGE)

III. Religious Reforms [8]

1. Allowances and subsidies for mullahs were reduced and in some cases abolished. (LAST STAGE)

2. *Muhtasibs* were abolished. These were religious enforcers and in many cases informers who made certain all religious observances were strictly complied with. (FIRST STAGE)

3. Schools for mullahs were established. (MIDDLE STAGE)

4. Educational standards for mullahs as a prerequisite for officiating as religious teachers were proposed in 1928. (LAST STAGE)

5. Secular codes of law, both penal and civil, in effect relegated Shari'a to a secondary place. (See Legislative Reforms, above.) (FIRST STAGE)

6. Graduates of the Deoband School of Islamic Theology in India were disqualified from acting as religious leaders in 1928. (LAST STAGE)

7. A school for qazis (religious judges) was proposed in 1928 with the proviso that only graduates would be appointed as judges. (LAST STAGE)

8. A secular school of law was proposed in 1928 and its graduates were eventually to replace religious qazis as judges. (LAST STAGE)

9. The day of rest was changed from Friday to Thursday. Friday was to remain the day of prayer. (LAST STAGE)

10. The pir and murid system in the army was abolished in 1928. Soldiers and officers often became disciples (murids) of certain holy men (pirs) and were under the influence of such religious leaders. (LAST STAGE)

11. Income from some Waqfs which had not been taken over by Amir Abdur Rahman were nationalized around 1920. (FIRST STAGE)

[8] It should be noted that this classification is of necessity somewhat arbitrary and artificial since in a traditional Islamic society such as that of Afghanistan, practically all the reforms had religious overtones and implications. Thus, secularization of education, changes in the marriage customs, or even the introduction of the telegraph could be considered by certain extreme traditionalists to be as much a danger to the religious way of life as the effort to regulate the education of mullahs or limit their activities in more direct ways.

IV. Economic Reforms

1. The entire tax structure was reorganized and rationalized in the early 1920's. (FIRST STAGE)

2. Collection of taxes was enforced and cash was substituted for kind in 1920. (FIRST STAGE)

3. Whimsical and arbitrary taxes were prohibited (e.g., the tax on shopkeepers to buy "oil for the Queen's hair"). (FIRST STAGE)

4. A new customs tariff was published to encourage imports and exports. Internal customs duties were abolished to simplify and stimulate domestic commerce. (FIRST STAGE)

5. Antismuggling and anticorruption campaigns in customs matters were initiated in 1920 and pressed during Amanullah's entire reign. (ALL STAGES)

6. Some special taxes were levied for specific purposes such as to pay for arms purchases (one month's pay from all officials) and to establish libraries (5 rupees from each student). (LAST STAGE)

7. A livestock census was started for tax purposes. (FIRST STAGE)

8. Cadastral surveys for assessment of land taxes were started. (FIRST STAGE)

9. Afghanistan's first government budget was instituted in 1922. (FIRST STAGE)

10. Government accounting systems were modernized starting in 1923. A double-entry system was required and later Western-type numerals had to be used. (FIRST AND MIDDLE STAGES)

11. The *Baqiyat* system was abolished. Under this system a government employee could be liable all of his life for old accounts and his family would inherit the liability. After 1923 all old accounts were closed. (FIRST STAGE)

12. The metric system of weights and measures was introduced in the mid-1920's but did not take hold. (MIDDLE STAGE)

13. A new unit of currency, the afghani, was introduced around 1923. (FIRST STAGE)

14. A National Bank and a Chamber of Commerce were proposed in 1928. (LAST STAGE)

15. Extensive communications projects were undertaken during the entire course of Amanullah's reign. New roads were opened, old ones improved; telephone and telegraph service was expanded;

postal facilities were improved and Afghanistan joined the International Postal Union; bridges were built and Afghanistan's first civil aviation program inaugurated. In 1928 a Franco-German firm began a survey to build railroads in Afghanistan. (ALL STAGES)

16. Large construction programs were launched. Two new capitals (in Dar-ul-Aman and Paghman) were built; public buildings were constructed; old palaces were refurbished; parks, fountains, royal gardens, markets, playgrounds, colleges, hotels, water systems, and even new jails were built. (ALL STAGES)

17. A broad small-industries program was proposed. A law to encourage investment was passed as early as 1923. In 1928 Amanullah purchased a number of small factories in Europe. The emphasis in this program was on small import-substitution industries such as textiles, matches, soap, hydroelectricity and the like. (FIRST AND LAST STAGES)

18. Extensive mineral development was proposed in 1928. Lapiz lazuli was to be exploited by a German firm; Krupp was to do an iron survey; development of coal and marble was started; oil exploration was to be done by Russia, and Afghan students were to be trained at the Baku fields. (LAST STAGE)

19. Commerce was actively encouraged. Commercial laws issued in 1922–23 gave merchants some protection. The first *shirkats* or joint-stock companies were started in Herat in the mid-1920's. Firms dealing in exports, transport, and medicines, among others, began to function profitably in the same period. (FIRST AND MIDDLE STAGES)

20. Agricultural development was undertaken. The King often attended agricultural fairs dressed in *deshi* (peasant) clothes. A large reforestation program was commenced. Public lands were sold cheap at 10 afghanis per *jerib* (about half an acre), creating a new class of peasant proprietors. The first Ministry of Agriculture was created as well as the first school of agriculture. (MIDDLE AND LAST STAGES)

The vast changes made or contemplated by these reforms certainly amounted to a major program of modernization. Indeed the avowed aim of this program, as proclaimed by Amanullah himself, was to alter completely the structure and nature of Afghan society. Amanullah described himself as a "revolutionary" and he seemed to be entirely conscious of the fact that he was engaged not in a simple program to "reform," that is, to ameliorate certain conditions, but rather to revolutionize the traditional character of Afghan life and transform the country into an entirely new kind of entity.[9]

We should not, however, accept the modernization program at face value on the basis of a mere comprehensive listing of the types of changes Amanullah sought to bring about. This would be falling into the same error of most writings about this period which take it for granted that all these projects were actually put into effect. From such a premise it is quite easy to conclude that such an indigestible mass of change would necessarily cause a social regurgitation in the form of national revolt. But, as shown in the listing, a large part of these reforms were merely proposals put forth when Amanullah returned from Europe a few months before he was deposed. In this sense a substantial part of his modernization program assumes more the aspect of a planning exercise than of an operational program rammed down the throats of a reluctant people. Moreover, a good many of the reforms that were put into effect were actually quite limited in scope and were based on rational objectives, although these might not be immediately evident. There is also clearly reflected here a breakdown in communication between the reformer and the reformed, about which I shall have further observations later.

Nowhere was this breakdown in communication better illustrated than in the misinterpretations and misconceptions created

---

[9] Fraser-Tytler, p. 213, states: "In the month of October [1928] he [Amanullah] delivered to a representative gathering of Afghans in Kabul a series of lectures covering in detail the various measures he proposed to adopt. *He boldly pronounced himself to be a revolutionary* and asked his countrymen to follow him in a programme which, if carried into effect, *would have entirely altered every aspect of Afghan social and official life*" (my italics).

by the so-called social reforms. The requirements for Western dress, for example, were applied only in certain areas and were intended, among other things, to lower the visibility of the self-conscious differences between ethnic and religious groups, particularly in the capital. It was the custom for Hindus, Sikhs, and Jews to wear distinctive clothing or headdress and of course the various ethnic tribal groups had their "national" costumes. If all could be got into a uniform Western costume the divisive elements in the Afghan population could be minimized and made less visible. This would, in Amanullah's view, be an important step in nation-building. The measure may have been an ill-advised one; certainly it was subject to misinterpretation by the people and to ridicule by poorly informed critics who did not investigate the reasons behind the measure.[10]

There were also economic reasons for some of the measures. The prohibition against wearing the *karakuli* (fur caps) and the *kulah* (turban caps) was based on the fact that the export of karakul (erroneously called Persian lamb) pelts had become an important earner of foreign exchange, and the turbans required several yards of imported cloth. Amanullah sought to increase exports and reduce imports by forbidding domestic consumption.[11]

In spite of Amanullah's good intentions regarding dress reforms, he does seem to have gone to unnecessary extremes. We must recall his dressing down of the Egyptians during his royal tour about their slavishly religious attitude toward clothing and

[10] I am indebted for these explanations of the dress reforms to several informants who were close to Amanullah. One of them pointed out that in urging the adoption of Western dress, Amanullah felt it impolitic to announce his real purposes since this would have fired the religious and tribal pride and particularism which he sought to abolish. His silence about the true rationale for this reform made it appear whimsical and even nonsensical to many. Interviews in Kabul, 1967–68.

[11] Interviews with three informants who were experts on the economic problems of the Amanullah era, Kabul, 1968.

headwear.[12] Tewfik Bey's description of Amanullah's going about with a pair of large shears and cutting up his courtiers' clothes if they violated his precepts is perhaps an amusing illustration of the King's sense of humor, but this practice surely did not add to his dignity. Moreover, the dress regulations were an extra expense for some citizens and cause of discomfort and embarrassment to many. One of my informants recalled that his mother and her circle of older women refused to wear the required Western dress and therefore had to give up the pleasure of walks in certain parks and attendance at certain public functions.[13]

Probably no single social reform was so misinterpreted and misreported as Amanullah's attempt to liberate women from some of the onerous customs which, in his view, had become encrusted onto the Muslim way of life. Contrary to most published reports, unveiling of women and emergence from purdah were not legal requirements, but this important fact was lost in the political propaganda that accompanied the rebellion against Amanullah.[14] Amanullah played into the hands of his enemies by his insistence on publicly campaigning against the veil. Sir Francis Humphrys, the British minister in Kabul, reported to his

[12] Melia, pp. 14, 15, quotes the following extract from Amanullah's speech in Egypt: "I am amazed to see the Egyptian people insisting on the wearing of the fez and believing that it is required by religion. Wearing this headdress is encouraged by despots so that Muslims should think they are Muslims just because they wear a fez even if they conserve nothing of Islam.

"We have also our national costume but we abolished it because it has no religious character. Islam teaches liberty, equity, practicing Koranic principles and traditions, respect for the prophet; it recommends all that can raise up and strengthen the nation. Religion imposes virtues and patriotism. The Muslim is free, after all that, to choose whatever dress he pleases." [My translation from the French.]

[13] Interview with informant, Kabul, 1968.

[14] Andrée Viollis, *Tourmente sur l'Afghanistan* (Paris: Librairie Valois, 1930). See also the report of Amanullah's speech in the *Aman-i-Afghan*, October 10, 1928, where it is made quite clear that the unveiling and emergence from purdah are to be purely voluntary acts.

6. Queen Soraya, about 1928.

government on Amanullah's famous four-day speech in October
1928:

It is significant that though the King's most passionate appeal was
directed towards the emancipation of women, none of the Ministers
outside the Royal family have yet permitted their wives to follow
the Queen's example in discarding the veil, while the acting Minister
of War has flatly refused to observe the new rule which requires
Government officials to abjure polygamy.

Humphrys then reports Amanullah to have stated:

"Religion does not require women to veil their hands, feet and faces
or enjoin any special type of veil (At this point the Queen who
since her return from Europe had worn a light transparent veil, tore

off her veil amidst applause and other women followed her example). Women should now discard the old *burqa* and either go unveiled or wear modest garments and a light veil. Outside Kabul, the decision of the whole matter must rest with the individual. But tribal custom must not impose itself on the free will of the individual." [15]

Delia and Ferdinand Kuhn have compared the more recent and more successful effort in 1959 by Prime Minister Daud to unveil the women and put an end to purdah with Amanullah's unsuccessful attempt; they point out that whereas Amanullah sought the full glare of publicity for his campaign, thereby flinging a challenge at his conservative enemies, Daud's reform was implemented with no publicity, no official announcement, but quietly: letting it be known by word of mouth that any woman who went abroad modestly dressed but unveiled would be protected by the full power of the government. [16] The Kuhns also note, on the basis of quoted interviews, that the urban population readily accepted Amanullah's arguments to unveil and abandon purdah even though the force of custom was such that few women actually cast off the garment or the institution. This was also the opinion of the informants I interviewed. [17]

Those who wanted to make political capital out of the deep-seated feelings of a tribal society about the proper position of women found the subject of unveiling and abandonment of purdah a ready-made issue. By propagating the false notion that unveiling and the end of seclusion of women was compulsory they made it appear an invasion into the rights, privacy, and chastity of the family and a violation of the modesty of women, which is highly valued in the Pushtunwali. Moreover, unveiling, polygamy, and purdah were connected, for purposes of political pro-

[15] Secret Despatch from the British Minister in Kabul to the Secretary of State for Foreign Affairs, London, cited in note 5, above.

[16] Delia and Ferdinand Kuhn, *Borderlands* (New York: Knopf, 1962), p. 268.

[17] Interview with informants, Kabul, 1967.

paganda, with religious beliefs which, whether doctrinally correct or not, were widely accepted in Afghan tribal society. These questions were also tied in the propaganda to the larger question of women's rights in general. As early as 1923 legislation assured Afghan women certain hitherto denied rights, such as the freedom to marry a man of their choice.[18] This legislation had already been used effectively as propaganda by mullahs in southern Afghanistan who during the 1924 Khost rebellion went about the tribal areas brandishing in one hand the Qur'an and in the other the Nizamnamah, inviting true Muslims to choose between them.[19]

Quite apart from the meagre legislation which he was able to pass on freedom for women, it is clear that during his entire reign Amanullah, aided and abetted by Queen Soraya, her mother, and various other members of the royal family and of the Young Afghan party, conducted an insistent campaign for the "liberation" of women. The formation of the Women's Protective Association (Anjuman-i-Himayat-i-Niswan) headed by Qubra Jan, one of Amanullah's sisters, in the mid-1920's was followed by publicity encouraging women to protest to the society against any injustices suffered at the hands of their husbands or other males.[20] The persistent drive to improve the education of girls, the dispatch of girls to Turkey for secondary education, and the proposal for coeducation in the primary grades all lent themselves to political propaganda which, though it often misrepresented and distorted the facts, quite correctly assessed the threat to the tribal society's insistence on keeping women in an idealized though essentially inferior status.[21] Given

[18] Nizamnamah-ye-'Arusi, Nikah wa Khatnasuri [Law Concerning Engagements, Marriages, and Circumcision], 20 Aqrab 1302 (November 11, 1923), Article IV.

[19] Pernot, p. 20.   [20] Interview with informant, Kabul, 1967.

[21] Dupree ascribes the secondary place of women in tribal society to the fact that "Afghan tribal organization is patriarchal, patrilineal and patrilocal (bride moves to groom's house and the preferred marriage is with the father's brother's daughter)" (Louis Dupree, "Tribalism, Re-

the very high proprietary value assigned to women in tribal society, the alarm and dismay of the men can well be imagined when they heard of the frequent feminist speeches made by Queen Soraya.[22]

Of all his social reforms probably none was dearer to Amanullah than his courageous attempt to remodel completely Afghanistan's educational system. He set about it in a systematic way and, contrary to his mercurial interest in some of his other schemes, he stuck with education to the bitter end. In fact the 1928 Loya Jirgah proceedings and his marathon speech on reforms in October 1928 were heavily loaded with educational plans. As early as 1920 he saw the need for a complete revamping of the curricula, which up to that time had been almost entirely in the hands of religious teachers whose chief method of instruction was rote learning of a few sacred texts and instruction from the Panch Kitab, or Five Books. The Panch Kitab contained a smattering of the three R's plus selections from classical writers such as Saadi and Jami.[23] This curriculum tended to produce, according to A. H. Waleh, an inward-looking, mystical, and highly romanticized view of life. Before Amanullah, generations of young Afghans were brought up on this fare. All this was brushed aside. Amanullah and a succession of French and British-Indian directors of education planned a completely new curriculum based on secular, rational values and on more realistic preparation for dealing with the problems of a new nation. Alfred Foucher, who came to Afghanistan to head the first French archeological team, was pressed into service by

---

gionalism and National Oligarchy," in K. H. Silvert, ed., *Expectant Peoples: Nationalism and Development* [New York: American Universities Field Staff, 1963], p. 261). This is probably a more elegant way of saying that women in tribal society are a valuable piece of property for composing conflict, making useful alliances, and improving the social, economic, and political position of the family, clan, or tribe.

[22] See, for example, the reports of two such speeches in *Aman-i-Afghan*, V, nos. 44 and 46.

[23] A. H. Waleh, "Five Books and the Old Curriculum," *Kabul Times*, June 1, 1968.

Amanullah in 1922, first to be the head of the new French school, Amaniyah, and later to direct the reshaping of the entire educational program. Foucher has left us a fine description of his educational efforts in which he speaks glowingly of the support he received from the King.[24] A number of French teachers were brought to Afghanistan to develop the educational program. Seeing them off in Paris, Mahmud Tarzi, at that time Afghan minister in Paris, declared in a public speech: "Our confidence in France is great, this France to whom we are grateful for having supported the legitimate cause of the Turks and who thereby has won the entire heart of the Muslim world." [25] Tarzi always found it difficult to keep international politics out of even educational affairs, and his pro-Turkish, anti-British feelings kept showing through at odd moments.

As we have seen from the list of educational reforms, Amanullah made a courageous effort to institute compulsory elementary education and was defeated only by lack of teachers and schools. Nevertheless by 1927 he had made substantial progress and in that year alone his budget provided for twenty-seven new primary schools for boys and three for girls, as well as for schools of agriculture and telegraphy.[26] He also realized that a certain number of Afghans would require university training and that it would not be possible for some time to provide such education in Afghanistan. This meant that students would have to be prepared in foreign languages so that they might continue their studies abroad.[27] This led to the establishment of additional foreign-language schools in Kabul. A plan to extend them to the

[24] Alfred Foucher, *Bulletin de la Chambre de Commerce Franco-Asiatique*, Special Number, January 1928. Alfred Foucher should not be confused with Maurice Fouchet, author of *Notes sur l'Afghanistan*, who was French Minister in Kabul during part of the same period that Alfred Foucher worked there.

[25] Quoted in Melia, p. 11.

[26] *Annual Register*, new series (Afghanistan) (London: Longmans, Green, 1919–1930).

[27] The only foreign-language school in Afghanistan at the time was Habibia College, established during Amir Habibullah's reign.

provinces was cut short by the 1928 rebellion. A number of young students were sent to Europe, among them Amanullah's oldest son Hidayatullah (by his second wife). The roster of the boys who went to France in this first group now reads like a register of top leaders of Afghanistan, for almost all of them, including Prince Daud who later as Prime Minister in 1953 assumed Amanullah's mantle of modernization, became prominent in Afghan public life.[28]

But Amanullah was not satisfied with merely developing the usual type of education on a large scale. His mind ranged in many directions. Just before his downfall he was able, with Loya Jirgah approval, to send a number of girls to Turkey for education. He encouraged Queen Soraya to develop girls' schools, thereby laying the foundation for the emergence of many women educators and leaders in Afghanistan. These women were ready for public life when in 1959 they at last were able to cast aside the encumbrances of veil and purdah. Amanullah made an important start in vocational education and began schools for specific occupations such as clerks and accountants and government administrators. He even tried an imaginative program to have itinerant teachers accompany the great nomadic migrations, but this program failed because the right kinds of teachers could not be found and because of the supreme disinterest of the nomads.[29] He also founded the Police Academy and the Pushtun Academy. He was very keen on adult education and started a fairly extensive literacy program; he even personally taught some of the classes.

His restless mind continued to explore many types of imaginative innovations such as sending young men to Europe to work in factories as apprentices at Afghan government expense so as to create a generation of middle-level technicians and sending boys to Persia to learn carpet-weaving, which he rightly

[28] *Aman-i-Afghan*, II, no. 18 (1922–23), 1–8, describes the elaborate ceremonies for the departing students and lists their names.

[29] Interview with informant, Kabul, 1968.

foresaw as a potentially important industry for Afghanistan. Nor was he sensitive only to the utilitarian aspects of education, as is shown by his 1928 proposals to set up art schools and libraries to supplement the museum which first saw light in Afghanistan under his aegis.

There can be little doubt, then, that of all of Amanullah's social reforms, his educational program was the most important, not only in his own eyes, but for the future of the country. His attitude toward the importance of education can perhaps be summed up in the fact that during his reign the Medal of Education became the highest decoration, civil or military, in the kingdom. The entire generation of present Afghan leaders fell directly or indirectly under the influence of Amanullah's educational program and had Amanullah not had the vision and courage to initiate and develop it, Afghanistan today would be many years further back on the road to modernization. One thing that neither intensive capital input nor forced-draft modernization can provide is indigenous educated and trained manpower.

Like his dress reforms, Amanullah's educational reforms were pilloried by latter-day commentators who claimed the Afghan people were not ready for advanced forms of secular education. It has also been claimed that the freedom-loving Afghan tribal society deeply resented the compulsory features of the educational reforms. But in fact compulsory education was never actually enforced simply because there were not enough schools or teachers to support such a program. Only in Kabul and to a lesser extent in provincial centers was an attempt even made to educate as many children as possible. No one who did not really want to send his children to school was ever forced to do so. This was especially true of the so-called compulsory education of girls.[30]

Among the other social reforms listed, the abolition of slavery and forced labor were of truly major importance but received

[30] Interviews with four informants who had been active in Amanullah's educational program, Kabul, 1967–68.

little attention because they did not lend themselves readily to political propaganda. The form of slavery practiced in Afghanistan, of course, was the traditional Islamic variety of familial incorporation and bore no resemblance to the plantation slavery of the United States. *Begir,* or forced labor, was more of a perquisite exercised by local tribal khans or village maliks as a feudal incident of tenure than a social custom. The abolition was apparently not deeply resented probably because it was not a major deprivation and because it was not vary effectively or widely enforced. Moreover, slavery and forced labor were not suited to the social climate of rugged tribal freedom prevailing in Afghanistan. These practices were probably grafts on the indigenous society from Arab, Persian Mughal, and Indian sources.

Some of the other social reforms are worthy of comment. Amanullah's wistful attempt to control excessive marriage and funeral expenses was, according to all reports, completely ignored even though it was enshrined in legislation; the problem of conspicuous consumption at ceremonies of this kind continues unabated to the present day.[31] Amanullah's attempts to regulate student life are interesting in the light of current student agitation in Afghanistan and elsewhere. His 1928 proposals were only partially put into effect. The students did go into uniform but the injunction to students at the foreign-language schools to address fellow students in French, English or German was, needless to say, ignored. The proposed prohibition on student marriages, which seemed somewhat whimsical and was attacked in propaganda as a violation of family sanctity, was actually intended to avoid students' being pressed by parents into premature marriages, which often resulted in school drop-outs with a consequent loss of scarce educated manpower. An attempt to

[31] Marriage law cited above; also *Nizamanamah-ye-T'aziadari* [Law Concerning the Conduct of Funerals], 32 Asad 1303 (August 14, 1924). A *Kabul Times* article of September 30, 1968, bemoans the same wasteful practices which Amanullah sought to curb thirty-five years earlier.

obtain approval from the Loya Jirgah for the imposition of minimum marriage ages, designed to cure the same social ills, was
summarily rejected in 1928.[32]

As for the balance of Amanullah's social programs, we need
only note that for the most part such projects as orphans' homes
and hospitals constituted the first effort to provide governmental administration of social welfare in Afghanistan. They were
intended first to supplement and later to displace similar but
much less effective charitable institutions under religious en-
dowments, (the waqfs). Amanullah made only a modest start in
programs of this kind. His intentions were large and his vision
long, and had he continued to reign these programs would most
likely have been extended from Kabul and one or two provincial centers into the countryside. The value of these projects lay
in their example, which later Afghan governments have sought
to emulate.

[32] *The Annual Register*, 1928, reporting on some of the proceedings of
the Loya Jirgah of August 1928. See also Sykes, Vol. II, ch. 56.

chapter iv

the amanullah reforms:
modernizing the nation-state

Judging from the development of his political program, Amanullah's thinking appears to have gone through considerable evolution in the ten years he ruled. At first he placed great faith in achieving political development through juridical means—that is, he seemed to feel that by providing the country with a liberal constitution, detailed codes of law, and parliamentary machinery, he could institute a modern political system. As time passed he became more sophisticated and realized, especially after the 1924 Khost rebellion, that having a model government on paper was a far cry from achieving the goal of a united and politically loyal nation in fact. He lost considerable faith in his French and Turkish legal advisers and in their sponsor, Mahmud Tarzi, and came to the perceptive conclusion that political unity, integration, and civic loyalty would require very extensive changes in the social system itself. He then began to advocate more strongly his programs of education, secularization, and economic development. This was a highly sophisticated assessment in the light of what we now know about the problems of political modernization. The fact that his plans did not have the opportunity to mature and allow the desired political realignments to take place does not detract from the sagacity of Amanullah's analysis.

But even if Amanullah had done nothing else, the juridical base he provided for Afghanistan was of considerable importance since it gave the country the skeleton of the government it was eventually to develop. In this sense the 1923 Constitution was unquestionably a landmark document.[1] Joseph Schwager, a recognized authority on constitutional law, is of the opinion that this constitution was the result of a Loya Jirgah called by Amanullah in 1921. Schwager states that the dates of its compilation and its coming into force are not known. He notes that in some versions the document is designated as a *qanun* or law. The Appendix copy, however, was labeled as a Nizamnamah or regulation, presumably in deference to the usage which reserves the term *qanun* for Shari'a (religious law). Schwager states that "in spite of the designations of the document as a *Qanun* or a *Nizamnamah*, there can be no doubt that it was in substance a judicially valid constitutional law, which by its provisions for legislation was designed to lead to an autonomous development of secular law-making and to show the way to the separation of secular from canonical jurisprudence." [2]

Although Amanullah employed some French advisers in his legislative program, he relied principally on Turkish jurists led by a "Young Turk," Badri Bey, who had been director of the Constantinople police. Badri Bey drew heavily on the Turkish codes, which were in turn based on the Code Napoleon. The extensive compilation of Nizamnamah, or Code of Government

[1] Nizamnamah-ye-Asasi-e-'Aliyah-e-Afghanistan [The Constitution of Afghanistan], 20 Hamal 1302 (April 9, 1923). The history of this document is obscure. It was apparently approved by a Loya Jirgah held in the Eastern Province and the original draft was in Pushtu. Later it was translated into Persian but apparently no English version was ever made. After Amanullah's overthrow the Constitution sank into oblivion. Though its provisions were extensively copied in the 1931 Constitution drawn up under Nadir Shah, no mention of the 1923 one was made and the document itself was found only after an extensive search in the Kabul booksellers' bazaar. The English translation included in the Appendix is, so far as I know, the only one in existence.

[2] Joseph Schwager, *Die Entwicklung Afghanistans als Staat und seine zwischenstaatliche Beziehungen* (Leipzig: Noske, 1932), p. 110. There appears to be some difference of usage in various Islamic countries for the term *qanun*. In some places it is apparently used freely to designate secular laws.

Regulations, proceeded between the years 1921 and 1926, both before and after the publication of the Constitution in 1923, but most of the legislation saw the light after the Constitution and indeed as a follow-up to its various provisions. The Nizamnamah were issued as individual booklets, each dealing with a specific subject and constituting a separate law. They were developed in the various ministries and government departments with the assistance of the French and Turkish experts. The drafts were then submitted to the State Council (the legislative body under the Constitution) for approval or emendation. The entire government and Council worked feverishly during 1922 and 1923, when the bulk of the legislation was promulgated. Amanullah personally directed the entire operation and checked all the laws minutely.[3] This became the first comprehensive legal code in Afghanistan.

In the autumn of 1924, when the Khost rebellion of the Mangal tribe was at its height, Amanullah assembled the second Loya Jirgah of his reign for the purpose of reconsidering some of the laws and certain provisions of the Constitution which the rebels allegedly objected to. As a result several laws were rescinded and the Constitution was amended.[4] Since we do not possess a complete collection of Nizamnamah it is not possible to pinpoint which laws were amended at that time.

There is considerable evidence that the real controversy which led to the Khost revolt was not Amanullah's progressive legislation but rather the growing encroachment of Amanullah's centralized authority into the Mangal areas. The tribesmen, abetted by local mullahs, raised the cry that the new legislation violated the Shari'a, using this as a propaganda move to enlist

[3] Mir Ghulam Mohammad Ghobar, *Afghanistan dar Masir-e-Tarikh* (Kabul: Government Press, 1967). This book is very critical of the present ruling dynasty. Only a few copies got off the press before it was banned. I was able to obtain the material from the chapter on Amanullah through the kindness of one of my informants. This information was confirmed in interviews with three other informants, Kabul, 1968.

[4] The amendments to the Constitution are detailed in Appendix B.

popular support and increase tribal resistance. The real causes of the rebellion are implied in the recommendations of the 1924 Loya Jirgah, which stress the suspension of the requirement for identification cards and the relaxation of the army draft in the tribal areas.[5]

The Khost revolt dampened Amanullah's enthusiasm for legislation as a panacea for Afghanistan's political ills. He realized that laws on paper may have an educational value but will not of themselves ensure political cooperation from fractious elements in the society. From 1925 until Amanullah's return from his trip abroad in 1928, legislative activity was almost at a standstill. His 1928 proposals to set up a constitutional monarchy with a separate cabinet and prime minister and to establish a political party and a bicameral legislature were consumed in the flames of the rebellion.

The Constitution and the legal codes do not appear in themselves to be outstanding models of modern political liberalism, but if we view them in the context of the social and political conditions prevailing in Afghanistan we can perhaps appreciate the startling and revolutionary political changes that these documents advocated. The seventy-three articles of the Constitution reaffirmed Afghan independence from all forms of foreign control. Article 2 proclaimed Islam to be the national religion but guaranteed freedom of worship to "followers of other religions such as Jews and Hindus." Article 6 set forth for the first time the principle of cabinet responsibility, and Article 7 enumerated

[5] The real cause of the revolt is, curiously enough, mentioned in a despatch from the British Foreign Office to its embassy in Moscow: "The Mangals of the Khost district of southwest Afghanistan, discontented with the centralizing policy of the Amir, his reforms of internal administration, enforcement of military service and his compliance with British demands in connection with search and arrest of murderers of British subjects, rose in revolt" (Despatch no. 712 dated May 31st, 1924, IOL, LPS/10/1112 P1360/1924). This information was presumably relayed from the British Legation in Kabul. *Aman-i-Afghan*, V, nos. 9 and 10 (14 Sunbula 1303), 5–6, contains the Loya Jirgah report.

the powers of the king, making them subject to existing laws
—a radical departure from the personal and sometimes tyranni-
cal rule customary in Afghanistan. There follow a series of articles guaranteeing civil rights "to all persons residing in the
Kingdom of Afghanistan without respect to religious or sectarian differences." The touchy question of who is an "Afghan"
was skirted by extending the rights to all persons "residing" in
the kingdom. The civil rights are the usual ones contained in
liberal Western constitutions: free press, free speech, petition,
free education (an Amanullah addition), the right to government employment (in accordance with vacancies and qualifications), security of property and equality of taxation, freedom
from searches and seizures, from forced labor, and from torture.

The problem of secular versus religious law was handled in
Article 21, which boldly stated that "all cases will be decided in
accordance with the principles of Shari'a and of general civil
and criminal laws." This apparent inconsistency was reconciled
by public declarations that the Constitution and all legal codes
were designed so as to be compatible with the dictates of
Shari'a.[6] These assurances, of course, did not go entirely unchal-
lenged, but only during the Khost rebellion were specific provisions of the penal code declared by rebel mullahs to be un-Is-
lamic, and, as we have noted, compromise amendments were
made.

The section on the cabinet established a Council of Ministers
with the king as chairman and vested it with collective responsibility for running the government. The work of the cabinet and
various government departments was to be subject to review
once each year by a special High Assembly (Darbar-e-'Ali)
composed of elders of the people chosen in the traditional manner of Loya Jirgah members. This was an interesting innovation
on the part of Amanullah, intended to serve not only as a popu-

[6] *Aman-i-Afghan*, V, nos. 11 and 12 (25 Sunbula 1303), 5–6, contains
Amanullah's proclamation assuring the nation that Islamic scholars had
checked all laws and found them in accordance with Shari'a.

lar check on government but also to incorporate into the formal juridical system in a modified form the tribal institution of the jirgah. In addition Article 33 provided for a special High Court (Diwan-e-'Ali) to try ministers for misconduct.

The Constitution then went on to prescribe in general terms the rights and duties of government officials and refer to specific legislation on these subjects. Articles 39 to 49 concern the establishment of the State Council and of Provincial Councils. These were composed of an equal number of appointed and elected members. Their duties and modes of appointment and election were spelled out in a Law on the Basic Organization of the Government of Afghanistan.[7] The next eight articles (50 to 57) established an independent judiciary, including trial and appellate courts and a High Court which convened only for trials of ministers. Free access to the courts was guaranteed to all.

General financial affairs, the establishment of an annual budget, and the imposition and collection of taxes were covered in Articles 58 through 62. The next five articles dealt with the administration of provinces, with Article 63 laying down the philosophy that "Provincial administration is based on three basic principles: (1) decentralization of authority; (2) clear delineation of duties; and (3) clear determination of responsibilities." In Article 67 the government reserved the right to impose military government "in any part of the country in which signs of disobedience and rebellion are such as to disturb the public security."

A series of miscellaneous articles at the end of the Constitution established compulsory education and provided for amendments to the Constitution; the final article, Article 73, forbade the post office to open private mail on the ground that "security of personal correspondence is one of the rights of all citizens."

[7] Nizamnamah-ye-Tashkilat-e-Asasiyah-e-Afghanistan [Law concerning the Basic Organization of the Government of Afghanistan], 15 Jauza 1302 (June 5, 1923).

The amendments recommended by the Loya Jirgah which met in Paghman in July 1924, during the Khost revolt, made the Hanafite religious rite official; added the provision that Hindus and Jews must pay the special tax and wear distinctive clothing and that "Afghan subjects are bound by the religious rite and political institutions of Afghanistan"; provided that penal offenses for which specific punishments were prescribed in the Shari'a would be so punished; and specified that taxation was the prerogative only of the state. It will bear repeating that the intent of the original constitutional provisions was to minimize the differences between Sunni and Shiah Muslims, as well as between Muslims, Hindus, and Jews. Here again the insistence of the orthodox forces on distinctive clothing for Hindus and Jews helps to explain Amanullah's later (and on the surface whimsical) insistence on Western-style clothing.

The controversy over punishment prescribed in the penal codes versus those provided under Shari'a was explained in the following terms by an informant who is a legal expert:

Amanullah's penal code prescribed maximum punishments, such as 5 years in prison, for specific offenses. Under Shari'a a *qazi* was free to impose a far wider range of punishments, anything from restitution to long imprisonment. This latitude created a far greater incentive to bribe the judge to gain his good will than where the offender knew exactly what the limits of the punishment were. Naturally the *qazis*, who, because of a shortage of secular judges, continued for the most part to judge criminal cases, strongly maintained that the penal code violated Shari'a and were able to convince the rebellious Mangal tribesmen that their revolt would be greatly strengthened by injecting this religious issue into their political struggle.[8]

Considering the *Zeitgeist* and the political complexion of Afghanistan, the 1923 Constitution was a very liberal document indeed and formed a good base on which to construct a secular code of laws. A detailed analysis of this legislation would, no

[8] Interview with informant, Kabul, 1968.

doubt, prove a fruitful subject for an entire book. For our purposes we need only note the very extensive effort to provide a tribal society, which had virtually no formal written laws, with a comprehensive written legal code. The task was worthy of a Justinian or a Hammurabi. Amanullah was neither, but we can gain some conception of the magnitude of his task by simply listing some of the laws encompassed by Amanullah's code.[9]

NIZAMNAMAH PROMULGATED DURING THE REIGN
OF KING AMANULLAH

1. Nizamnamah-ye-Tashkilat-e-Asasiyah-e-Afghanistan, 15 Jawza 1302 (June 5, 1923). Law Concerning the Basic Organization of the Government of Afghanistan.

2. Nizamnamah-ye-Wazayef-e-Mustufiyan wa Sarishtah Daran-e-'Ala, 7 Jaddi 1302 (December 28, 1923). Law Pertaining to the Duties of Provincial Finance Officers.

3. Nizamnamah-ye-Hazari-e-Mamurin, 28 Qaus 1302 (December 19, 1923). Law Concerning the Attendance of Civil Servants.

4. Nizamnamah-ye-Estafaye Mamurin-e-Mulki, 15 Dalwa 1302 (February 4, 1924). Law Regarding the Resignation of Civil Servants.

5. Nizamnamah-ye-Wakil-e-Tijarat, 19 Jaddi 1302 (January 9, 1924). Law Concerning Trade Agents.

6. Nizamnamah-ye-Wazayef-e-Mamurin-e-Zira'at, 25 Qaus 1302 (December 16, 1923). Law on the Duties of Agricultural Officials.

7. Nizamnamah-ye-Khazanah Jat-e-Daulat, 17 Jaddi 1302 (January 7, 1924). Law on the Operation of Government Treasuries.

8. Nizamnamah-ye-Tafriq-e-Wazayef-e-Katiban-e-Dakhl-e-Qeta'at, 31 Mizan 1302 (October 23, 1923). Law on the Duties of Clerks in Army Units.

[9] This is only a partial list since many of the laws are now lost. I was able to locate only two volumes, although I was assured by various informants that there were at least four. The date indicated after each law is the date it was sanctioned by King Amanullah. More than one date indicates a revision. Some laws were undated and others did not indicate the day or month, only the year. This partial list probably represents a fair random sample of the total scope of legislation.

9. Nizamnamah-ye-Baladiyah, 25 Dalwa 1302 (February 14, 1924). Law Concerning Municipalities.

10. Nizamnamah-ye-Usul-e-Mahakimat-e-Jazayah-e-Mamurin, 20 Hut 1302, 10 Qaus 1306 (March 11, 1924, December 1, 1927). Law Concerning the Trials of Public Officials.

11. Nizamnamah-ye-Idarah-e-Layiliah, 21 Jaddi 1302 (January 11, 1924). Law Concerning the Operation of Student Hostels.

12. Nizamnamah-ye-Mahikamah-ye-Shari'a Darbab-e-M'amelat-e-Tijarati, 1301 (1922). Law Concerning Commercial Cases in Shari'a Courts.

13. Nizamnamah-ye-Tazkirah-e-Nufus wa Usul-e-Pasaport, 5 Jawza 1302 (May 6, 1923). Law Concerning Identity Cards, Citizenship, and Passports.

14. Nizamnamah-ye-Tashwiqiah-e-Sana'aye', 1 Sawar 1302 (April 21, 1923). Law for the Encouragement of Private Industry.

15. Nizamnamah-ye-Furush-e-Amlak-e-Sarkari, 17 Sawar 1302 (May 7, 1923). Law Concerning the Sale of Government Property.

16. Nizamnamah-ye-Mudiriyatha-e-Mamurin-e-Wizarat, 25 Saratan 1302 (July 16, 1923). Law Concerning Personnel Offices in Ministries.

17. Nizamnamah-ye-Muhajarin, 18 Saratan 1302 (July 9, 1923). Law Concerning Immigration.

18. Nizamnamah-ye-T'aziadari, 30 Hamal 1301, 32 Asad 1303 (April 2, 1922, August 14, 1924). Law Concerning the Conduct of Funerals.

19. Nizamnamah-ye-Taqawi-e-Tijariyah, 1 Aqrab 1301 (October 23, 1922). Law Concerning Credits for Trade.

20. Nizamnamah-ye-Nashanat-e-Ma'arif, 1302 (1923). Law Concerning the Medal of Education.

21. Nizamnamah-ye-Rukhsati-ye-Mamurin, 12 Hamal 1302, 12 Qaus 1302 (April 1, 1923, December 3, 1923). Law Concerning Leave for Civil Servants.

22. Nizamnamah-ye-Mudiriyat-e-Daftar-e-Awraq wa Mudiriyat-e-Maktub, 14 Qaus 1302 (December 5, 1923). Law Concerning Offices of Archives and Correspondence.

23. Nizamnamah-ye-Zar'at-e-Lalmi, 27 Sumbula 1302 (September 18, 1923). Law Concerning Dry Farming.

24. Nizamnamah-ye-Furush-e-Amwal-e-Takhawilhanaha-e-Sar-kari, 15 Aqrab 1302 (November 6, 1923). Law Concerning the Sale of Government-Procured Commodities.

25. Nizamnamah-ye-Maktab-e-Khanagi, 9 Mizan 1302 (October 1, 1923). Law Concerning Private Schools.

26. Nizamnamah-ye-Naqlin be Samt-e-Qataghan, 4 Mizan 1302 (September 26, 1923). Law Concerning Land Settlement in Qat-aghan Province.

27. Nizamnamah-ye-Mahsul-e-Mawashi, 17 Mizan 1302 (October 9, 1923). Law on the Administration of the Livestock Tax.

28. Nizamnamah-ye-Tawqifkhanaha wa Mahbuskhanaha, 10 Mizan 1302 (October 2, 1923). Law Concerning the Operation of Prisons.

29. Nizamnamah-ye-'Arusi, Nikah wa Khatnasuri, 20 Aqrab 1302, 1 Sumbula 1303 (November 11, 1923, August 23, 1924). Law Concerning Engagements, Marriages, and Circumcision.

30. Nizamnamah-ye-Mudiriyat-e-Mahsabah Wizarat-e-Jalilah-e-Kharijah, 14 Aqrab 1302 (November 5, 1923). Law Concerning the Accounting Office in the Ministry of Foreign Affairs.

31. Nizamnamah-ye-Jazayi-e-'Umumi, 1 Mizan 1303, 30 Jawza 1306 (September 23, 1924, June 20, 1927). General Penal Code.

32. Nizamnamah-ye-Jazayi-e-Askari, 14 Dalwa 1302 (February 3, 1924). Military Penal Code.

33. Nizamnamah-ye-Tafriq-e-Wazayef-e-Hukam wa Mamurin-e-Mut'aleq-e-an, 18 Mizan 1302 (October 10, 1923). Law on the Duties of Governors and Their Subordinate Officials.

34. Nizamnamah-ye-Taqsimat-e-Mulkiyah-e-Afghanistan, un-dated. Law Delimiting the Provincial and District Boundaries of Afghanistan.

35. Nizamnamah-ye-Layiha-e-Adariya-e-Masakin, 15 Hut 1303 (March 6, 1925). Law Concerning the Relief and Care of the Poor.

36. Nizamnamah-ye-Akhz-e-Rasum-e-Gomrok, 1 Hamal 1300 (March 21, 1921). Law Concerning Customs Duties.

37. Nizamnamah-ye-Matabu'at, 10 Jaddi 1303 (December 31, 1924). Law Concerning Publications (Press).

38. Nizamnamah-ye-Wazirat-e-Jalilah-e-Harbiya, 25 Aqrab 1302 (November 16, 1923). Law Concerning the Ministry of War.

39. Nizamnamah-ye-Ijraat-e-Tasfiyah-e-Mahasibah-e-Maziyah, 5 Jaddi 1302 (December 26, 1923). Law Concerning the Clearing of Past Accounts.

40. Nizamnamah-ye-Budjah-ye-'Umumi, 25 Jaddi 1302 (January 15, 1924). Law Concerning the General Budget.

41. Nizamnamah-ye-Maqyasat, 23 Hut 1304 (March 14, 1926). Law Concerning Units of Measurement.

42. Hidayat-e-Surat-e-Faizalah-e-Qatt wa Habs-e-Diwan, 10 Jaddi 1303 (December 31, 1924). Regulations Regarding Decisions in Cases Involving Life Imprisonment or the Death Penalty.

43. Nizamnamah-ye-Layihah-ye-Taliqat-e-Daulat, 8 Dalwa 1303 (January 28, 1925). Law Concerning State Decorations.

44. Nizamnamah-ye-Konsulgari-e-Daulat-e-'Ali-ye-Afghanistan, 1 Aqrab 1302 (October 23, 1923). Law Concerning Afghan Government Consulates.

45. Nizamnamah-ye-Abriyah-ye-Shahr-e-Dar-ul-Aman, 19 Asad 1302 (August 10, 1923). Law Concerning the Construction of the City of Dar-ul-Aman.

46. Nizamnamah-ye-Takhfif-e-Ebarat-e-Alqab, 25 Jaddi 1305 (January 15, 1926). Law Concerning Abbreviations of Official Titles.

47. Nizamnamah-ye-Khidamat-e-Dakhliya-e-Askariyah, 1305 (1925–26). Law Concerning Domestic Military Service.

48. Nizamnamah-ye-Tarbiyah-e-Atfal Yatim, 23 Jaddi 1305 (January 13, 1926). Law Concerning the Welfare and Training of Orphans.

49. Nizamnamah-ye-Mamelat-e-Nahr-e-Razak Samt-e-Shimali, 26 Dalwa 1305. (February 15, 1926). Law Concerning the Razak Canal in the Northern Province.

50. Nizamnamah-ye-Dar-ul-M'olaminha wa Dar-ul-Malimat-e-Markaz, 1302 (1923–24). Law Concerning Teachers' Training Colleges for Men and Women in the Capital.

51. Nizamnamah-ye-Karguzari-e-Maliya, 20 Dalwa 1302 (February 9, 1924). Law Concerning Job Descriptions for Finance.

52. Nizamnamah-ye-Tamirat-e-Daulat, Saratan 1301 (July 1922). Law Concerning Government Buildings.

53. Nizamnamah-ye-Nishanha, 1299 (1920–21). Law Concerning Medals (Decorations).

54. Nizamnamah-ye-Tamirat-e-Paghman, Saratan 1301 (July 1922). Law Concerning Buildings in Paghman.

55. Nizamnamah-ye-Klub Siah, Surkh-o-Sabz, Sumbula 1307 (October 1928). Law Concerning the Black, Red, and Green (Military) Club.

56. Nizamnamah-ye-Farqah-ye-Isteqlal wa Tajdid, 1307 (1928–29). Law Concerning the "Independence" Division and (Military) Modernization.

57. Nizamnamah-ye-Jamia't-e-Taiarah-e-Afghanistan, 1307 (1928–29). Law Concerning Aircraft in Afghanistan.

58. Nizamnamah-ye-Wizarat-e-Ma'arif, 1305 (1927–28). Law Concerning the Ministry of Education.

59. Nizamnamah-ye-Azuqah, 1305 (1927–28). Law Concerning Supply.

60. Nizamnamah-ye-Talimgah-ye-Amiran wa Zabetan, 1305 (1927–28). Law Concerning Training Centers for Superior and Junior Military Officers.

61. Nizamnamah-ye-Rutbaha-ye-Askari, 1305 (1927–28). Law Concerning Military Rank.

62. Nizamnamah-ye-Khurd Zabetan, 1301 (1922–23). Law Concerning Noncommissioned Officers.

63. Nizamnamah-ye-Maliyah, Hamal 1299 (March 1920). Law Concerning Finance.

64. Nizamnamah-ye-Dak-khanah, 1300 (1921–22). Law Concerning the Post Office.

This list gives some idea of the scope of the Code Amanullah. Some of the subjects covered may seem rather trivial for legislation, such as maintenance of government buildings or vacations and leave of civil servants, and would probably be handled by departmental regulations in most countries. But this presupposes a degree of administrative sophistication which Afghanistan did not possess, and we must keep in mind that Amanullah wanted to dignify these new rules with the legislative imprimatur since in many cases they called for radical changes from the ways of the old bureaucracy.

Some of the laws deserve brief commentary since they tell us a good deal about the problems of modernization faced by Amanullah and the philosophy underlying his program. Item 12 indicates an attempt to secularize the handling of commercial cases even when heard in Shari'a courts. Item 13 caused bitter resentment in the tribal areas, where it was judged correctly as an attempt by the central government to limit freedom of movement across borders and to obtain personal data for purposes of control and taxation. Item 18, as we have already noted, was a hopeful attempt by Amanullah to curb foolishly extravagant expenses at funerals. Item 20 is further evidence of the great importance he ascribed to education. As previously noted, the Medal of Education was the highest decoration in the kingdom and was dignified by means of a special law. Item 25 again shows Amanullah's firm decision to secularize education even in the private (for the most part, religious) schools. Item 27 was another reform that was resented in rural and especially in tribal areas where livestock had often escaped taxation. In many cases, particularly among the warlike and nomadic Ghilzai, livestock was the principal source of wealth. Item 35, dealing with care of the poor, has a modern ring to it. It illustrates Amanullah's concern for welfare, previously a strictly religious responsibility. Items 38 and 58 make it appear likely that each ministry had a law to cover its own administration. Item 46 was an attempt to curb the use of lengthy and flowery titles of address in correspondence, which, in the Persian tradition, sometimes occupied half the document. Item 47, as will be seen later, was another serious source of conflict with the tribes and the rural population, who resented the new lottery system of conscription. Item 50 setting up teachers' colleges for men and women again demonstrates Amanullah's sincerity in the matter of education and his intention to develop teachers of both sexes.

Item 1 is an especially important law which details the organization of the government, at the central, provincial, and local
levels, as conceived by Amanullah. This was a major and eventually a successful effort to institutionalize the government machinery and provide it with a functioning and permanent bureaucracy. Amanullah's purpose in providing for a healthy
development of provincial and local government was "to provide a linkage between the government and the people." [10]

If Amanullah had done nothing more than undertake the reorganization of the government and give the nation a new constitutional charter and a body of laws, all of which have
survived or re-emerged virtually intact in the present-day Afghan state, his accomplishment would have been noteworthy as
a pioneering effort. Yet these programs have been largely disregarded by historians and critics of his regime who prefer to ridicule some of his more dramatic social and religious reforms.
Amanullah eventually realized that merely providing the country with a formal-legal system of government was not enough
and was driven to pursue an accelerated program of social and
economic reforms. The entire edifice tumbled under the attack
of traditional tribal separatism but the idea of providing these
legal foundations, first put forward by Amanullah, re-emerged
in recent years when the social and political climate became
more favorable.

Amanullah also saw the need for an independent judiciary but
was faced with a vacuum of secular legal talent. When Amanullah ascended to the throne there was not a single Afghan lawyer
trained in secular jurisprudence.[11] Until a corps of secular law-
yers could be developed Amanullah had to rely on religiously

[10] Ghani, ch. 4. Ghani, who was a member of the State Council (legislature) which passed on all laws, was in a good position to know Amanullah's mind on this question. This law runs to 116 pages in the Persian
text. It was reprinted serially in *Aman-i-Afghan*, II, nos. 5 to 34 in 1923.

[11] Interviews with four informants in Kabul, 1967–68.

trained *qazis* (judges) and *muftis* (legal counsellors) to operate
the judicial system. This at once raised the question of the place
of Shari'a in the courts' decisions; Amanullah tried to solve this
problem with the assistance of liberal members of the ulema
who could be induced to approve the legislation in a back-
handed manner by issuing *fatwas* (religious opinions) to the effect that the legislation was not contrary to Shari'a. Amanullah
made this a basis for a campaign to convince the *qazis* and *muftis* that they could apply the secular codes with a clear conscience. For example in his *Id* speech in 1922, traditionally given
annually at the principal mosque in Kabul, Amanullah, explaining the basis of his proposed judicial reforms, assured the
congregation of religious leaders that all the laws to be promulgated would be based on Shari'a and the spirit of progress and
that the purpose of the laws was to protect the weak from the
powerful and from the whims and abuses of rulers so that the
government would be one of laws and not of men. According
to Amanullah these laws were simply a codification to make
Shari'a understandable and easy to apply and to control the actions of officials and even of the king.[12]

On the whole the judicial reforms were well received by the
people, though many *qazis* and *muftis* found their powers curtailed and their bribe value reduced.[13] As we have noted, some
adjustments were made in the matter of punishments in criminal
cases as a result of pressures generated during the Khost rebellion in 1924. According to Franz Schlegelberger, by 1928
Amanullah was convinced that the situation was ripe for a further and far-reaching modernization of the judicial order, espe-

[12] *Aman-i-Afghan*, II, no. 2 (15 Mizan 1301) (October 7, 1922), 2–3.
[13] Louis Dupree, "Constitutional Development and Cultural Change,
Part IV: The 1964 Afghan Constitution," *American Universities Field
Staff Reports*, South Asia series, IX, no. 4 (1964). Dupree points out that
in the 1964 Loya Jirgah held to ratify the present Afghan constitution,
delegate after delegate rose to complain of arbitrary, unjust, and corrupt
practices by *qazis*. There is little reason to suppose that most Afghans
felt very differently in Amanullah's time.

cially of civil and criminal law; because of the outbreak of the 1928 revolution, these plans were never implemented.[14] That Amanullah felt the need for further moves to modernize the judicial system seems to indicate that his attempts to secularize it, to eliminate corruption, and to expunge all traces of tribal customary law from judicial practices had not been altogether successful. This estimate was borne out by responses from most of the informants questioned. An additional bit of evidence was the specific proposal made to the 1928 Loya Jirgah to prohibit "blood money" in judicial settlements. That such a proposal would even have to be made after nearly a decade of judicial reform is ample proof of the stubborn persistence of tribal notions of justice.[15]

In addition to constitutional, legislative, and judicial modernization, Amanullah also instituted a number of reforms through executive action. The development of extensive foreign relations and the admission of substantial numbers of foreign technicians into the country were matters of policy. So too was the abolition of ranks and titles, a personal decision of the king aimed at democratizing the regime of the *sardars* (royal chiefs), khans, and maliks and intended as a pseudo-egalitarian gesture which is often an earmark of nationalist revolutions. This attempt to deprive the tribal aristocracy of the symbols of privilege did much to alienate the chiefs from Amanullah, such is the secret power of vanity, egotism, and *amour propre*. One informant assured me that some of Amanullah's staunchest admirers lost their en-

[14] Franz Schlegelberger, *Rechsvergleichendes Handwortbuch für das Zivil und Handelsrecht des in- und auslandes* (Berlin: F. Wahlen, 1927). See also Julius Magnus, *Die hochsten Gerichte der Welt* (Leipzig: W. Moeser, 1929), Part IV, Asien-Afghanistan.

[15] According to the unwritten code of Pushtunwali, one of the ways to settle a claim for *badal*, or retribution, is by the payment of an agreed sum to the victim or to his kinsmen. This so-called blood money concept is often extended to what would be considered civil wrongs or torts in our society such as vehicle accidents, accidental killing of livestock, or alienation of affections. It is used in Afghanistan to this day.

thusiasm for him when he abolished the tradition of sending food from the royal kitchens to favored courtiers.[16]

Amanullah also curtailed other perquisites and fringe benefits of the tribal aristocracy. He ordained that remuneration had to be based on work of value to the nation. This was incomprehensible to the tribal chiefs around him. Their loyalty depended upon their privileged position and they in turn bound their families and clans and tribes in a web of loyalty dependent upon the dissemination of largesse all along the feudal chain of command. This was the service that they performed, which Amanullah seemed either not to understand or not to appreciate. To ask them to perform constructive work in addition to their service as power brokers was an imposition that violated the terms of Pushtun tribal relationships.

Amanullah, nevertheless, backed by his enthusiastic and inexperienced Young Afghans, proceeded not only to deflate the pride of the heads of leading families but—far worse—to deflate their purses as well by abolishing or drastically reducing many of their stipends, subsidies, and gratuities.[17] To add insult to injury he launched his anticorruption campaign and gave every evidence of being serious about enforcing it.

Western notions of corruption do not translate readily into the terms of most underdeveloped societies. The values tend to coincide in the extreme cases, but many fine gradations and shadings must be distinguished to be understood. Thus an outright bribe to obtain a favorable decision from a judge would be condemned in both cultures but a suitable present to have one's case heard more promptly might be quite acceptable in Afghanistan and a criminal act in England. A great deal of what is termed corruption by Western standards is, in other cultures, merely a lubricant to overcome the friction of inept bureau-

[16] Interview with informant, Kabul, 1968.

[17] For a similar situation which led to the revolt of the tribal chiefs against British occupying forces in 1841 see the study by M. E. Yapp, "The Revolution of 1841–42 in Afghanistan," *Bulletin of the School of Oriental and African Studies*, XXVII (1964), Part 2, 333.

cracies staffed by incompetent and underpaid officials. To the extent that bakhshish (gratuities) serves this purpose it can be argued that it is functional in the society. If pushed to the extreme where payment must be made simply to avoid harassment or as "protection," i.e., to avoid negative actions, it may be regarded as dysfunctional.

The subject of corruption and its relationship to the modernization process is far too complex for full discussion here. But when Amanullah decided, in effect, to apply Western standards of probity to the intricate system of payment and support through which power was transmitted in Afghan tribal society, he was not only threatening the economic position of many of his loyal supporters but was also unwittingly undermining his political "machine" without providing an alternative system of financial and political rewards. Tribal and political leaders at first viewed the anticorruption drive with skepticism, thinking it would be aimed at the small fry of the bureaucracy and conducted principally for public-relations purposes. But their doubts turned to shock when Amanullah showed by his actions that he was after bigger game. C. Morrish recollects that "Amanullah made the first serious effort in Afghanistan to eradicate bribery and corruption from the public services and in this laudable effort he was forced to relieve influential personages from their offices." [18] One such "influential personage" was the police commandant of Herat who was tried for dishonesty and sentenced to twelve years in prison, "public exposure," and a fine of about 100,000 rupees.[19] The last straw was put on the camel's back when Amanullah did not hesitate to jail one of the top Barakzai (Durrani) tribal *sardars*, Shahgasi Mohammed Sarwar Khan, who was his own mother's stepfather.[20] Tribal leaders were outraged at this manifest violation of kinship obligations. In spite of these Draconian measures, Amanullah did not

[18] C. Morrish (pseud.), *Afghanistan in the Melting Pot* (Peshawar and Lahore: Civil and Military Gazette Press, 1930).

[19] *The Times* (London), November 29, 1928.

[20] Reported in the *Annual Register*, 1923.

succeed in eliminating or even in substantially reducing the bakhshish system. Writers like Sorab K. H. Katrak, Lowell Thomas, and others who traveled in Afghanistan during that period reported that at every turn they had to grease palms in order to get simple cooperation from government clerks and officials. Indeed, British reports as well as accounts written by Afghans such as Ali Ahmad are so explicit about the extensive corruption even among the top officials of the period that we are led to speculate whether the anticorruption drive did not have the opposite effect of frightening those who normally drew reasonable profits from the system into trying to make killings while there were still some opportunities left. Amanullah's extensive proposals in 1928 to step up the campaign and put more teeth into its enforcement by creating teams of independent inspectors, forcing all officials to list their assets, and establishing special tribunals to try offenders, indicate that his previous efforts had met with little success.

The extent to which the anticorruption reforms actually undermined Amanullah's political support when the rebellious challenge from the tribes came, is somewhat unclear. Ali Ahmad is of the opinion that the revolt was directly fomented by Amanullah's officials, who felt their dishonest gains threatened by his puritanical approach to politics.[21] We must bear in mind that Amanullah also attacked nepotism, one of the most hallowed institutions of the tribal kinship system.[22] It is certainly fair to say that at the very minimum Amanullah's unyielding stand on corruption and nepotism won him few friends, made him some enemies, and diluted the loyalties of the traditional aristocracy which was the principal link between the monarchy and the tribes.

[21] Ali Ahmad, pp. 5–7.

[22] For example, in Amanullah's famous marathon speech of October 2 to 6, 1928, he asserted that thenceforth all diplomats proceeding abroad would not be permitted to recruit their staffs from among their relatives, a practice considered not only acceptable until then but the proper thing to do (IOL, LPS/10/285, 1929).

chapter V

the amanullah reforms:
modernizing the soldiers
and the mullahs

Most observers of the Amanullah period have asserted that he handled his military problems very badly. Many are of the opinion that he neglected the army and some even say that he treated it shabbily. All agreed, however, that the army was no match for the tribal rebels and indeed had neither the means nor the *esprit* to put up a good fight. There were certainly many cases of desertion during the 1928–29 rebellion and several ignominious surrenders (at Charikar the entire garrison turned the fort and all its armaments over to the Bacha-i-Saqao without firing a shot). The assertion, however, that Amanullah's military reforms were intended to weaken the military and that this eventually cost him his throne does not ring quite true. Amanullah had been raised in a military tradition. He was the only son Habibullah sent to the Military Academy for his education. When the crisis of Habibullah's assassination came, Amanullah instinctively turned to the army to support his bid for the throne, and the army made his accession possible and thwarted the ambitions of his uncle Nasrullah. It was on the army that Amanullah first relied in launching the Third Afghan War of Independence. True, the army disappointed him, and only when Nadir Khan was able to raise the fierce Wazir and Mahsud tribes could the Afghans give the British as good as they got. Amanullah had to call on the army again when the Mangals revolted in Khost in 1924, and again the army gave a very poor account of itself. Amanullah, therefore, would have been dull indeed, which he certainly never was, not to have perceived that he needed a strong and reliable army to back up his programs at home and abroad.

There is substantial evidence that he did realize this and that he made consistent though fruitless efforts to build a strong military establishment within the system of national priorities which he had set for himself. This explains most of the military reforms, which have been severely criticized. Amanullah believed he could obtain the political loyalty he needed to support modernization by rational persuasion, by convincing his subjects that what he was prescribing was good for them and for Afghanistan. The use of force or coercion to achieve his national goals was therefore assigned a low priority. He wanted to avoid a swollen military establishment that would consume large portions of the national revenues. Amanullah's high priorities were education and economic development, but this did not mean, as some allege, that he held the military forces in contempt or that he deliberately weakened them. It simply means that he tried to develop the kind of armed forces that seemed to him best suited to the kind of modern state he was trying to build. We can question the effectiveness of his means but should not cavil at the worthiness of his ends.

A more accurate and objective assessment of Amanullah's military reforms is needed. He relied heavily on Turkish military advisers, led first by the redoubtable Jamal Pasha, later by the gallant defender of Medina, Fakhri Pasha (who doubled in brass as Turkish ambassador), and finally by General Kazim Bey.[1]

[1] Telegram from His Majesty's Minister in Kabul to the Secretary of State for Foreign Affairs, London, no. 32, January 12, 1929, IOL, LPS/10/1288 P53, Part 5, 1929. See also Lowell Thomas, p. 230. According to several informants interviewed in Kabul in 1968, the Turkish military mission was not very effective at first and met considerable resistance and jealousy from Afghan officers. A new and more high-powered Turkish mission headed by General Kazim Bey, one of Ataturk's top officers, was sent to Afghanistan after Amanullah's meeting with Ataturk in 1928. Unfortunately this mission arrived after the revolution

7. King Amanullah (*left*) with Turkish military adviser Jamal Pasha.

Amanullah's concern for military affairs was consistent and constant. For example, one of the principal clauses he inserted in the Turco-Afghan treaty signed in Moscow in 1920 provided that Turkey would send a military mission to Afghanistan to reorganize the Afghan army and to remain there at least five years or for as long as the Afghans requested. Again, as we shall see in the chapters on foreign relations, Amanullah strove during his entire reign to play his cards with the Russians and the British in such a way as to obtain a maximum amount of military aid from both and did in fact succeed in getting substantial amounts

that brought about the abdication of Amanullah was already out of hand.

of both Russian and British arms, including airplanes, from both sides.[2]

It would seem, then, that Amanullah's attempts to bring about changes in the military structure reflect an intense concern with the difficulties of creating the kind of army he felt a modernizing state should have, rather than the lack of interest or failure to appreciate the importance of military strength with which he is so often charged. One knowledgeable informant declared that Amanullah wanted a small but efficient and cohesive disciplined army, drawn from the population as a whole rather than from tribal levies—a fighting force thoroughly professional and capable of developing complete loyalty to the central government and capable of maintaining internal security.[3] This was what his Turkish advisers counseled, and it made both political and fiscal sense to the King. Unfortunately in order to produce such an organization the old army would have to be completely remade from the ground up, and this, of course, meant cracking up all the vested interests and power cliques as well as imposing a great deal of individual hardship in many cases.

If we view Amanullah's military reforms not as attempts to harass the army but as efforts to remake the system along the lines mentioned above, then his reforms begin to make fairly good sense. For example, he wanted an army that would be representative of the country as a whole. Under the old system instituted by Abdur Rahman, conscription was by the *qaumi* system in which each tribe or village was required to furnish a certain number of recruits. Habibullah modified this to the so-called *hasht nafari* system whereby each "eighth man" in a given village or tribe was called up. Under these two systems the recruits were often the dregs or rejects of village and tribal

[2] The text of the Turco-Afghan Treaty may be found in Adamec, Appendix, pp. 192–193. *The Annual Register*, 1925, reports Amanullah's purchase of planes from Russia and his plans to send fifty officers for pilot training to the USSR.

[3] Interview with informant, Kabul, 1967.

life, selected, and at times paid for "volunteering," by the local elite. In both cases they maintained their primary ties and loyalties to their group of origin. Amanullah tried to institute *pishk*, a fairer and more representative system of national service by lottery. But the older systems were based on an open and public selection controlled by the traditional power elite of the village or tribe. Everyone understood this and knew just where he stood. Manifest inequities became a subject for negotiation and pressure within the group itself. The introduction of a lottery system transferred control of recruitment to external boards outside the local power structure and susceptible to pressures and types of corruption other than those to which the people were accustomed and which they knew how to manipulate. This challenged and offended the influential chiefs and maliks, particularly when some of their own sons began to be drafted. Widespread discontent in the rural and tribal centers of political power became rampant and charges of bribery, corruption, and blackmail flew in all directions.

This is a classic example of how even the best-intentioned move toward modernization can backfire when it is imposed without an understanding of the internal power structure and the political dynamics of the group on whom the "benefits" are conferred. The situation was aggravated in 1928 when Amanullah, in an attempt to improve the army by extending the period of training, announced that the already unpopular draft system would thenceforth require three instead of just two years of army service. It should be borne in mind that the conscription reforms were among the very few which actually affected the rural and to some extent the tribal areas as well as the urban population centers, and conscription had been one of the few grievances of the Khost rebels in 1924 which had to be satisfied to restore peace. And yet the revolt itself showed more clearly than ever the need for a completely new kind of army. Thus the circle became ever more vicious.

Similar misunderstandings and difficulties attended most of

the other attempts to reform the military structure. Soon after
their arrival in 1921 the Turkish military advisers strongly
urged that most of the men already in the army were too set in
their ways and many of them too old to change. They recommended discharging these men and drafting a younger generation which could be trained from scratch. These new men
would be paid much less (5 rupees per month instead of 20) but
would be provided with a package of fringe benefits, such as
cooked food, uniforms, and better quarters, which would more
than make up the difference in pay and would bind the new
men into a paternalistic system and ensure their loyalty to the
government. Nadir Khan, the Minister of War, strongly opposed this scheme. Mahmud Tarzi, who was very pro-Turkish
and who had masterminded the close relations between Afghanistan and Turkey in the first place, supported the Turkish advisers. Most of the Afghan army officers, who resented the superior air of the Turks, sided with Nadir Khan, while a number of
Amanullah's civilian officials backed Tarzi. The result was the
formation of pro- and anti-Turkish factions and a serious schism
in the Amanullah cabinet which eventually resulted in the complete alienation of Nadir Khan and his influential Musahiban
family.[4]

Nadir Khan and his allies believed that the changes advocated
by the Turkish advisers were not in accord with the requirements of a tribal society which the Turks did not quite understand. It was neither politic nor desirable to reject soldiers with
a record of seniority and loyalty simply in the interests of effi-
ciency. Nadir did not oppose modernization of the army. In
fact he favored it, but he argued it had to be done far more
gradually and with full respect for tribal sensibilities. On the
Turks' side were ranged men like Mahmud Sami, an Arab who
had intrigued his way into the Afghan military hierarchy during

[4] See the Secret Report on the Kabul Mission by Sir H. R. Dobbs,
IOL, LPS/10/809, 1919, for a contemporary documentation of the military reforms controversy.

Habibullah's reign. At that time, as a Mesopotamian, he had claimed Turkish citizenship. He actually hated the Turks but pretended to support their recommendations for modernizing the army in order to undermine Nadir Khan's position. He had been Amanullah's instructor at the Military Academy and therefore wielded a good deal of influence. He and Nadir Khan detested each other. Mohammed Wali Khan, who later was appointed regent by Amanullah during the latter's absence in Europe, also sided with Tarzi and Sami.[5] Nadir finally took the issue to Amanullah himself but made the tactical error of reminding Amanullah that he owed his throne to the army, a debt of gratitude binding by the code of Pushtun honor. This reminder apparently did not go down well with Amanullah, and Nadir, whose relations with Amanullah had for long been strained over family differences, became further alienated.

The result was that the Turkish proposals were approved. As an intermediate step, army pay was reduced from 20 rupees per month to 14 (remember that Amanullah won the army to his cause in taking the throne by raising pay from 14 to 20), apparently in the hope that many soldiers would be dissatisfied and leave. This apparently did not happen, and the pay was further cut to 5 rupees.[6] In the meantime the improved conditions and fringe benefits such as food instead of cash (*makulat*) did not entirely materialize. The army bureaucracy and top brass dragged their feet and became demoralized. Officers pocketed the money that was supposed to go for cooked food and the sol-

---

[5] *Ruyidad-e-Riasat-e-Diwan-e-'Ali-e-Hukmat-e-Shahi-e-Afghanistan* [Record of Proceedings of the High Court of the Royal Government of Afghanistan] (Kabul: Government Press, 1930) describes the trial of Mohammed Wali Khan and Mahmud Sami. When Nadir Khan became king, both men were tried and convicted of treason against the government (of Amanullah) for having aided and abetted the rebel Bacha-i-Saqao. Mohammed Wali was condemned to imprisonment. Sami was condemned to death and hanged. Some of the background information on the activities of Mohammed Wali Khan and Mahmud Sami was obtained in an interview with an informant in Kabul, 1967.

[6] Ghani, ch. 4.

diers got neither cash nor food. Old, unsanitary barracks were torn down with promises to build shiny new ones that failed to materialize and winter found men in tents. The Turks valiantly tried to untangle all this and were supported by Amanullah, but they soon discovered what many a foreign adviser has since learned: that once the "system" goes sour on the technical advice tendered, difficulties multiply and passive resistance causes even the most worthy projects to sink deeper and deeper into the morass.[7]

Against this background, the Mangal tribesmen of Khost rebelled in the spring of 1924. The army was totally unprepared to deal with this threat and Nadir Khan refused to lead it into battle, preferring to retreat into relative obscurity as minister to France. The Turks had managed to form some of the young recruits into "model battalions," some of which were thrown in against the Mangals, but they were new and untested and their performance was unsatisfactory.[8] Amanullah's efforts to remodel the army into an effective instrument continued during his entire reign but success somehow eluded him. It is incorrect, however, to assert that he neglected the army.[9] It was not that he did not *try*, merely that he did not *succeed* in imposing

[7] I am especially indebted to two informants interviewed in Kabul in 1968 for this enlightening and heretofore unrecorded exposition of the politico-military controversy surrounding the reforms proposed by the Turkish Military Mission.

[8] Fletcher, p. 208. Bacha-i-Saqao, later to become the bandit king who deposed Amanullah, received his military training in one of these model battalions, which were called Qita Namunas (Telegram from His Majesty's Minister in Kabul to the Secretary of State for Foreign Affairs, London, no. 84, January 23, 1929, IOL, LPS/10/1288 P53, 1929). An informant interviewed in Kabul in 1967 told me that the traditionalist army command sabotaged the effectiveness of the new units by withholding ammunition and rations when the model battalions were in exposed forward positions.

[9] See, for example, Fraser-Tytler, p. 206; Fletcher, p. 207; and Louis Dupree, "Mahmud Tarzi: Forgotten Nationalist," *American Universities Field Staff Reports*, South Asia series, VIII, no. 1 (January 1964).

sound military reforms on an army which after all was but a microcosm of the larger tribal society.

Amanullah's religious reforms were even more controversial and more subject to political intrigue than his military reforms. In this case his means and his ends were more closely related. His goals were quite clear. He had no quarrel with religion as such—indeed, as we have seen, he was a devout believer. But he felt, as Amir Abdur Rahman had felt before him, that the religious establishment was on the whole composed of ignorant and selfish men who used their religious hold on the people to further their political and economic ends. The means which Amanullah chose to alter the situation were characteristic: he sought to educate the religious leaders, especially the rural mullahs, and at the same time to curb their powers in those fields in which he felt modernization required secularization, mostly in education and in the judicial process.

To understand the magnitude of the problem facing Amanullah it is necessary to remember the ubiquity of the religious establishment in Afghanistan. Not only was it firmly entrenched in the urban centers, where the higher ulema made their influence felt directly on the elite and on the centers of intellectual and political power, but in the rural areas hardly a village or hamlet or small nucleus of population could be found where a mullah was not the local teacher, the dispenser of folk Islam, and often a person of economic and political power. Mullahs were well represented in the tribal areas as well, and even nomadic or seminomadic tribesmen were in close contact with mullahs who either traveled with the group or were based in the villages where most nomads had some kind of home base. The army not only had a "chaplain corps" of mullahs but was committed to the popular practice of adopting special spiritual leaders with whom individual soldiers and officers established the relationship of pir and murid (master and disciple). Thus the religious establishment permeated all strata of Afghan society, shared to a considerable degree the values and ideology of each stratum, and maintained a system of informal but effective communications through which ideas and propaganda could be rapidly disseminated throughout the entire Afghan population.[10]

One of my most knowledgeable informants put the situation facing Amanullah thus:

Amanullah's difficulties with the religious leaders were essentially political rather than religious. In the beginning, the mullahs were all in favor of Amanullah because of his support for Turkey, his anti-British posture, and his help to Pan-Islamic causes.

Gradually the attitude of some of them began to change, not because of Amanullah's lack of religion—on the contrary he was very devout and they knew it—but because his attempts to end corruption, curb privilege, demand hard work, and establish an ordered administration began to bite into the prerogatives of the religious leaders. This happened at two levels.

In the urban areas the religious leaders usually held honored and remunerative posts. *Qazis*, scribes, and *muftis* made money from handling disputes, often took bribes, etc. They began to realize that law and order offered by Amanullah would seriously affect their economic and political influence. The choice he offered was to transform many of their activities along more secular lines, become more expert in their traditional duties, and in other ways pay their own way and help carry the load of state administration. A few saw that these reforms were necessary for the nation and cooperated with Amanullah. These were the more enlightened ones. Curiously enough they were often the older men who had already established reputations. On the other hand, younger religious leaders who were greedy for quick profits saw nothing but a hard road full of work ahead for them in what Amanullah offered.

In the rural areas the situation was even more difficult. Education, as demanded vigorously by Amanullah, threatened to challenge the position of the village mullah. Moreover the village maliks were also being adversely affected by some of the administrative reforms— for example, the collection of taxes and the system of conscription.

[10] See Louis Dupree, "Political Uses of Religion: Afghanistan," in K. H. Silvert, ed., *Churches and States: The Religious Institution and Modernization* (New York: American Universities Field Staff, 1967).

The local mullahs were the natural allies of the entrenched village power structure so they were affected by many changes which had nothing to do with religion. They however sought to put their grievances in religious terms.[11]

The result of these political and economic conflicts was eventually a struggle for power between the more reactionary religious leaders and the central government, a struggle which Amanullah sought at all times to keep on secular terms but which the religious leaders, knowing where their strength lay, insisted on making into a religious controversy. Essentially this was a struggle between "church and state." [12] It was the same struggle which existed in the days of Amir Abdur Rahman, except that Abdur Rahman was content with repression whereas Amanullah hoped for conversion. An important premise underlying the effort to modernize Afghanistan, discussed in Chapter II, was that the burden of the great task of modernization should be borne jointly by an enlightened Muslim leadership composed of the religious and the ruling elites. Under Amanullah, with his liberal "democratic" ideas and his preference for persuasion over force, therefore, the religious leaders had more leeway and less to fear in a physical sense than under the repressive regime of the Iron Amir. This gave them more room to maneuver and attack Amanullah over petty points of orthodoxy

[11] Interview with informant, Kabul, 1968.

[12] It is fascinating to note that Benito Mussolini, who later was to become Amanullah's host in exile, analyzed Amanullah's problems as being essentially an Eastern version of the old European church-state conflicts. In a copyrighted article in the *Daily Express* of February 13, 1929, Mussolini, writing as Premier of Italy, stated *inter alia:* "We have come to regard it as a fixed governmental principle that the ecclesiastical authority shall be completely distinct from the civil." Mussolini then traces the bloody European history of church-state conflict and winds up by saying: "Yet, in comparison with what has happened in Afghanistan, these are mere incidents in religious feeling, for with a stroke of the pen the youthful Afghan king has decreed a complete religious reversal. . . . When he attempted his reforms he found the religious and civil life combined in a maze of intricate entanglements."

and over the lack of religious sanction for his social reforms, especially those affecting the status of women. While some outstanding religious leaders continued to support Amanullah to the end, others became more and more alienated and hoped to goad him into a show of force which would stir up popular indignation. But Amanullah for a long time was too wise to fall into the trap and met each controversy with persuasion and by bringing to his aid those members of the ulema who supported his views.

During the 1924 Khost revolt, for example, in which the Mullah-i-Lang ("Lame Mullah") was one of the principal rebels, Amanullah countered the rebels' contention that their cause was a religious one by dispatching a delegation of respected ulema to argue the religious case with the tribal mullahs at Baidak in the Logar Valley. The rebel mullahs, headed by the Mullah-i-Lang, confined themselves to trying to convince the government delegation to join the revolt. It was not a discussion but an attempt at intimidation, the rebels boldly stating that they had already selected a new amir and that Amanullah must go. The meeting served two important purposes: the government realized at last that compromise was not possible and that only defeat in battle would squash the uprising, and the moderate and loyal ulema became convinced that the rebel mullahs' claims were entirely political and not religious.[13] As a result of this confrontation, Amanullah's religious advisers recommended the calling of a Loya Jirgah to consider all the religious complaints. This Jirgah on the whole endorsed Amanullah's reforms but recommended some changes in the legislation regarding the powers of *qazis* to fix punishment and several other matters which we have already noted in the discussion on judicial reforms. Amanullah accepted these modifications reluctantly but did agree willingly to name a "Committee of Islamic Scholars" to sanction all future laws and

---

[13] *Aman-i-Afghan*, V, nos. 13 and 14, 8–13.

to certify that they did not offend the dictates of Shari'a.[14] In return for this concession he received sufficient support from religious leaders to permit him to rally loyal tribes against the rebel Mangals and Jajis. With these tribes helping the ineffective army, the Khost rebellion was quelled.

Amanullah's insistence on extending religious freedom and eliminating discrimination based on religious differences was a cause of considerable controversy between him and the religious community. Amanullah persisted because he was convinced that the task of nation-building could not go forward so long as tribal and religious differences separated large sections of the inhabitants. Nevertheless, after the Khost revolt he was forced to give ground to religious pressure. It will be recalled that the 1923 Constitution had to be amended to require Jews and Hindus to wear distinctive dress and to limit freedom of religion so as to prohibit apostasy from Islam. The Hanafite rite was also adopted as official and this discriminated against the substantial Shiah community, most of whom were members of the large and depressed Hazara tribe. It seems clear that at times Amanullah was frustrated by his inability to disentangle religion from politics or to make his followers measure up to the high ideals of national unity which he advocated. To Joseph Castagne he unburdened himself in private conversation: "I ask of God that he help me in serving my people well and also the cause of Islam. I am ready to give my life for Islam but I want to abolish all religious prejudices which are the cause of the weakness of the Muslim world. Whoever dares to talk of Shiites or Sunnites will be severely punished." [15] Yet he found that his advocacy of

[14] *Annual Register,* 1929. When Nadir Khan became king he institutionalized this idea by establishing a body called the Jamia'at-ul-'Ulema, which was given virtual veto power over legislation. The 1931 Constitution provided that "no laws approved by the National Assembly may be in contradiction with the doctrines of Islam and the policy of the State." See Article 65 of the *Constitutional Law of Afghanistan,* 1931.

[15] Joseph Castagne, *Les Basmatchis* (Paris: E. Leroux, 1925), p. 27.

tribal and religious unity often alienated powerful Pushtun and orthodox Sunni elements whose political support he needed for his modernization program as a whole. At times, therefore, he had to bow to their pressure, as in the case of the stoning of the Qadiani missionaries.

The Qadianis, a branch of the Ahmadiya sect of the Punjab, are considered by most orthodox Muslims as heretics because they allegedly deny that Mohammed was the Seal (that is, the last) of the Prophets. Unlike most other Muslims, the Qadianis are active missionaries and proselytizers. Some of their religious leaders entered Afghanistan under cover of the Hijrat movement when the Indian Khilafat party sponsored a Muslim exodus from British India as a protest against the subjugation of Turkey. These Qadianis soon were busy preaching in the bazaars and successfully gathering converts into the fold. They preached a liberal form of Islam, being strong believers in education and literacy, and in many ways worked along lines which Amanullah could not help but approve. In spite of this, in 1925, shortly after the Khost revolt, a Qadiani named Nimatullah and his missionary assistant were stoned to death in the Kabul bazaar at the instigation of orthodox Sunni mullahs. The liberal press in India protested vigorously, stating that such persecution was inconsistent with the Afghan constitutional right of freedom of religion. To these charges the Afghan government felt compelled to reply in the *Aman-i-Afghan* that the constitutional freedom of religion referred to the rights of followers of other religions but was not a license for so-called Muslims to preach heretical doctrines. This was considered by most observers as a sop thrown out by Amanullah to the orthodox clergy whose political loyalty he wanted to keep. As justification for this violent act it was given out that the Qadianis had helped to foment the 1924 rebellion.[16]

The first show-down of power between the religious leaders

[16] *Aman-i-Afghan*, V, no. 13, 1–5, *Annual Register* 1925.

and Amanullah during the 1924 Mangal revolt was followed by an armed truce during which Amanullah's modernization program gradually made inroads into the privileged positions of the mullahs. Secular laws began to be applied. Amanullah tried to develop more liberal religious schools, and the day of rest was changed from Friday to Thursday. This last measure was later used effectively as propaganda to accuse Amanullah of profaning the Muslim holy day. In fact, like a number of other Amanullah reforms, it was intended to do just the opposite. Amanullah had noted that most people used the Friday day of rest for taking holidays rather than for prayer. By making Thursday the official day of rest from work, the people could spend it in their leisure pursuits and then on Friday they would take officially sanctioned time off, closing shops and offices to perform their religious duties and then return to work. This intention was later deliberately misrepresented by the mullahs as an attempt to destroy the sanctity of the Jum'a (Friday), and the error was solidified by the foreign press and later writers.[17]

Between 1924 and 1928 Amanullah was winning the campaign against the more backward religious leaders and they had not been able to goad him into abrupt repressive measures. But what the mullahs were not able to accomplish, Amanullah's trip to Europe, which had glaringly driven home to him how advanced and "civilized" the Western world was in comparison to Afghanistan, did succeed in doing. He returned convinced that the orthodox religious leaders could not be won over, that they were a drag on modernization that could no longer be tolerated, and that fairly extreme actions would have to be taken to break their power. It was for this reason that the new plan for modernization, announced to the Loya Jirgah and amplified in his four-day marathon speech in the fall of 1928, was highly charged with proposals which aimed at the heart of clerical power. The proposals for the education of mullahs, the *qazi*

---

[17] Interview with informant, Kabul, 1968.

school, the secular law school, the complete liquidation of the waqfs, the abolition of pirs and murids in the army, and the banning of all mullahs educated in Deoband were correctly interpreted by conservative religious leaders as a declaration of war.[18]

The conservative religious leaders were now convinced that this time they could provoke Amanullah to an overt act against the religious establishment which would evoke national indignation. The challenge was issued by one of the most powerful religious families in Afghanistan, that of the Hazrat of Shor Bazaar. Amanullah's relations with this family of conservative but respected Muslim religious leaders offer an excellent example of his problems with the more orthodox hierarchy. The Mojadidi family, claiming Arab descent, had been traditional pirs of Sirhind, where they had established a shrine highly revered by the great Ghilzai tribe. After moving to Kabul, the head of the family was given the title of Hazrat of Shor Bazaar, one of the city's important commercial quarters. This family claimed the hereditary right to crown Afghan kings at their coronations. They maintained close ties and influence with the Ghilzai tribes, especially with its very warlike and powerful subdivision, the Suleiman Khel. They thus exercised great power in the amir's court. The two principal members of the family at this time were Fazl Rahim, the Hazrat Sahib himself, and his able and ambitious brother, Fazl Umar, better known as Sher Agha.

The Mojadidi family had been strongly pro-Turkish and hence anti-British when Amanullah was a prince during World War I. They cooperated with Amanullah as members of the so called War party led by Amir Habibullah's brother, Nasrullah. They had also supported Amanullah's accession to the throne and had put their entire weight, particularly their tribal influ-

---

[18] According to two informants interviewed in Kabul, 1968, many of the most conservative religious leaders in Afghanistan had been trained in the well-known madrassah of Deoband in northern India. Amanullah, rightly or wrongly, believed that many of them had been recruited by British intelligence.

8. The Hazrat Sahib
of Shor Bazaar, leader
of the religious
opposition against
Amanullah.

ence, behind the Third Afghan War which brought Afghanistan independence from British suzerainty. For this Amanullah
had rewarded them with lands and honors. The Hazrat of Shor
Bazaar also supported Amanullah's Pan-Islamic policies. But dis-
illusion set in when Amanullah was unable to obtain, in the
peace treaty with the British, annexation, amnesty, or even assured protection for the tribes east of the Durand Line.[19] The

[19] See the secret Report from the Chief British Representative, Indo-
Afghan Conference, to the Foreign Secretary to the Government of
India, Simla, August 6, 1920, Public Records Office, London, F.O.
371/5381. Following the temporary peace treaty of Rawalpindi signed in

Hazrat Sahib felt this was a betrayal of the tribes and a threat to his own influence over them. The breach between Amanullah and the Mojadidis widened as his modernization program more and more stressed secular values and was aggravated by Amanullah's unceremonious behavior toward the revered Hazrat. When Amanullah announced his intention to adopt stronger measures against the recalcitrant mullahs in 1928, the Hazrat responded with a gesture of active opposition. In the meantime Amanullah had become convinced that the growing opposition of the Hazrat of Shor Bazaar was caused by his having become an agent of British intelligence and that he and his family were plotting a revolt.[20]

Accordingly, when in September 1928 the Hazrat of Shor Bazaar obtained the signature of 400 mullahs opposing Amanullah's proposals for additional reforms, Amanullah took a very serious view of this activity. He summoned Abdur Rahman, the chief *qazi* of Kabul and a onetime teacher of the Hazrat of Shor Bazaar, and put pressure on him to obtain a recantation under pain of dismissal and grievous punishment. Caught in this predicament the Hazrat and Abdur Rahman tried to escape to British India, passing through the tribal areas in Khost where the revolt had started in 1924. Amanullah interpreted this as intention to raise a revolt against him and had the Hazrat, Abdur Rahman, and thirty other mullahs arrested and brought back to Kabul where Abdur Rahman was found guilty of treason. He and four other mullahs were executed and the Hazrat and other

---

1919, the Afghans sent a delegation to Mussoorie, India, in 1920 to negotiate a final settlement. While the conference was in progress the British moved into Waziristan to pacify and punish the tribes which had risen and joined General Nadir Khan's advance into India. Afghan protests went unheeded and the conference eventually broke up. But the Wazirs were taught a bitter lesson about supporting Afghanistan against British India.

[20] I am indebted for hitherto unpublished details about the relations between Amanullah and the Mojadidi family to an informant interviewed in Kabul in 1967 who generously shared his personal knowledge with me.

members of his family thrown into jail.[21] This was the kind of incident which the most conservative religious leaders had been hoping to provoke. From that point most of the Muslim religious leaders, including many of the more moderate supporters of Amanullah, turned against him. A few of the better educated and more liberal ulema continued to support the King, but they tended to be revered, scholarly, devout, and gentle men, whereas those in opposition to Amanullah were activists with the political power to influence the people in general and especially the tribes.[22]

As a result, when a minor tribal revolt broke out in Shinwari country in November of that year, the vast majority of mullahs immediately gave it a religious sanction and launched an effective propaganda campaign against the government and king. They used religious symbols and incantations to defend their secular interests. Their reputed fanaticism was a fanaticism not of religion but of political and economic power, and as propagandists they enjoyed an access to word-of-mouth communication which the government's meagre technical facilities could not begin to match.[23] Amanullah was declared to be a kafir, to have gone mad as a result of having been defiled by eating pork and drinking wine in Europe. His modernization program was declared to be in contravention to the dictates of Islam, particularly those measures that forced women to bare themselves and to reject the authority of their husbands and fathers. Photographs which had appeared in European newspapers of Queen Soraya in low-cut evening gowns with European kafir men in

[21] Telegram from His Majesty's Minister in Kabul to the Secretary of State for Foreign Affairs, London, no. 132, September 11, 1928, IOL, LPS/10/53, 1929, Part 3.

[22] Interviews with three informants, Kabul, 1967–68. See Louis Dupree, "The Political Uses of Religion."

[23] M. E. Yapp, "Disturbances in Eastern Afghanistan, 1839–42," *Bulletin of the School of Oriental and African Studies*, XXV (1962), 499. Yapp notes the use of religious propaganda to cover up the essentially political issues of tribal resistance against Anglo-Saddozai government during the First Afghan War.

attendance were circulated in the tribal areas, and stories of atrocities against religious leaders were manufactured and passed from bazaar to bazaar.[24]

In sum, the ultimate result of the religious reforms, however well-intentioned, was to lose for Amanullah the political support of the large majority of the religious community. This lack of support was converted into active disloyalty as soon as a typical but minor tribal revolt broke out and the religious leaders helped to fan the flames of this uprising into a major conflagration with all the overtones of a religious war. Other factors were also at work, of course, but there can be no doubt that the political activity of the mullahs was most effective in spreading the revolt. Eventually Amanullah awoke to the implications of this religious agitation and tried to defuse the bomb by publicly retracting nearly all the religious reforms (most of which were only proposals in any case). On January 6, 1929, he issued a proclamation in which he offered to release the religious leaders, to reinstate Friday as the day of rest, to close the girls' schools, to cancel the ban on the Deoband mullahs, to forego the requirement of teaching certificates for mullahs, to agree to the reappointment of *muhtasibs* (religious inspectors) and to cancel the restrictions on pirs and murids in the army.[25] But the recantation came too late to have any political effect. Within a week Amanullah had abdicated the throne.

[24] The *Daily Express* (London), March 7, 1929, contains a typical example of this kind of propaganda in a story allegedly written by a Colonel Ghulam Nabi Khan, describing Amanullah's summary executions of many innocent mullahs. The author of the piece was unknown to any of my informants. There was a *General* Ghulam Nabi Khan, the distinguished head of the Charkhi family, who during that period was Amanullah's ambassador in Moscow and completely loyal to the king. It is probable that the *soi disant* colonel deliberately used this well-known name to gain foreign credibility.

[25] Melia, p. 56, reports that the proclamation appeared in the *Official Gazette* of January 7, 1929. I was unable to locate the *Gazette* for that date. The recantation is also summarized in the secret Telegram from His Majesty's Minister at Kabul to the Secretary of State for Foreign Affairs in London, no. 19, January 6, 1929, IOL, LPS/10/285, 1929.

chapter VI

the amanullah reforms: modernizing the economy

Amanullah's program of economic modernization is probably the least known but perhaps one of the most important contributions he made to the continuing change and transformation of Afghanistan. It escaped much of the noxious critical propaganda because it was much less subject to emotional distortions than the social or religious reforms. The economic program was initiated early in Amanullah's reign and proceeded at a fairly steady pace throughout the period of his administration. Basically it consisted of two parts: clearing away old practices which stood in the way of progress and substituting new methods and systems. Thus, for example, his tax reforms at first emphasized the elimination of anachronistic and dysfunctional imposts (such as taxes "for oil for the queen's hair"), which amounted to a little more than meaningless extortions by the state. In the same category was the "tea and sugar money" which had to be paid to many government officials simply to get them to perform their duties. The abolition of *baqiyat*, the system whereby officials and their heirs were liable in perpetuity for small irregularities in accounts, falls under the same rubric. *Baqiyat* caused officials to shun responsibility and avoid all actions or decisions through which they might even remotely incur some liability. Amanullah also abolished all internal customs duties, thus stimulating the flow of goods in domestic commerce and giving the country a feeling of greater political unity.[1]

[1] Ghani, ch. 4; interview with informant in Kabul, 1967. So deeply ingrained was this nefarious system of *baqiyat* that it lingers on even

Along with this clearing of ancient debris went the more constructive task of initiating new procedures and practices. Thus new systems for maintaining government accounts were instituted with double-entry reckoning. Cadastral surveys on a limited scale were introduced so that land taxes might be more equitable and based on something more tangible than ancient fictions of ownership. Even the use of "Western" (Arabic) numerals was attempted and made modest progress. All this, of course, required a rather extensive educational and training program, which was to be conducted by various schools for government employees which Amanullah founded. In these schools government clerks were gradually weaned away from the old Persian system of symbolic entries on scrolls and taught to keep accounts in a numerical system on ledgers. The progress on all this was predictably slow, but the foundations were laid; though interrupted by the revolution, many of these same reforms were gradually reintroduced under Nadir Shah and his successor.

Perhaps the most important of these economic reforms was the reorganization of the system of taxation. Although previous amirs had made spasmodic attempts to convert from a system of collecting revenue in kind to one of collecting in cash, little permanent progress along these lines had been made until Amanullah tackled the problem with his usual energy and resolution. The reason the old system had proved so durable was that it favored graft and corruption at all levels of government administration. In the rural areas, for example, the farmer had to bring the percentage of the crop owed to the government to central collecting points at his own expense. Already the amount due had been the subject of haggling and crossing of palms with silver when the government officials came to look over the crop

today as one of the curses of Afghan bureaucracy in the form of the responsibility of the so-called *tawildar*, "the man who keeps the keys." It often takes many signatures and countersignatures before the *tawildar* will issue any of the precious objects in his charge which may range from an urgently needed spare part for an airplane to a mere government form.

and assess its value. Now when the grain was brought to the depot the official in charge would perhaps declare it to be of bad quality and would underweigh it until "tea and sugar money" changed hands. The grain then had to be stored in government warehouses, sometimes for many months. The question of spoilage formed the basis for more spoils. An inspector had to verify the amounts spoiled, money would pass again. A vast amount of paperwork and record-keeping was involved in handling the grain, and the more modest demands of the clerks and accountants had to be met. In the end everyone made some profit up and down the long line except the government, which often registered a net loss in the transaction.[2]

The reforms in the system of taxation were of fundamental importance in a number of ways. In the first place the change to cash transactions tended to monetize the economy, which most economists agree is one of the basic steps on the road to economic development. Monetizing the economy greatly improves and accelerates the distribution of commodities and is a general stimulant to all forms of commerce and trade. There is no doubt that this fundamental reform survived the Amanullah period, and Afghanistan's internal revenue and trade have been principally on a cash basis ever since. Then again, the new tax system increased the revenues collected by the central government, and, together with the currency reforms initiated by Amanullah, it changed the entire fiscal picture of the government, enabling it to support the staggering expenditures involved in some of the other programs such as education, roads, buildings, and communications.[3] Another important result of the tax reform was that it created confidence in the agricultural sector. The farmer knew for the first time with some certainty what his tax

[2] This description is based on Ghani, ch. 4.

[3] Interview in Kabul in 1968 with an informant who was well-informed about the economic problems of the Amanullah period; also Amalendu Guha, "The Economy of Afghanistan during Amanullah's Reign, 1919–1929," *International Studies* (New Delhi), IX, no. 2 (October 1967), 161–182.

liability was and could plan accordingly. This was a stimulant to production, particularly when coupled with the modest but ameliorative effects of the campaign against corruption. Finally, the rationalization of the tax system enabled the Afghan government to operate on a budget for the first time in its history and to control its expenditures and to husband its resources in a more efficient manner.

The budget itself became something of a *cause célèbre* during Amanullah's time. So novel was the idea and so completely had government finances in the past been the personal prerogative of the amir, that when Mir Hashim, Amanullah's finance minister, with the help of the Italian expert Bernardi, tried to explain the principles of a budget to the cabinet and the Royal Council, it became clear that a considerable educational effort would have to be undertaken if the concept were to be accepted and acted upon at all levels of government. In fact, the whole idea was widely misunderstood and it became quite common for government servants and the people in general to blame the "boojit" for all sorts of failings and misadventures. Amanullah was wryly amused when on one occasion he stopped by the wayside as was his wont to ask a peasant about his problems and was promptly informed that the crops that year had been very bad because of the "boojit." [4]

Amanullah felt that some of the most promising and immediate opportunities for economic development lay in agriculture, and reforms in this field occupied a very important position in his modernization program. Not only did he encourage agriculture through his taxation program—after abolishing many irritating small taxes and extralegal exactions, this program increased the land tax by only 1 afghani per *jerib* (½ acre), plus ½

[4] This tale, whether apocryphal or not, was recounted to me by two informants in Kabul interviews in 1967–68. "*Se non è vero è ben trovato*." The *Annual Register*, 1927, reports new budget procedures adopted in July 1926 refining previous practices. See also *Aman-i-Afghan*, II, no. 35, 305, for a revealing article explaining what a "budget" is.

afghani as an education tax—but he also stimulated interest in agriculture by sponsoring the first agricultural fairs and live-stock shows, many of which he personally attended. He also initiated an extensive reforestation program in a land which for centuries had known only indiscriminate denudation by man and beast.[5]

Amanullah also conducted the only major land reform program in Afghan history. Although Afghanistan, for historical reasons, has not had the problem of large landlordism to the same extent as other Asian countries, it did have a large class of landless peasants who had little incentive to produce more or better. Amanullah alleviated this problem by selling large tracts of public lands at the very low price of 10 afghanis per *jerib* of irrigated land. He thus created a class of peasant proprietors, increased agricultural production, and minimized peasant dissatisfaction. This enlightened program made it possible during the last part of Amanullah's reign for Afghanistan to become for the first time a net exporter of surpluses of wheat, rice, and other grains to Soviet Russia, thereby earning substantial quantities of foreign exchange.[6]

Amanullah's fiscal policy fitted neatly into his other economic reforms. He issued a new currency consisting of new afghani coins, 90 per cent silver, which immediately became a much more acceptable medium of exchange than the previously some-what debased Afghan rupee. This confidence in the currency stimulated internal and external trade, and for the first time in history the Afghan coinage enjoyed a favorable rate of exchange

[5] *Aman-i-Afghan*, V, no. 1 (28 Hut 1302), reports the King's Nauroz (New Year) speech dedicated to agriculture. Amanullah is described as wearing a locally made indigenous costume and exhorting his listeners on the importance and nobility of agriculture. Viollis, p. 49, comments on the extensive reforestation program.

[6] This information was obtained in interviews with two informants in Kabul, 1967–68. Unfortunately no reliable economic statistics are available for the Amanullah period and these judgments must remain somewhat impressionistic. The general prosperity during the reign of Amanullah was remarked upon by most informants.

with the Indian rupee, even though the latter was backed by the economic power of the British Empire.[7]

Amanullah wanted to buttress the country's economic independence and he felt that a national bank would help accomplish this purpose as well as ensure congruency between policies of credit, capital formation, and currency reforms. Judging from statements made in *L'Afghanistan Nouveau*, the idea of starting a bank began to be considered as early as 1924. No private or public banks existed in Afghanistan at that time. However, there was religious opposition to the bank because of the Islamic prohibition against interest. This coincided with the aftermath of the Khost revolt and the need to pacify religious feelings, so the scheme was dropped. It was revived shortly before the 1928 revolution when Amanullah asked a British concern to study the possibility of starting a bank in Kabul. The proposal was supported somewhat reluctantly by the British Foreign Office but was aborted by the 1928 revolution.[8]

Connected with Amanullah's fiscal reforms and his desire for economic independence was his remarkable feat of financing the extensive development program described below almost entirely from domestic capital. Aside from small loans for arms and planes, a German credit shortly before the rebellion, and small sporadic Soviet grants, Afghanistan received no direct foreign aid during Amanullah's reign. The British had terminated their annual subsidy on signing the peace treaties of 1919 and 1921. Later proposals for economic aid in lieu of the subsidy came to naught. The Russians had promised an annual subsidy of one million rubles in the 1921 Russo-Afghan treaty but made only

[7] MacMunn, pp. 311-313, and interview with informant in Kabul, 1967.

[8] *L'Afghanistan Nouveau*, ch. 5, pp. 49-51. The first bank in Afghanistan was not opened until 1931. Pernot, p. 39, notes the resistance to the bank on religious grounds and the fact that most of the trade and credit transactions were in the hands of Hindu and Jewish moneylenders.

partial and intermittent payments.[9] One of the favorite subjects of speculation in British official reports of the period was the possible sources of financial support for such items as Amanullah's spectacular program of new cities and public buildings. The usual conclusion was that the country was going bankrupt and the treasury was empty.[10] But these same prophets of doom saw the programs moving forward and not grinding to a halt for shortage of funds. Many of these same "empty treasury" critics later asserted that Amanullah had made off with millions of pounds from the same "empty" treasury.

We are now better able to judge that Amanullah's financing of the development program was not based on alchemy but rather on previous savings accumulated by the amirs Abdur Rahman and Habibullah, on sound fiscal reforms, on better systems of taxation and collection, on a generally rising gross national product, and lastly—and least known—on a very generous, albeit wholly involuntary, foreign aid program from Soviet Russia. This took the form of a great infusion of wealth when hundreds of thousands of Turkmen, Uzbeg, and Tajik refugees fled into Afghanistan from the communist reign of terror in Russian Central Asia which accompanied the Basmachi rebellion. They brought with them large numbers of sheep, horses, and other livestock. Especially important were the great flocks of karakul sheep that gave Afghanistan a completely new and still highly valuable export: the prized karakul (or so-called Persian lamb) skins. There had been a few of these valuable sheep in Afghanistan before, and

[9] The text of this treaty is given in the Appendix to Adamec, pp. 188–191. According to one informant interviewed in Kabul in 1967, a large number of foreign specialists were employed by the government and for the most part were paid by Afghanistan. The Russians provided some military pilots for training and the Turks paid the salaries of their military mission, but local costs were borne by the Afghan government.

[10] See, for example, Sir Francis Humphrys' prediction of bankruptcy in the Telegram from His Britannic Majesty's Minister at Kabul to the Secretary of State for Foreign Affairs, London, no. 87, July 14, 1928, IOL, LPS/10/285, 1929.

some skins had been exported through Bokhara, forming part of the Russian world trade in "Astrakhan," as the fur is known there. But by the 1920's Afghanistan was able to begin export of large quantities of karakul directly to German and English markets. The carpet industry also received a great boost from the immigration of skilled weavers such as the Tekke and Mervi Turkmen tribes. There was thus a very considerable net input of wealth, talents, and skills which had an impact both on the domestic economy and on foreign trade.[11]

Needless to say, Amanullah did not neglect the important question of foreign trade. One of his first steps was to reorganize the customs service and completely rewrite the customs tariff so as to encourage exports and nonluxury imports.[12] Afghanistan also negotiated trade agreements with as many countries as showed any interest in increasing mutual trade. To stimulate exports, in addition to fiscal and customs measures, Amanullah encouraged the formation of joint-stock companies or *shirkats*. Commercial agents and missions were sent abroad with considerable success. Trade with Persia and Russia was greatly increased. As we have already noted Afghanistan became a net exporter of food grains to Russia, and in the years 1920–1923 it exported substantial amounts of dried and fresh fruits, vegetable dyes, skins, wool, silk, and rugs. According to one source, Afghanistan's exports rose from fifty million francs in 1920 to one billion francs by 1925.[13]

The obverse of this policy was Amanullah's resolve to conserve his foreign exchange by establishing import-substitution

----

[11] Interview with an informant in Kabul, 1968. This informant, without statistics to aid him and based on his own experiences in the export-import trade, estimated that during Amanullah's decade the yearly export of karakul rose from around 60,000 to over a million skins and the export of carpets may have increased by as much as 500 per cent.

[12] Ghani, ch. 4 and Appendix.

[13] *L'Afghanistan Nouveau,* ch. 5, pp. 49–51; Melia, p. 25. Melia cites no source for these figures and they must, therefore, be taken as an educated guess.

industries. One of Afghanistan's principal imports was textiles, and it caused Amanullah pain to see some of his "enlightened" countrymen spending large sums on imported cloth. He ascertained to his own satisfaction that the local homespun could be cut and put together into acceptable modern costume and, though most sartorially informed critics disagreed with this judgment, he mercilessly chivied members of his court who persisted in wearing imported cloth. But some of the habits of his less sophisticated countrymen also disturbed him. He remarked, for example, that a normal country turban required seven and one-half yards of cloth, usually imported, and that this multiplied by some six million male Afghans came to fifty million yards of imports per year. This was the reason he wanted to abolish turbans in favor of hats and not, as the religious propaganda later insisted, in order to prevent the faithful from pressing their foreheads to the ground in prayer.[14] In any case, Amanullah wanted as soon as possible to have his own textile mills and he accordingly contracted for the machinery during his sojourn in Europe.

Indeed, as Mir Ghulam Mohammad Ghobar points out, Amanullah's whole program of light industries was aimed at import substitution, thereby freeing his earned foreign exchange to fuel his over-all development program. The list of industries for which Amanullah bought machinery during his European tour make this very clear: tanning, gunpowder, cement, soap, textile, stone and woodworking, ice-making, vegetable oil, sugar, dairies, foundries, and so on. He also sensed the need to develop sources of adequate industrial power and for this reason started his search for coal and began to develop the considerable hydroelectric potential of the country.[15] In this field, as in so many

[14] This clarification was vouched for by a knowledgeable informant in Kabul, 1967.

[15] Ghobar. See also *Aman-i-Afghan*, V, no. 22 (7 Jaddi 1303), which reports the opening of a new hydroelectric plant for Kabul and announces that electricity would now be available at rates cheaper than kerosene or candles.

others, Amanullah was an Afghan pioneer. C. Morrish points
out that, contrary to the claims of many critics, Amanullah's
tour of Europe was by no means a pleasure jaunt:

He worked all the time and completed many contracts for extensive development work which was to start after his return. . . .
Amanullah previous to his abdication had ordered large quantities of
machinery from Germany. His purchases included mills for cotton
and wool yarn, electric light plants, paper-making machinery, complete laundries, printing presses, and a match factory. The cost
amounted to many *lakhs* of rupees and under an arrangement with
the German government and the firms supplying the goods, payment was to extend over a period of years. The machinery arrived
in Karachi immediately before the fall of Kabul to Bacha-i-Saqao
and in consequence it remained at that port incurring huge expenses
for demurrage, storage, port fees, etc.[16]

Thus, Amanullah's plan for developing a light-industries sector
to substitute for imports never got the chance to develop as
planned.

Of all the economic reforms, probably none had more significant economic and political long-run effects than the extensive
program to develop communications. Roads, air service, telegraph, telephones, and improved postal facilities were the begin-
nings of an economic and political infrastructure that continued
to develop during the half century which started with Amanullah's reign. None of these systems of communication reached a
high degree of completion or perfection during Amanullah's decade but an important start was made in all of them. The Great
North Road was conceived by Amanullah as the first all-
weather connection between northern and southern Afghanistan. Until 1932 Afghanistan was effectively cut in two by the
Hindu Kush which rises like a wall, with peaks reaching nearly

[16] Morrish. Morrish is a pseudonym probably for M. A. Hakim, a
wealthy Afghan merchant living in Peshawar, who was anti-Amanullah
and later acted as liaison between the British and Nadir Khan. (A *lakh*
is one hundred thousand.)

20,000 feet, sixty miles north of Kabul. Caravans slowly wound their way through that labryinthine barrier and during winter the routes were often completely closed. Amanullah tried a breach across the Salang Pass, the narrowest point, but failed. In 1932 Nadir Shah chose a circuitous route and succeeded. Finally in the early 1960's Prime Minister Prince Daud used Russian engineering skill to return to Amanullah's Salang route and by means of a long high-altitude tunnel saved hundreds of miles of travel. Another Amanullah project which Prince Daud resurrected was the route from Kabul to Peshawar through the gorge of the Kabul River. Amanullah made motorable other important roads, such as those between Kabul and Kandahar and between Kandahar and Herat. With these roads and their branches came increased mobility, gradual penetration of isolated areas, better government control, and more effective distribution of commerce and trade. These objectives were strengthened by telecommunications, which gave the central government rapid contact with distant provincial administrators and sped information and news to and from the capital and remote outposts.

These communications facilities and the beginning of a commercial air service began to break up not only the internal isolation of the country but its external remoteness as well. The Russians pioneered the air service flying between Tashkent and Kabul in Junkers planes. Later Lufthansa signed an agreement to extend its services from Tehran, and in 1928 the British were negotiating with Amanullah for an air service between Kabul and India.[17] All these projects were casualties of the 1928 revolution and it was not until nearly two decades later, after World War II, that they were revived in any significant form. But the breakout to the outside world had been made and the British

[17] Imperial Airways was doing a survey of a proposed Lahore-Kabul route in April 1928. See the secret Telegram from the Secretary of State for India, London, to the Government of India, no. 1057, April 20, 1928, IOL, LPS/10/1203 P135, 1927.

had dramatically demonstrated the new dimensions of air power in a remarkable pioneering airlift that evacuated the entire British community and most other Europeans from Kabul when Bacha-i-Saqao invaded the captial.[18]

One of Amanullah's most cherished projects was the construction of a railroad. The route from Kabul to Kandahar was his first choice and he hoped to extend it from Kandahar to Herat. During his visit to Europe he negotiated with German and French firms on this matter and persuaded a French syndicate headed by the famous and notorious arms magnate, Sir Basil Zaharoff, to undertake a survey of the railroad project. The survey was conducted in the summer of 1928 by a team of engineers headed by Michel Clemenceau (son of the Tiger) and Pierre Makcheef. The British, always sensitive to the subject of railroads through Afghanistan in terms of a possible Russian invasion of India, arranged to be kept informed of the progress of the survey by both Zaharoff and Clemenceau. In September Clemenceau and Zaharoff informed the British Embassy in Paris that Makcheef had satisfactorily completed the survey from Kabul to Kandahar to Herat.[19] What the ultimate result of this project might have been had not the revolution intervened, it is difficult to say. At any rate, Afghanistan does not have a railroad to this day.

[18] Great Britain, *Parliamentary Papers,* Vol. XXIII (*Accounts and Papers,* vol. 6), "Report on the Air Operations in Afghanistan, December 12, 1928, to February 25, 1929," Cd. 3400, 1929–30, p. 813.

[19] The correspondence between Makcheef, Clemenceau, and Zaharoff concerning the railroad survey was enclosed in a demiofficial letter from Sir Trevor Dawson, British Chargé d'Affaires in Paris, to Sir Edward Crowe, Director of the Foreign Division of the Department of Overseas Trade, dated September 18, 1928, IOL, LPS/10/1928, Afghan Series, Serial no. 117.

chapter VII

the amanullah reforms: why did they fail?

In a very important sense any inquiry into the causes of failure of the Amanullah reforms really begs the question. The full development of the modernization program was certainly cut short by the revolution that deposed Amanullah, but this does not mean that the reforms themselves were failures unless it can be shown that they caused the revolution in a very direct way. In attempting an objective evaluation of the reforms we must stand at some distance from the individual programs and from the events and take a broader and longer look at the entire complex situation. First of all we should note the coherent and integrated nature of the reforms and the fact that they were designed as a transforming national experience. It is this that makes the reforms a program of modernization rather than a mere attempt to bring a few governmental or social institutions up to date. Good examples of this integrated approach are the economic reforms in which the tax and customs measures reinforced and supported the fiscal, commercial, and agricultural innovations. At a higher level, the economic reforms reinforced and supported the educational reforms and vice versa, while economic, social, religious, and military reforms were necessary adjuncts to the political formation of a constitutional state governed by laws, which in turn formed the overarching framework within which all the other modernizing influences could operate freely. There is unfortunately no direct documentary evidence that Amanullah or his advisers conceived of the program in such precise terms. There is, however, abundant indirect evidence in the nature of the reforms themselves and in Amanullah's statements which shows a consciousness that he was dealing with a social system as a whole and that, as he said, he desired "a revolution in every phase of national work and life." [1]

Amanullah's modernization plan, therefore, was integrated, grandiose, and bold. To a certain extent it required movement along all fronts simultaneously and all within a very short time span. To put such a grand design into operation under even the most favorable circumstances would have required the combined talents of a gifted innovator, a brilliant administrator, and a master politician. Amanullah was amply endowed with the first requirement but deficient in the other two.

The administrative irregularities caused largely by Amanullah's mercurial and unpredictable temperament and the political incongruities between what was planned and the end product made it possible for critics of the Amanullah regime to discredit the entire modernization program. It is interesting to note, however, that the critics often wrote *after* Amanullah's downfall and tended to place blame on Amanullah as a person rather than examine objectively the modernization program itself.

A disinterested inquiry into the linkages between the reforms and the revolution must commence with an examination of the social and religious reforms since these were singled out by propagandists and commentators as the principal source of popular dissatisfaction. Of the social reforms, the most controversial were those referring to dress, women's rights, and familial customs such as marriages and funerals. Did these reforms indeed provide the explosive mixture for social revolt? A re-examination based on contemporary sources and materials answers the question in the negative. Dress reforms were unpopular, but they were applied only in a few places. Most people disregarded

[1] Fraser-Tytler, p. 213.

them and enforcement was lax to say the least. The campaign to liberate women was presented in an unsophisticated and aggressive fashion and met with considerable resistance, but it was largely based on persuasion rather than enforcement and was on the whole rather ineffective. The attempts to reform marriage and funeral customs, even though they took the form of enforceable laws, were ignored by the population at large and none of the informants interviewed could recall an instance of prosecution under these laws.[2]

Three important elements of the social reforms should be kept in mind. First, most of them had a primary impact on the urban population and reached the rural and tribal areas more via the route of rumor and gossip than through any meaningful application or demand for compliance. Second, even within the urban groups the impact of these measures was primarily on the upper classes. The balance of the urban groups were relatively unaffected and unconcerned. Thus Humphrys reported to his government as late as July of 1928 about the proposals to relax the purdah system: "There are no indications so far that the general public is taking this question very seriously." The *Times*, in an article reviewing the modernization program, stated:

To the peasant woman, wearing her loose baggy trousers and long regulation coat, her hennaed pigtails tucked into a muslin veil, and working with bovine patience in her husband's fields, emancipation for the moment means nothing. She cannot read, she hardly thinks, she merely feels. But to her richer sister, comfortably, even luxuriously, situated, an outlet for energy must be welcome after the everlasting boredom of close confinement and conforming to endless conventions.

Third, there is considerable evidence that even the classes affected by the social reforms were not altogether opposed to

---

[2] All informants interviewed in Kabul in 1967–68 were asked about this and their responses were uniformly negative.

them and soon adapted to the new mores involved. The Kuhns, speaking in 1962 with a survivor of the Amanullah days, obtained this reaction: "People got used to it rather quickly. At the start we boys used to hang around the girls' school to watch them come out. But after a month we took them for granted." [3]

If the social reforms affected relatively narrow strata of Afghan society and were not especially resented by them, why did the myth develop that the revolution against Amanullah was caused by resistance to these measures? The answer is that the program of social modernization made superb propaganda material with which to excite, threaten, and frighten the inhabitants of rural and tribal areas—that is, those classes who were not primarily affected by the reforms, who knew very little from firsthand experience what the reforms were all about, and who could therefore be deceived into believing all kinds of outrageous and distorted stories. Moreover the social reforms dealt with intimate family matters dear to a tribal society based on kinship, and they touched at many points on sensitive questions of religion and faith. It is not strange, therefore, that Amanullah's opponents seized on the social reforms as the key issues in their propaganda campaign nor that this handy and simplistic explanation of the revolution was picked up by the sensational foreign press and was eventually solidified into doctrine by more serious writers who failed to look below the surface.

The political, military, and religious reforms were linked to the revolution in a different way. The formal-legal government framework promulgated by Amanullah was no more suitable for transforming the political patterns of tribal conflict than was the "best butter" in *Alice in Wonderland* for lubricating the watch. Amanullah's ideal patterns of government, which were beyond the capacity of the political culture of his time to assimilate,

---

[3] Telegram from His Britannic Majesty's Minister at Kabul to the Secretary of State for Foreign Affairs, London, no. 87, July 14, 1928, IOL, LPS/10/285, 1929; *The Times* (London), December 12, 1928, p. 13; Kuhn, pp. 247–248.

came to partial fruition only in the present day.[4] During Amanullah's reign the political system and the power structure were
hardly affected by the constitutional and formal-legal reforms.
They were, however, affected by political reforms which
strengthened the administrative grip of the central government
on the tribal areas, by measures aimed at removal or control of
corruption and special privilege, by the curtailment of subsidies
to tribal chiefs, by the requirement of personal identity cards
and the extension of the draft lottery into tribal areas, and by
the entire thrust of Amanullah's efforts to substitute merit for
ascription. The perception of threat on the part of leaders of lo-
calized centers of power explains, in large part, the withdrawal
of loyalty and allegiance from the king at critical moments in
the course of what started out as a minor tribal uprising.

The parochial leaders, both within and outside Amanullah's
court, who saw in the penetration of the tribal areas a threat to
their autonomy and power as well as a loss of personal privilege,
were only too happy to ally themselves with religious leaders
who perceived in Amanullah's religious reforms a similar threat
to their position and prestige. The religious reforms had sought
to form an alliance between the ulema and progressive government and intellectual elements in order to eliminate religious
and tribal differences, popular ignorance, and resistance to the
modernization program. Amanullah did not want to destroy the
religious leaders, he wanted to educate them and convert them
to his gospel of modernization. This turned out to be impossible

---

[4] *Afghanistan dar Pinja Sal-e-Akhir* [Afghanistan in the Last Fifty
Years] (Kabul: Book Publishers Association, 1347 [1968]). In this book,
published on the fiftieth anniversary of Afghan independence, Amanullah is given credit for having laid the base of the modern Afghan state.
See also King Zahir's speech made on the same occasion in which he acknowledges Amanullah's contribution to Afghan independence and
modernization (*Kabul Times*, August 26, 1968). This was significant in
view of the feud between Amanullah and the present ruling family,
which since 1933 has resulted in an almost total blackout of the history
of the Amanullah period.

in a country in which the threat of tribal separatism hung constantly over any attempt to achieve national unity. The resentful ulema saw this inviting alternative to modernization and readily became the collaborators of the separatist tribal leaders. They found their most useful role as propagandists, a role in which their vocal talents and their natural advantages of propinquity and communication could enjoy full play.

Similarly, the military reforms, whose goal was to transform a loose, tribally based rabble into a compact, professional, and efficient army, succeeded only in alienating most of the officers and men who were not yet ready to exchange their privileges and kinship ties for the impersonal loyalties of a professional service and who deeply resented the intrusion of foreign (Turkish) military "experts" into what they considered a "family" affair. Nadir Khan wanted to achieve the same goals, but his superior knowledge of the tribal ethos led him to recommend a gradual and more indirect indigenous effort of the type his nephew, Prince Daud, was to launch so successfully in the decade from 1953 to 1963. The military reforms, then, were in no sense a cause of the revolt, but to the extent that they created political turmoil and dissension within the army, they left it unfit to meet a widespread tribal uprising.

The most severe criticism of Amanullah's economic reforms comes from Soviet sources which have been meticulously examined by Vartan Gregorian.[5] The Soviets saw in Afghan socioeconomic conditions a situation ripe for exploitation by British imperialism. The Soviet view is that Amanullah left the essentially feudal economic structure unchanged and that his taxation and agricultural policies laid heavy burdens on the peasants. These contentions are not borne out by an examination of the economic reforms themselves nor by interviews with contemporaries.[6] Another telling argument against the socioeconomic the-

[5] Gregorian, pp. 266 ff.

[6] The excellent and well-documented article by Guha, which utilizes both Russian and other sources, describes Amanullah's economic pro-

sis is the unquestionable fact that it was not the peasants who rose in revolt but the tribes, whose socioeconomic conditions had not deteriorated and indeed had substantially improved during Amanullah's reign.

The evidence now available on the economic reforms strongly indicates that they succeeded in their primary mission: they increased national income, expanded commerce and trade, and created the base for sound developments in public works, communications, mining, and industry.[7] The principal criticisms of the economic program were directed against the ambitious construction projects, the tax increases, and the schemes to develop light industries. A good deal of material has been written about Amanullah's heavy taxation and extravagant expenditures and the bankruptcy of the central treasury. The extensive program of construction and beautification of public buildings, gardens, and the like and especially the building of the new capital at Dar-ul-Aman were characterized as extravagant and megalomaniac. The attempt to set up small factories to manufacture items which were normally imported was also classified as wasteful. W. K. Fraser-Tytler has this to say:

While the essential services were being starved, large sums were expended on the purchase of aeroplanes which would not fly, on

---

gram in favorable terms. Unfortunately it does not attempt an over-all evaluation of the effectiveness of the program and in a short and somewhat hasty conclusion seems to lean in the direction of the Russian socioeconomic explanation of the rebellion.

In an interview in Kabul in 1967, an informant who had firsthand knowledge of Amanullah's economic programs commented: "It is completely untrue that Amanullah's taxation program was onerous and caused resentment among the people. In fact his program brought great relief to most taxpayers because he abolished many irritating small taxes, brought a measure of predictability to tax liability and increased the land tax by only 1½ afghanis per *jerib* with part of that earmarked for education. The tax reforms were popular except for the few corrupt who lost thereby. Unfortunately these were often the people who had local political power."

[7] Ghobar, and interviews with three informants in Kabul, 1968.

furnishing for the great new capital and on industrial implements and equipment which, in the absence of suitable arrangements for housing and repair, were rapidly rendered unserviceable until Afghanistan became a mausoleum of derelict machinery and abandoned factories.

Humphrys, reporting on a conversation with a German colleague about Amanullah's purchases of machinery during his visit to Germany, states: "I was informed by my Germany colleague that he considers all machinery purchased in Germany as absolutely of no use." [8]

Like many of the criticisms of the Amanullah modernization program, these comments seem to be compounded of a bit of bias, a bit of misinformation, and a bit of half-truth. No doubt taxes were raised and more efficiently collected but no mention is made of the fact that per capita income was apparently rising faster. It is true that the Amanullah construction programs were on a grand scale, but a backward country like Afghanistan badly needed a psychological boost to help overcome its sense of inferiority toward more advanced nations. The construction programs were esthetically excellent, the product of first-class French architects and German engineers, and they were all paid for out of Afghanistan's own resources. Afghans still point to them with pride. [9]

It was probably true that Afghanistan lacked the technical capacity to maintain the factories in top condition. However, Amanullah expected to employ foreign technicians to train Afghans. Both Mohammed Ghobar and C. Morrish mention the industrial program as well-conceived and indeed essential to a

---

[8] Fraser-Tytler, p. 206; Telegram from His Britannic Majesty's Minister in Kabul to the Secretary of State for Foreign Affairs, London, no. 151, October 6, 1928, IOL, LPS/10/285, 1929. See also George B. Scott, *Afghan and Pathan* (London: Mitre Press, 1929), p. 52; Fraser-Tytler, pp. 202 and 206.

[9] An article in the *Times* (London) of February 15, 1928, praises the conception and the architectural quality of the new capital at Dar-ul-Aman.

nation intent on husbanding its foreign exchange.[10] It is also surprising to note Fraser-Tytler's reference to Afghanistan as a "mausoleum of derelict machinery and abandoned factories" when the bulk of this machinery was only bought by Amanullah in 1928 during his European trip and did not reach Afghanistan until many months after Amanullah was deposed.[11] Finally it seems difficult to believe that the German Minister in Kabul would speak so critically of German machinery purchased with German government and commercial credits and after full consultation with German engineers and specialists.

It is certainly true that some economic programs had politically undesirable side effects. The attempt to conduct a livestock census and extend the livestock tax to the nomadic Ghilzai undoubtedly further enraged this traditionally independent and warlike group who in the end administered the *coup de grâce* to Amanullah's attempt at a comeback. I have already remarked that the change in the tax system short-circuited many of the maliks and khans who had acted as tax collectors and had in other ways profited from the slackness and corruption which characterized the traditional tax system. Moreover the communications program, particularly the extension of roads into the tribal areas, was looked upon with fear and suspicion by the tribes not only as an opening wedge in the campaign to extend the tax system to them but also as an instrument of government control and administration. We shall see in Chapter VIII that the most probable explanation of the incident that set off the rebellion is that it was an attempt by the central government to control the collection of road tolls by the Shinwari tribe.

Having now examined some factual and objective data about the modernization program, we are better prepared to inquire

[10] Ghobar, pp. 223 ff., and Morrish, p. 67.

[11] See the quotation from Morrish in Chapter VI, above, on the question of delays in the delivery of industrial machinery bought by Amanullah.

into the larger question of whether the reforms caused the revolution that overthrew Amanullah. To a considerable extent the problem is a semantic one. If by the "reform program" we mean principally the social and religious measures introduced by Amanullah, then we must disagree with most critics and writers who have claimed that the Afghan people revolted against such reforms and that Amanullah, having deliberately weakened his army, was in no position to resist the rebellion. Such a version of what occurred simply does not agree with the facts. On the other hand, if we understand that the rebellion was primarily political in nature and was merely an aggravated recurrence of tribal separatism, then we can agree that certain political aspects of the modernization program weakened the central government, strengthened the tribes, and accentuated the scope and fury of the rebellion. In other words, social change or religious liberalism did not destroy Amanullah so much as his efforts to create a strong central government. It was this possibility that smelled of death to the tribal leaders and mullahs, and this classical struggle between centralized power and tribal separatism was resolved in blood and in the downfall of a dynasty. This fundamental political conflict was inherent in the fractured structure of Afghan national power and would have made itself felt whether a modernization program existed or not. Basically the same situation had faced every Afghan amir since Ahmad Shah had asserted the claim to being "king" of all the tribes. Because of this same conflict Abdur Rahman was involved in almost constant tribal warfare during what Dupree calls his period of "internal imperialism." [12] In this same work Dupree traces through Afghan history the process of what he calls "fusion and fission": a strong charismatic leader arises, welds a strong government, subjects the tribes and rules (fusion) until *for any reason* his hold is weakened and the process of break-up (fission) takes place with the various tribal groups returning to a

[12] Louis Dupree, *Afghanistan.*

state of insolence and anarchy. In earlier times the central power was usually weakened by the death of the charismatic leader whose personal rule could not be duplicated or by dynastic struggles in which princelings scrabbled for the throne, whereas in Amanullah's case the erosion of political power resulted from a number of complex factors, many of which were side effects of his modernization efforts. We must now examine these factors in more detail.

First and foremost we must consider the lack of political experience that characterized Amanullah and most of his advisers. Until 1928 the King had no firsthand knowledge of the modern world; his chief mentor, Tarzi, knew the modern world well but, as a long-time exile, had little experience with the realities of tribal politics. Both Amanullah and Tarzi failed to take into sufficient account the political fact that they were not dealing with a united and loyal national entity. This disadvantage was perhaps not sufficiently impressed upon the consciousness of the Afghan leaders of the period because of their lack of experience with any form of protracted colonial occupation. As Dupree has pointed out: "Where there has been no colonial occupation to create over-arching interest groups and unifying centralized administration, the extreme stubbornness of tribal and regional interests cannot be easily broken by imported techniques of centralizing power." [13]

Amanullah's blindness to the need for a strong political foundation on which to build his modern state is difficult to understand, especially after the experience of the 1924 Khost revolt which nearly cost him his throne. Here, again, perhaps the personality and character of the man offer some explanation. His intense patriotism which at times bordered on chauvinism and his ideals for the progress of his country seemed to blind him to the possibility that many of his compatriots might be

[13] Louis Dupree, "Tribalism, Regionalism and National Oligarchy" in K. H. Silvert, ed., *Expectant Peoples: Nationalism and Development* (New York: American Universities Field Staff, 1963), p. 207.

motivated by more parochial and selfish interests. Amanullah, in his own mind, knew that modernization was good for Afghanistan and that indeed his country could not survive without it. Therefore, he reasoned, if the program was good it should be gratefully embraced and actively promoted by all Afghans regardless of what to him must have seemed petty political considerations. Amanullah never lost this faith, even in exile.

Amanullah's reaction to the rebellion that overthrew him was bitter surprise that a rebellion could have taken place. No other amir before him would have been surprised, for that had been the history of Afghanistan since the days of Ahmad Shah Baba. Clearly Amanullah did not understand the internal political dynamics of his own country. The perceptive Tarzi, on the other hand, had by 1925 sensed that Amanullah's political power was being seriously undermined. He apparently came to realize that the basic political structure necessary to support the modernization program did not exist. He aptly remarked: "Amanullah has built a beautiful monument without a foundation. Take out one brick and it will tumble down." [14]

Amanullah's political naïveté is best demonstrated by (1) his failure to build a political apparatus that would have provided adequate communication with his people and replaced the tribal linkages which he was dismantling, and by (2) his underestimation of the power of the tribes. Surely a more sagacious politician would have realized that the modernization program which he himself had declared revolutionary in nature required a dedicated and pervasive group of political activists to spread the gospel and elicit popular understanding and participation or at least compliance. The sycophants who surrounded him could hardly fulfill this important role since outside of intimate court circles they were for the most part held in contempt. His only other sources of political cadres were the few Westernized Young Afghans who tended to be idealists rather than prag-

[14] Quoted in Dupree, "Mahmud Tarzi: Forgotten Nationalist," p. 35.

matic politicians. He also desperately needed a stirring ideology and at first hoped to find it in a revivified and dynamic Islam. During his Pan-Islamic period, which lasted for approximately the first four years of his reign, he was able to command the support of the religious leaders, but, as we have seen, when his Pan-Islamic charisma faded and his reforms began to cut into the privileged political position of these leaders, the honeymoon came to an end.

In addition to some kind of political organization and a suitable ideology with which to inspire it, Amanullah badly needed an adequate web of political communication. We have seen that many of his best-intentioned reforms were misunderstood or deliberately misrepresented by his opponents and he lacked the means of correcting these incoherencies in the political system. He had partially opened up the country by means of roads, telegraph, and telephones, but in a largely nonliterate society he lacked the human elements to spread his message. His newspapers were read by only a small literate minority in the principal urban centers, and the remainder of the population continued to rely on bazaar rumors and other word-of-mouth systems which often produced distorted versions of what the government was trying to do. It is interesting to note that Amanullah never had the equivalent of a ministry of information. He seems on the whole to have taken the attitude that his intentions and work were so clear and right that no government propaganda effort was required. The only concession he made in this direction was the holding of the three Loya Jirgahs in 1921, 1924, and 1928, where he charged the representatives to spread the word of the transactions and discussions in their respective districts. But these men were not disciplined party members; many of them had no great love for the central government and little reliance could be placed on their rendering favorable reports to their constituents.[15]

[15] It is interesting, though perhaps idle, to speculate that if Amanullah had had access to the radio, then in its infancy, so that he could have

We have already noted Amanullah's unwitting undermining of the supportive tribal power structure of the monarchy through his fight against corruption and nepotism as well as his denial of special privileges to the tribal aristocracy. Some of the alienated tribal chiefs were removed even further from the circle of royal favor and influence through family feuds and the machinations of sycophants newly come to power. The elimination of tax intermediaries and the system of conscription by lottery left many disaffected maliks and khans in their wake. The plans to introduce conscription and taxation into the tribal areas and to require identity certificates of all Afghans became more menacing to the tribes as roads and telecommunications penetrated into more remote areas and raised the normal level of disaffection among the explosive tribesmen. And finally the threat to the secular political power of the mullahs led first to the loss of their political support and finally drove the activists into treasonable alliance with the rebellious tribesmen.

Amanullah's political naïveté was also evident in his underestimation of the power of the tribes. In spite of the many lessons with which Afghan history is replete and the dire warnings left behind by the Amir Abdur Rahman, Amanullah seemed not to take the tribal threat seriously. Strangely enough, as we shall see in Chapter XI, he maintained an active Tribal Affairs Department which indulged in extensive propaganda and payment of subsidies to the tribes, but this activity was aimed mostly at the British, and its considerable success in stirring up anti-British

---

conveyed his zeal and his considerable personal magnetism directly to his people, the modern history of Afghanistan might have been quite different and today Afghanistan, with a head start on both independence and modernization, might be one of the most advanced nations in Asia. An informant interviewed in Kabul in 1968 told me that Amanullah did in fact establish a radio station and imported several hundred crystal receiving sets at some time late in his reign. Gregorian, p. 312, also mentions this. But my informant assured me that only a few members of the elite had access to receiving sets and Amanullah did not have time to develop this new instrument of instant communication.

sentiment tended to obscure the fact that the tribes did not care much more for the central government than they did for the British.[16] So far as the tribes were concerned the decision which of these two enemies to attack depended almost entirely on which was the weaker and therefore offered the easier target for prey and loot. In this situation the alienation of the tribal aristocracy was crucial because not only did they fail to restrain the tribes but even more importantly their loss of communication with Amanullah prevented them from giving him adequate warning of the rising temperature in the tribal areas.

Besides Amanullah's political myopia, which was undoubtedly a contributory cause, the fundamental reason for the revolt was the political fragmentation of the country as manifested by the resistance of the tribes to the unifying forces of central administration and authority. The best contemporary statement of the problem was written by an anonymous author in an article in the *Modern Review* of Calcutta in April 1929. This perceptive author wrote:

Another reflection which will occur to the reader is that the reforms cannot be the only cause of Afghan unrest: there were troubles under previous rulers who had no thought of reforms. This is perfectly correct. Another cause has been at work, based on the geographical and ethnological features of the country. The northern part of the kingdom is separated from the southern by the formidable barrier of the Hindu Kush, running from the Pamirs in the east to near Persia in the west. Similarly the people of the country are divided into two main divisions, Afghans and "other Pathans," and "non-Afghans." But these two main divisions are by no means consolidated. The first named, it is true, all speak Pushtu and belong to the Sunni sect of the Moslem religion; but there are considerable differences between them—witness the many "other Pathan" revolts against the Afghan domination. The "other Pathan" have intertribal feuds, while the Afghans are divided into the two hostile Durani and Ghilzai confederations, and the former into two rival

[16] Interview with informant in Kabul, 1967.

sections, the Barakzai, to which Amanullah belongs, and the Sado-zai. The "non-Afghans" are of Persian, Turkish, Tartar, and Mongol origins, talk various languages and dialects, and belong, many of them, to the Shiah sect. Though a good deal has been done, partly by pressure from outside and partly by the internal efforts of the Amirs, to weld together these different races and tribes, the process is still incomplete. *Afghanistan is not yet a full national entity.* She has *not that homogeneity, for example, which is possessed by Persia or present-day Turkey,* and it is precisely this want of homogeneity which is one of the most serious causes and features of the present troubles.[17]

Other forces that had nothing to do with the modernization program also eroded the power of the central government. We have already noted the question of the legitimacy of Amanullah's accession to the throne, his erratic character traits, the sycophants who surrounded and isolated him, and the general impression of softness and weakness created in a tribal society accustomed to harsh rulers by Amanullah's insistence on the use of reason and persuasion rather than force as a means of securing compliance. In addition, his inability to impose his tribal policies on the British Raj or even prevent progressive British penetration of tribal areas played some part in convincing the tribes that the central government was a soft target. Also in the picture were a number of foreign policy considerations which I shall treat in subsequent chapters.

In sum, then, the 1928 rebellion which overthrew Amanullah and destroyed much of the progress made under his modernization program was essentially a tribal revolt in the classical pattern. It began in the tribal areas that were the least affected by the modernization program. The people in the urban areas most affected by the program did not rise in revolt and to an overwhelming extent remained loyal to the central government. Indeed they were the victims of tribal looting as the revolt spread. The modernization program as a whole was not the proximate,

[17] Pp. 318–319 (my italics).

necessary, or sufficient cause of the rebellion. The irritations, resistances, and alienation of loyalties generated by the modernization program were tangential to the basic conflict.

The fact that the revolution closely followed the modernization program in time, along with the misleading propaganda which accompanied the conflict, has led most writers on the subject to fall into the fallacy of *post hoc, ergo propter hoc.* Two events closely connected in time and space need not necessarily have a causal connection. The primary cause of the rebellion was tribal separatism and bellicosity.[18] The modernization program was more the victim than the cause of the revolution.

[18] Another contemporary writer who explicitly ascribed the Amanullah disaster to tribal politics was the Bokharan refugee, Mustapha Chokaiev, "The Situation in Afghanistan," *Asiatic Review,* XXVI (1930), 324–330. The fragmenting effects of tribal politics on national unity during an earlier period of Afghan history has been noted by M. E. Yapp in his trilogy of articles dealing with tribal revolts during the First Afghan War, "Disturbances in Western Afghanistan, 1839–41," *Bulletin of the School of Oriental and African Studies,* XXVI (1963).

chapteR VIII

the ReBellion:
tRIBal poweR pRevails

In November 1928 a section of the Sanghu Khel (subtribe) joined by a small detachment of the Alicher Khel of the Shinwari tribe, acting out the historical tribal pattern of defiance of government authority, set off the chain of events which was to cost Amanullah his throne, plunge Afghanistan into chaos, and dislodge the precarious fingerhold which the country had managed to secure in its struggle toward modernization. Fewer than three hundred tribesmen attacked and looted two small villages and an army post at Pesh Bolak and Achin in the Khyber Pass region of eastern Afghanistan.[1] The small army detachment surrendered without firing a shot and the reaction of the governor at Jalalabad, the provincial capital, was timid and vacillating. He merely reported the incident to Kabul and awaited orders. The tribal raiders, flushed with success and displaying their loot, were soon joined by other Shinwari malcontents and began to move toward Dakka, a larger and more important town, gathering more tribal levies as they went. They were led by two Shinwari tribal leaders, Muhammad Alam and Muhammad Afzal, who claimed they had support for their rebellious action from top political leaders in Kabul. They had religious support from a noted tribal Muslim divine, the Hafiz Sahib of Fakirabad.[2]

Ali Ahmad asserts that Ghulam Siddiq, a member of the pow-

[1] *Military Report, Afghanistan* (Simla: Government of India Press, 1941), pp. 168 ff.
[2] Diary of Events from November 15, 1928 to February 28, 1929, NAI, Foreign Political Files, 182-F, 1929.

erful Charkhi family and one of Amanullah's favorites at court, had instigated Alam and Afzal to start a revolt. According to this version, a struggle for political survival followed Amanullah's announcement of his intention to form a true constitutional monarchy and his asking Sher Ahmad, the old and conservative President of the Legislative Council (Rais-i-Shura), to form a cabinet with Sher Ahmad as prime minister. Siddiq and his supporters opposed this move, wanting power for themselves, and decided to create a diversion in the tribal areas. According to Ali Ahmad's scenario, Ghulam Siddiq would then go to the Eastern Province as an emissary from Amanullah and cover himself with glory by restoring peace. The prime ministership would then fall into his hands.[3]

Several other explanations of the Shinwari raid have been put forward. According to Arnold Fletcher, the match was lit by a small party of Ghilzai nomads. Passing through Shinwari territory they mistook some Shinwari for brigands and killed several. The Ghilzai were captured and turned over to the army for punishment. They were able, however, "either to convince the local commandant of their innocence or to satisfy his avarice, and were released." In revenge the Shinwari attacked the army post. Another version, widely believed in Afghanistan, is that the Shinwari revolted because of British instigation, gold, and promises of support. A far more convincing explanation is furnished by C. Morrish, who seems to have had a masterly knowledge of tribal politics, especially among those tribes along the eastern border. He ascribes the Shinwari rising to rivalry with their neighboring enemies the Mohmand over the collection of border tolls and the ill-advised attempt of Amanullah's government to inject itself into this controversy.[4]

[3] Ali Ahmad, pp. 25 ff.

[4] Fletcher, pp. 115 ff. A similar version is found in Ikbal Ali Shah. Neither author cites sources for his account. The theory that the Shinwari were encouraged by the British was stressed by an informant in Kabul, 1968. The problem of British involvement will be discussed in Chapter XI. Morrish, pp. 7 ff.

Contiguity and even kinship of tribal groups often tend to increase rather than diminish enmity and friction. The Shinwari and the Mohmand are close neighbors, both tribes straddling the strategic Khyber Pass. Most of the Shinwari live within Afghanistan while the Mohmand are divided by the Durand Line. Both tribes from time immemorial practiced the lucrative system known as *badraga* (roughly, "protection"). As applied to caravans transiting the Khyber it was little more than a thinly veiled system of extortion. Any *caravanbash* setting forth from Peshawar or Jalalabad found it prudent to contract for a tribal guide and escort and pay for *badraga*. When this was done, caravans were generally not attacked; the rare one that declined *badraga* seldom arrived at its destination unscathed. The attackers, as often as not, turned out to be the same tribesmen who had offered to supply *badraga*. In this deadly game the Mohmand and the Shinwari, like rival Mafiosi, were ancient competitors and at the same time collaborators. At times one tribe would attack the caravans under the other's protection. Once *badraga* had been arranged, Pushtunwali imposed an obligation of honor to protect the escorted party and, if necessary, to avenge any outrages perpetrated by any attacker. This naturally often led to armed clashes between Mohmand and Shinwari. On the whole a *modus vivendi* pregnant with submerged hostility prevailed.

Such a state of affairs galled Amanullah and his Young Afghan administrators who were keen on enforcing law and order in every corner of the realm. Moreover, the growing merchant class, whose influence had increased under Amanullah's encouragement of commerce, as noted in Chapter VI, began to demand relief from the system of *badraga*. According to Morrish, Amanullah returned from Europe deeply impressed with the modernizing influences of active commerce, the rapid flow of goods, and the freedom of the seas. He was outraged at the thought that the principal gateway of commerce in his own kingdom should be still subjected to what, in his new vision, seemed little more than tribal piracy. Accordingly he ordered

his governor in Jalalabad to enforce law and order on the caravan route and abolish *badraga*. To underline the seriousness of
his decision he dispatched to Jalalabad an additional army division under General Mohammed Gul.

The governor announced to Shinwari tribal leaders at Jalalabad in October 1928 that *badraga* would be discontinued, that
law and order would henceforth prevail in the Eastern Province, and then heaped coals on their heads by adding that all
tribesmen would have to register for identity cards in accordance with a law which had been on the books for some years
but never strictly enforced even in urban areas. These regulations were evidently not applied, or at least were not enforced
for the moment, among the Mohmand. Naturally this doubly
infuriated the Shinwari. The governor apparently thought it
would be better to take on one tribe at a time; that if he got
into serious trouble with the Shinwari he might have to call on
their traditional enemies, the Mohmand, for help; and that in any
case the Mohmand, who had their feet in both the Afghan and
British Indian camps, were more strategically placed and had
best be handled more softly. There had recently been a sharp
flare-up of Mohmand-Shinwari resentment when some Mohmand women were allegedly stolen during a Shinwari raid and
the Shinwari had come out on the short end of the fight. Now it
seemed their hated rivals were to receive preferential treatment
while the Shinwari would be deprived of their legitimate liveli-
hood.[5]

Was the Shinwari attack, then, the product of a political
cabal in Amanullah's court? Was it a British plot? Was it the
result of a Shinwari-Ghilzai clash and a military commandant's
venality? Or was it a reaction against Mohmand rivalry and

[5] This version of the immediate cause of the Shinwari rising is advanced by Morrish, pp. 7 ff. It was amply supported by documents and
reports contained in the volumes dealing with the rebellion in the IOL,
LPS/10/1288 P53, Part 5 (1929). Even Roland Wild in his otherwise in-
accurate book states (p. 97): "The Shinwari rebellion was a revolt
against tax collectors sent to oppress them."

government interference in the *badraga* system? Evidence, logic, and what we have learned of tribal politics favor the last explanation, though it seems likely that intrigue in Amanullah's court may well have added to the explosive mixture. In a sense it makes little difference which of these versions we accept because the real significance of the various explanations put forward for the outbreak of conflict lies in the fact that *not one of them mentions Shinwari opposition to the social or religious reforms.* Only later did this become the accepted explanation of the revolution.

Rather than a mass rising of fanatical Shinwari against the unveiling of women (their own women went habitually unveiled) or against wearing Western dress (which was only required in certain parts of the Kabul area) or against the Thursday holiday (outside of Kabul everyone continued to observe Friday as the day of rest), the Shinwari revolt followed the historical and normal pattern of tribal conflict with the central government. The authority of the central government had become unduly oppressive in a tribal area already rendered sensitive by intratribal or intertribal conflict. The more extreme members of the tribe then struck out almost blindly at the nearest government target. At that point firm resistance by the government and prompt punitive action would have restored the balance. Instead the Shinwari found they had struck a "soft" target. The army detachment promptly surrendered and the tribesmen were presented with ample loot and arms and ammunition, always among the most prized items in the tribal areas. The response of higher government officials in the provincial capital and in Kabul was hesitant and weak. The tribesmen had craftily timed their attack to coincide with the withdrawal of the Jalalabad division, which was out of touch in the mountain passes on its way to Kabul. The provincial governor merely reported the attack to the Ministry of the Interior and warned the Shinwari that if they did not behave, artillery and planes would be used against them and *"other tribes would be asked to help against them."* [6] This clear admission of the government's inability to handle the crisis with its own troops was just what the Shinwari wanted to hear. The successful *lashkar* (raiding party) proudly displayed its loot to the rest of the tribe and pointed contemptuously to the government's impotence. This brought many more of the young tribal "hotheads" into the ranks of the rebels. Apparently something more was needed before the conservative tribal elders, the *rish-i-safed* ("white beards") would throw the weight of their authority behind the risky venture of open conflict with the king, because at first the rebellion spread very slowly.

The missing element—religious sanction—was supplied by the mullahs. Now the carrion birds, which were released into the air when Amanullah and the religious leaders reached the point of open conflict,[7] came to roost among the tribal jirgahs which were debating peace or war. The mullahs were able to assuage the consciences of the more conservative tribesmen by assuring them that they would be fighting against a kafir king, an unbeliever who would defile women's modesty, traduce the tenets of Islam, and thus destroy the very bases of tribal society. The call to take up arms against a weak government from which much loot would be easily wrested and to do so in the holy name of Islam proved irresistible even to those same tribesmen wo had joyously responded to the call for jihad against the British raised by this very same king some years before. The Shinwari now rose en masse and were soon joined by other tribes, first the Khugiani, who lay between them and Kabul, and soon by tribes in the Kunar area. From there the rebellion began to spread to the south and soon reached Khost where the garrison deserted and surrendered to a force of Zadran and Jaji. From that point onward the entire machinery of delicately

[6] *Aman-i-Afghan*, X, nos. 51 and 52, pp. 1–3 (my italics).

[7] See the analysis in Chapters V and VII of the development of the conflict between the government and the religious community.

poised tribal checks and balances flew to pieces and eventually
the central government found itself invested by the active hostility of many thousands of tribesmen.

In such a situation the normal riposte of the central government would have been to exploit the ancient conflicts between
the tribes, to cash its political IOU's with the scions, khans, and
religious leaders of powerful tribes like the Durrani, which were
allied to the king through kinship or tribal fealty, and confront
the rebellious tribes with a combination of tribal and government counterpower which would force them either to sue for
peace or to face humiliating and disastrous defeat. This was the
way Abdur Rahman had handled tribal rebellions and Amanullah had found that the 1924 Khost rebellion of the Mangal, in
the end, had to be handled the same way. In 1924 Amanullah
still had political credit with the tribal leaders and heads of families attached to his court, but by 1928, for reasons explained in
previous chapters, the traditional network of political loyalties
and pay-offs linking the monarchy and the tribes had been dis-
mantled. Nothing stood in its place. The tribal leaders were
alienated, the army and state officials were disaffected and only
halfheartedly loyal, the religious leaders were actively hostile.[8]

The internal political situation in Afghanistan when the Shinwari revolt broke out was as follows: Amanullah had returned
to Kabul from his trip abroad on July 1, 1928.[9] His trip had
been a great success in a number of ways. Europe, in the midst
of the exuberance of the late 1920's, welcomed this exotic Muslim monarch and his charming, cultivated queen with open
arms. They moved with ease and poise in the highest circles, received homage from the top political leaders of the day—
Doumergue and Clemenceau of France, von Hindenburg of

[8] *Military Report, Afghanistan*, p. 167.

[9] The full and documented account of Amanullah's trip can be found
in the volume on this subject in IOL, LPS/10/285, 1929. A less accurate
but useful source is the series of articles by F. Taillardat in *L'Asie
Française* in the issues for February, May, and September/October,
1928.

9. King Amanullah (*second from left*) and Queen Soraya (*right*) at a state banquet with President and Frau von Hindenburg, during their European tour in 1928.

Germany, Victor Emmanuel and Benito Mussolini of Italy, as well as the reigning monarchs of Belgium and Great Britain. In England the British outdid themselves with hospitality, staging special events and military displays and even permitting Amanullah to operate one of their new submarines. After firing off a torpedo, Amanullah is reported to have exclaimed, "I feel more than half an Englishman already!" [10]

Even the Soviets, who found the visit by a Muslim "oligarch" a bit awkward, were cordial and almost obsequious. In Turkey and Persia, Ataturk and Reza Shah made special efforts to encourage and advise the young reformer king. Amanullah and Soraya captivated official hosts and people alike by their open and democratic manners and their personal attractiveness. Politi-

[10] Marshall McLuhan, *Understanding Media: The Extension of Man* (New York: McGraw-Hill, 1964), p. 340. McLuhan is making the point that direct contact with technology influences cultural perceptions. It seems clear that something of the sort happened to Amanullah as a result of his European tour.

cally and economically the visit was a success and Afghanistan acquired an international exposure and prestige it had never previously enjoyed. Treaties of friendship and commercial relations were signed with Belgium, Poland, Austria, and Italy and others. Amanullah worked assiduously during the entire trip generating interest among foreign governments and private enterprises for various schemes of economic development in Afghanistan. He purchased large quantities of machinery for factories and in Germany, among other places, he managed to obtain long-term loans to finance his purchases.

Amanullah drove from Iran to Kabul in his own Rolls Royce, passing through Meshed, Herat, and Kandahar—a noteworthy feat in 1928. Although during his seven months' absence there had been some restlessness among his subjects, he was welcomed back with joyous acclamation at all his stops en route and the very fact that he could have absented himself from his kingdom for a long period and return to find himself still on the throne startled many observers familiar with Afghan history and the precariousness of Durrani rule. In spite of this royal welcome, both king and subjects had changed during the trip. The web of political loyalties between ruler and ruled had become further frayed, especially in the tribal and rural areas, as evidenced by sporadic restlessness, increased brigandage, and a whispering campaign encouraged largely by the mullahs as well as general public grumbling at the prevalence of official corruption. The King's attitude toward his subjects had also undergone a subtle change. The impact of Western civilization, seen from the social heights in which he moved, convinced Amanullah more profoundly than before that Afghanistan was actually losing ground in the race for modernization. He suddenly seemed to see with great clarity that it was Afghan society itself, not the trappings of governmental insitutions or modern machinery, which needed to be made over. He returned to Afghanistan bursting with plans for bold new moves and revolutionary undertakings.

The first manifestation of Amanullah's new and impatient mood was in a speech he made on June 27, 1928, on his arrival in Kandahar. In this, the first address to his people on his return, he took them to task for their lack of interest in self-help and their unwillingness to work. In an excerpt from this speech we note his impatience as he castigated the officials of the Kandahar province for their apathy and laziness:

Now, take the telegraph. The line to Farrah has been left incomplete and the work postponed. Why? Because it is too hot and the men cannot work. . . . Simply because of the slackness on the part of the officials. . . . Is it not shameful that the women of Europe are more laborious and more active than the men of Afghanistan? I have personally witnessed in Europe that the women there work on equal terms with men . . . On the other hand the women of Afghanistan only know how to sit idly in the houses and they do nothing more.[11]

Amanullah sequestered himself in Paghman during July and August 1928, leaving the conduct of all government business in the hands of his regent, Mohammed Wali Khan. Surrounded by some of his Young Afghan advisers, he worked on his new plans for modernizing the country at an accelerated pace. On September 1, 1928, he convoked the third Loya Jirgah of his reign at Paghman. Nearly a thousand representatives from the tribal, rural, and urban areas of Afghanistan gathered at this meeting, which was later to be ridiculed by writers because all the delegates were required to wear Western clothes. Before this motley audience Amanullah unveiled the main outlines of his new reforms. Although the Loya Jirgah adopted most of his recommendations, the delegates dispersed in a puzzled mood. The religious leaders viewed some of the proposed reforms as a challenge to their entrenched political and economic power. The Hazrat of Shor Bazaar obtained the signatures of four hundred

[11] Despatch from His Britannic Majesty's Minister in Kabul to the Foreign Secretary, London, no. 67, July 21, 1928, IOL, LPS/10/285, 1929.

religious leaders to a petition opposing many of the proposed reforms and presented it to the King on September 7, 1928. This
led to the flight and subsequent arrest of the Hazrat and a number of his supporters, some of whom were executed.[12]

The battle lines between the King and the religious leaders
were now clearly drawn but the tribes had yet to make their
moves. On October 28, 1928, Amanullah undertook, in a marathon four-day speech, to expound the philosophy of the proposed programs, hoping still to persuade most of his subjects,
but during these talks he made no further effort to mollify the
mullahs. He castigated them for their self-seeking attitudes.
Within three weeks, on November 12, 1928, the Shinwari made
their first small-scale raid against Achin in the Eastern Province.

The response of the weakened government in Kabul was slow
and timid. Amanullah finally decided to try to conciliate the
Shinwari and to threaten them at the same time with aerial bom-
bardment of their villages. It was nearly the end of November,
however, before Ghulam Siddiq Charkhi, recently appointed
foreign minister, and Sher Ahmad, the president of the Legislative Council, were sent to the Eastern Province to placate the
Shinwari. By that time the minor tribal revolt had blossomed
into much wider rebellion involving other tribes such as the
Khugiani. Siddiq and Ahmad were political and tribal rivals.
Their mission was therefore almost doomed to failure since they
were working at cross-purposes. According to Ali Ahmad, Siddiq was actively disloyal to Amanullah and incited rather than
calmed the tribes.[13] The situation was aggravated by the ill-advised bombing of some Shinwari villages by Russian-supplied
planes of the Afghan Air Force piloted by Russians. The bombing was half-hearted, and instead of frightening the tribes this

[12] Report of Sir Francis Humphrys to Mr. Arthur Henderson, July
15, 1929, IOL, LPS/10/1289 P53, Part 6, 1929; Telegram from His
Britannic Majesty's Minister in Kabul to the Secretary of State for Foreign Affairs, London, no. 132, September 11, 1928, IOL, LPS/10/285,
1929.

[13] Ali Ahmad, p. 25.

attack succeeded in polarizing the more cautious tribesmen who had been holding back. By the end of November 1928 a large *lashkar* of tribesmen was laying siege to the provincial capital of Jalalabad and the demoralized garrison had taken refuge in the citadel.

By now the mullahs had generated a good deal of propaganda to the effect that the uprising was a holy war against an infidel king. In early December 1928, when Siddiq and Ahmad returned to Kabul to report their failure to calm the tribes, they bore with them a set of demands couched largely in religious terminology but transparently political in nature. In addition to demands for the cancellation of reforms in dress, purdah, and Shari'a, Amanullah was to divorce Queen Soraya, banish the entire Tarzi family, reduce all taxation, and abolish all foreign legations except the British.[14] Faced with these "nonnegotiable" demands, Amanullah realized that a strong combination of diplomatic and military pressure would be required to extinguish the flames of revolt. Accordingly, on December 6, 1928, he dispatched Ali Ahmad Jan (also known as Ali Ahmad Khan), a relative on his mother's side, to negotiate a truce and at the same time denuded the Kabul garrison of troops in order to send a strong force to the Eastern Province under the general direction of an old and trusted adviser, Mahmud Khan Yawar. Ali Ahmad Jan was a clever and ambitious man, an expert in dealing with the tribes, with whom he enjoyed great influence. Unfortunately he drank excessively and was accused of venality, and as a consequence his behavior tended to be brilliant but er-

[14] Telegram from His Britannic Majesty's Minister at Kabul to the Secretary of State for Foreign Affairs, London, December 29, 1928, IOL, LPS/10/285, 1929. The curious favorable treatment demanded for the British Legation has been cited as evidence of British incitement of the Shinwari. On the other hand, the Shinwari were living next to British territory and were keenly aware of the wisdom of staying in the good books of the British. This did not prevent them, however, where loot was involved, from sacking and burning the British consulate in Jalalabad.

ratic. His loyalty to Amanullah seems to have been questioned by all except Amanullah.

Ali Ahmad Jan arrived in Jalalabad on December 8, 1928. With the help of religious leaders he managed to arrange for a truce of the siege and he bribed the Mohmand to stay out of the revolt. What he needed now was a strong contingent of loyal government troops to back up his diplomacy. Unfortunately these were not forthcoming in time. The logistics and mobilization capabilities of the demoralized Afghan army were so poor that Yawar was not able to get his troops under way at once. Troop movements were also complicated by a new threat from the north, by the treachery of a Ghilzai chief, and by the injection of a dynastic element into the revolution.

The threat from the north took the bizarre form of a Tajik bandit leader, Habibullah by name, but widely and popularly known as the Bacha-i-Saqao ("Son of the Water Carrier")—a reference presumably to his father's erstwhile occupation. The Bacha's career is still something of a mystery.[15] He had had some army experience as a soldier in one of the Turkish-trained Qita Namunas (model battalions) but he had deserted during the 1924 Khost rebellion, taking his rifle with him. He escaped to British India and is said to have run a tea shop in Peshawar. He then disappeared for several years and resurfaced in the Koh-i-Daman, the fertile mountain plateau north of Kabul, as the leader of a small band of Tajik robbers. His fame as a dead shot, his personal bravery, his bold defiance of authority, and his reputation for helping the poor Tajiks of that area against government oppressors won him renown as a sort of Afghan Robin Hood even though his appearance and operations were far more reminiscent of a Pancho Villa.

Whatever the Bacha's antecedents, at this particular moment

[15] His so-called autobiography, *My Life from Brigand to King* (London: Sampson Low, Marston, n.d.), is highly colored, contains many obvious errors of fact, and is considered apocryphal by some scholars. It must be put down as one more misleading secondary source, of which so many plague the researcher of this period.

10. The Bacha-i-Saqao, "Son of the Water Carrier" (*left center in white*), during the campaign that overthrew King Amanullah in 1929.

in history his bell rang; hearing of the Shinwari attack in the east he became active in the north launching large-scale raids against government posts. Amanullah, harassed by the Shinwari, decided to win the Bacha to his side. In the first days of December he sent Ali Ahmad Jan to offer the Bacha arms and a commission as colonel if he would help put down the Shinwari. The Bacha agreed and oaths of loyalty were exchanged on the Qur'an but that evening he called Amanullah directly on the telephone, pretending he was Ali Ahmad Jan, and told him he had the Bacha surrounded. Amanullah, making a snap decision and a very serious error of judgment, said the Bacha should be executed forthwith. The Bacha then identified himself and told Amanullah he would first have to catch him, and fled.[16] His re-

[16] Interview with informant in Kabul, 1967. The explanation that Amanullah is supposed to have given of the Bacha's rise is reported in Ali Ahmad, p. 29. The incident of the Bacha's ruse in calling Amanullah on the telephone has been incorporated into the folk literature of the Tajiks as discovered by Louis Dupree when he was collecting ballads and folklore in the Tajik area (Louis Dupree, *Afghanistan.*)

sponse to what he considered Amanullah's Pushtun treachery was to launch a bold and unexpected attack on December 10, 1928, on Jabal-us-Seraj, a large garrison in the Koh-i-Daman. The 900-man garrison surrendered without firing a shot. The Bacha captured large stores of arms and much loot. His band of outlaws was now joined by hundreds and later thousands of non-Pushtun tribesmen from Kohistan. Most of them were Tajiks who had been quiescent for years under Pushtun domination and now smelled the chance to settle a few scores. On December 14, 1928, the Bacha again pursuing his bold tactics made a direct attack on Kabul. Much of the fighting took place around the British Legation in the outskirts of the city and the Legation was severely damaged, mostly by shelling from government artillery. The Bacha's attack was repulsed and he retired to Qala Murad Beg in the Koh-i-Daman. Government troops sent to pursue him were ambushed and cut to pieces. Kabul lay now virtually defenseless.

At this point another colorful villain enters the scene. Ghaus-ud-din, an Ahmedzai Ghilzai chief, turned up in Kabul offering his services to Amanullah and promising to recruit Ghilzai tribesmen if given money and arms. The measure of Amanullah's desperation at this point can be taken from the fact that he would trust a Ghilzai (traditional enemies of the Durrani) and one whose father had been defeated and humiliated by government troops under Nadir Khan in the course of a revolt during the reign of Habibullah. Ghaus-ud-din, having received arms and money, promptly absconded to his tribal area where he raised a band of Ghilzai cutthroats. They free-lanced throughout the course of the rebellion and were a thorn in the side, first of Amanullah, later of the Bacha, and finally of Nadir Khan.[17] Moreover, at one point Ghaus-ud-din, in possession of the stronghold at Ghazni, proclaimed himself amir at a time when there were already four other claimants at large. The news of

[17] *The Rebellion*, series of volumes of documents in IOL, LPS/10/1288 P53, 1929.

Ghaus-ud-din's defection seriously affected the morale of the few troops remaining to defend Kabul from the Bacha.

A further complication during this critical month of December 1928 was the escape from British surveillance in India of another claimant to the Afghan throne. Mohammed Umar Khan, a nephew of the exiled Amir Yakub, entered the tribal areas and declared himself leader of the revolt against Amanullah. That Amanullah realized his extreme peril in the face of these complications is shown by the fact that on December 21, 1928, he evacuated by air most of his immediate family, including Queen Soraya, his mother the Ulya Hazrat, his father-in-law Tarzi, and other prominent members of his government, sending them in one of the Russian planes to Kandahar, there to await the issue.

Kabul, at the start of the New Year of 1929, presented a dismal and wintry appearance as the city and the government prepared to make a last stand against attacks from the east, north, and south. Amanullah began to take measures of desperation which must have caused him deep discomfort. On January 7, 1929, he freed the Hazrat of Shor Bazaar hoping to take some sting out of the religious propaganda. Just a week earlier (but more than a month after the original rising) the Shinwari had issued and widely distributed a so-called manifesto addressed to the entire Muslim world in which the revolution was justified on purely religious grounds. Though purportedly written by Muhammad Afzal Shinwari and signed by his partner in revolt Muhammad Alam Shinwari, the manifesto bears unmistakable signs of being the emanation of religiously trained minds. Here for the first time appears the propaganda indictment against the Amanullah religious and social reforms, cunningly woven out of half-truths, which from that point onward would emblazon the standards of the revolution and become enshrined in popular mythology as the cause of the revolt.[18] All the themes that were

[18] Express Letter from NORWEF, Peshawar, to Government of India, no. 9 P.S., January 3, 1929, IOL, LPS/10/1288 P53, 1929.

later to become so well known are developed in this manifesto: violation of Shari'a, abolition of polygamy, immoral baring of women's bodies, forcible divorce, removal of purdah, export of girls to Europe, change of the Friday holy day, and the encouraging of bribery and corruption.

Wild as these assertions seemed, they were effective when propagated by the very efficient word-of-mouth communications system of the mullahs. The government had nothing to match it and Amanullah *in extremis* tried to minimize the effects of this propaganda by issuing a counterproclamation on January 8, 1929, in which he rescinded most of the actual and proposed reforms.[19] He also revealed that he was prepared to add an upper house or senate (Majlis-e-Ayan) to the Legislative Council which would be composed of conservative elements, i.e., tribal chieftains and ulema. At about the same time Amanullah issued another proclamation to the people of the Koh-i-Daman denouncing the Bacha as a common thief, accusing him of having violated his oath, on the Qur'an, of loyalty to Amanullah, and, more importantly, declaring that no reprisals were intended against the people of the Koh-i-Daman who had joined the Bacha if they would only turn him in and collect a reward of 40,000 afghanis.[20]

But these last-minute efforts were in vain. The tribes now had the bit in their teeth and the central government had few, if any, resources left with which to restore order. The end came quickly. On January 11, 1929, the sizable contingent of troops sent to the relief of Jalalabad under Mahmud Khan Yawar was tricked at Jagdalak (the scene of a British disaster in the First

[19] A summary of this proclamation was carried in two successive issues of *Aman-i-Afghan*, X, nos. 73 and 74 for 15 and 17 Jaddi 1307 (January 8 and 10, 1929). It is curious from a propaganda point of view to note that Amanullah felt obliged to "rescind" a number of reforms that had never been put into effect and were mere proposals at that time. The full proclamation is printed in five successive issues of *Aman-i-Afghan*.

[20] *Aman-i-Afghan*, X, no. 66, 7 Jaddi 1307 (January 1, 1929).

Afghan War) by Jabbar Khel Ghilzai and Khugiani tribesmen who had captured a smaller detachment, dressed themselves in army uniforms, and infiltrated Yawar's camp, taking the army completely by surprise and destroying or scattering the entire force.[21] No sooner had news of this disaster reached Amanullah in Kabul than the Bacha, also having heard the news, attacked Kabul again. Only the king's personal troops led by the recently arrived Turkish military mission were left to defend the town. On January 14, 1929, it became clear that the fall of the city was imminent and Amanullah now took the calculated political risk of abdicating in favor of his older half-brother, Inayatullah, and escaping secretly by car to Kandahar. Amanullah's tribulations during this flight are a fascinating tale but unfortunately beyond the scope of this work. Several days later Amanullah arrived in Kandahar to try to put together the bedraggled remains of his scattered government.[22]

Amanullah's flight from Kabul produced disastrous effects on the already demoralized army. It also had serious political and international implications which will be discussed in a later chapter. Mass desertions from the army units located in key areas such as Jalalabad, Laghman, Dakka, and Kahi meant that for all intents and purposes the central government's capacity to impose its will on the rebels had evaporated. This left Inayatullah in desperate, indeed hopeless, straits. Only small detachments of the military cadets and the palace guards, in some cases led by Turkish advisers, now stood between him and the Bacha who, by January 15, had occupied Kabul, laid siege to the Arg (the citadel), and demanded harsh terms of surrender. The Hazrat of Shor Bazaar now surfaced again, serving as intermediary between Inayatullah, the Bacha, and Sir Francis Humphrys, the

[21] Interview in Kabul, 1968, with an informant who had accompanied the field force.

[22] Eyewitness Statement of Haji Muhammad Amin Jan, contained in Confidential Memorandum from the Chief Commissioner, North-West Frontier Province, to Government of India, January 22, 1929, IOL, LPS/10/1288 P53, 1929.

British minister. In return for an instrument of submission by Inayatullah and most of the besieged *sardars*, the Hazrat arranged for safe conduct for Inayatullah and members of his family and top officials for evacuation via a special British plane to India on the understanding that the refugees would then proceed directly to Kandahar. Other officials and followers of Amanullah also made their submission in return for their lives. On January 16, 1929, the Bacha entered the Arg and proclaimed himself king of Afghanistan and the following day Inayatullah and his cortege left by air for Peshawar whence they proceeded by special train to Chaman and thence back into Afghanistan to Kandahar.[23]

While these events were taking place in Kabul, Amanullah was holding durbar in Kandahar in an effort to rally his Barakzai kinsmen to oppose the Bacha and the rebels in the eastern provinces. But his pleas, though forcefully backed by those of his influential mother, the Ulya Hazrat, fell on deaf ears. The ties of loyalty and confidence between the monarch and his tribal kinsmen had been severed. The intermediate power brokers—the chiefs, khans, and mullahs—had been alienated. When Amanullah turned to them they were apathetic, if not hostile. In many cases they too had lost the capacity to influence the behavior of their fellow tribesmen. Learning of Inayatullah's flight from Kabul, Amanullah again sought to wear the robes of legitimacy by rescinding his abdication on January 25, 1929. Inayatullah himself arrived in Kandahar on January 27 and at once tendered his submission to Amanullah, again reiterating that he had never wanted to be king. Laboriously now Amanullah tried to rebuild a power base within the apathetic but potentially strong Barakzai. His most potent rallying cry was the fact that a Tajik king

[23] Confidential Memorandum Concerning Recent Events in Afghanistan, prepared by the Northwest Department, Foreign Office, London, June 10, 1929, IOL, LPS/10/1292 P53, 1929, Part 13. See also Confidential Report from Sir Francis Humphrys to Mr. Arthur Henderson, July 15, 1929 IOL, LPS/10/1289, Part 6, 1929.

in Afghanistan (and a former bandit at that) could not be tolerated by the ruling Pushtun tribes.[24]

The same call to Pushtun tribal pride was being made at that
time by Ali Ahmad Jan to the eastern tribes but not in support
of Amanullah. Ali Ahmad Jan saw in Amanullah's flight from
Kabul a unique opportunity to fulfill his own ambitions. On
January 20, 1929, he called together a large jirgah; supported by
fatwas issued by influential mullahs such as the Naqib Sahib of
Charbagh, the Chaknaur Mullah, and the Hadda Mullah, declaring Amanullah to be a heretic, Ali Ahmad Jan had himself declared king of Afghanistan. He sought to unite the eastern tribes
behind his banner, but the eastern tribes did not unite.[25] They
were enjoying their new-found freedom from government authority, and they distrusted Ali Ahmad Jan, not only because of
his alcoholic bouts but because they suspected he might be a
stalking horse for Amanullah, who would reassume power once
the Bacha was defeated and would surely punish the early rebels
of the eastern provinces. The Khugianis, for example, playing
the old tribal game secretly, sent a delegation headed by Malik
Mohammed Shah Khan to dicker with the Bacha in Kabul. The
Bacha, having captured the royal treasury (in spite of false propaganda that Amanullah had made off with it), was able to pay
handsomely for Khugiani support. The Khugianis, who formed
a large contingent in the "united" tribal *lashkar* which Ali
Ahmad Jan was leading toward Kabul, treacherously attacked
from within on February 7, 1929, when the *lashkar* reached the
notorious narrow defiles around Jagdalak. Ali Ahmad Jan
barely escaped with his life and the clothes on his back, made
his way as a pursued fugitive to Peshawar, and threw himself on
British mercy. Thus ended Ali Ahmad Jan's brief bid for power.

[24] *Military Report, Afghanistan*, pp. 103 ff.

[25] *Ghairat-i-Islam*, no. 1 (January 28, 1929). See also Secret Memorandum from Chief Commissioner, North-West Frontier Province to the
Government of India, February 6, 1929, IOL, LPS/10/1288 P53, 1929.
These sources contain the proclamation of Ali Ahmad Jan declaring
himself amir and branding Amanullah as a kafir.

In Peshawar he consoled himself with alcohol, tried to attach himself to Nadir Khan when the latter passed through en route to Afghanistan, and eventually was forced by the British to go to Kandahar. There Amanullah's severity was mitigated by the intervention of the Ulya Hazrat on behalf of her nephew. But even this respite was short-lived, for when the Bacha's troops captured Kandahar, Ali Ahmad Jan was sent to Kabul and mercilessly hanged by the Bacha.[26]

After the disaster at Jagdalak, the other tribal elements which Ali Ahmad Jan had succeeded in uniting temporarily now retreated to Jalalabad hungry for loot and fell on that defenseless city where less than four hundred troops had remained loyal, all others having deserted on news of Amanullah's flight from Kabul. The city was now gutted. In an excess of last-minute zeal some loyalist officers blew up the magazine killing nearly a thousand innocent citizens. The tribesmen, like jackals at a kill, fell into violent disputes over the loot and eventually skulked off to their hills leaving a dead city behind them. A period of tribal pillage and chaos prevailed in the Eastern Province until late spring when Hashem Khan, Nadir Khan's brother, appeared to make his bid for tribal unity in support of Nadir.

Meanwhile Amanullah's February campaign to rally the Barakzai was meeting with some success. The undisputed rule of the Bacha, an upstart Tajik bandit, in Kabul was galling to Pushtun pride. His success in destroying all resistance from the Eastern Province alarmed the southern Pushtuns. Among the large numbers of Indian Muslims and Pushtun tribesmen on the British side of the Durand Line a wave of revulsion against the Bacha was expressed in sentiments of support for a comeback by Amanullah. The largest fly in the ointment was the attitude of the Ghilzai. A large portion of the Ghilzai tribe was in India on its periodic winter migration to the Indus plains. No one was

---

[26] *Military Report, Afghanistan*, pp. 182 and 205.

certain what their attitude would be on their return in the spring. Amanullah tried to win assurances of their allegiance by dispatching a mission headed by Sahibzada Mohammed Umar Jan. It was a total failure. The emissary returned to report that, as ever, the Ghilzai would resist their old enemies the Durrani. The Ghilzai still remembered that Amanullah had, in their view, betrayed their trust, violated their safe-conduct, and inflicted severe punishments on the Ghilzai after the 1924 rebellion.[27] Amanullah then worked harder on the Barakzai, seeking to win back the support of the mullahs whose Pushtun antipathy for the Bacha equaled their dislike of Amanullah. On February 24, 1929, Amanullah made his all-out bid to win back religious support in an impassioned speech at the Mosque of the Robe of the Prophet (Da Kherqa Sharif Ziarat), one of the holiest shrines in Afghanistan. He disclaimed any plans to destroy the religious leaders, declared himself a loyal and orthodox Muslim, roundly condemned the Bacha as a heretic and bandit, and made it clear that if he did not receive the support of the people of Kandahar in his bid to recapture the throne he would leave that city to its fate and seek help elsewhere. He then dramatically opened the casket containing the sacred robe and lifted it above his head, demanding from his audience whether Allah would permit a heretic or apostate to perform this sacred act. This was Amanullah at his dramatic best and it set in train an emotional reaction among the Barakzai, who rushed to him with promises of support and pledges to fight to the death for his cause.[28]

Now in the spring of 1929, as the snows began to melt in the rugged passes, activity quickened in the stricken land. In particular the tribal cauldron bubbled and boiled. In March a number of important developments took place. Nadir Khan and two of his brothers, Hashem and Wali, returned from France complete

[27] *Ibid.*, p. 182.
[28] Ali Ahmad, p. 39. See also *Military Report, Afghanistan*, p. 186.

with British diplomatic visas.[29] During brief halts in Bombay and Peshawar, Nadir consistently refused to commit himself publicly to any of the claimants to the throne. He would only say that he himself did not seek the throne, that it was a matter for the Afghan people to decide, and that he had returned simply to try to restore peace and order to his troubled country. Both the Bacha and Amanullah were well aware of Nadir's influence with, and his expert knowledge of, the tribes. They both, therefore, sought to command his loyalty.[30] Nadir refused to comply with either summons. Technically, of course, he owed allegiance to Amanullah as the rightful king, but Nadir seemed to feel that loyalty to Amanullah had now become a liability with most of the tribes, and he preferred to enter the lists unencumbered and with maximum freedom of action. On

[29] Secret Telegram from the Foreign Office, London, to Legation, Kabul, no. 32, February 2, 1929, IOL, LPS/10/1288, 1929, Part 5. The issuance of diplomatic visas to prominent Afghans for transit through India was more or less standard practice and did not necessarily mean that these individuals were singled out for British favor.

[30] Amanullah did so in a letter summoning Nadir to Kandahar (IOL, LPS/10/1288 P53, 1929). The Bacha had sent envoys to France to summon Nadir but they crossed with Nadir's party on the high seas. Returning to Peshawar, they delivered the Bacha's letter asking Nadir to proceed to Kabul and promising him a high position; his negative reply is quoted in Shah Wali Khan, *Yaddashtha-i-man* [Memoirs] (Kabul: Government Press, n.d.). Later the Bacha made another attempt to win Nadir over by sending one of Nadir's brothers, Shah Mahmud Khan, who had remained in Afghanistan serving Amanullah and had been taken into the Bacha's service, to convince Nadir to submit. Shah Mahmud met Nadir Khan in Parachinar just as Nadir was preparing to enter Afghanistan. There is some evidence that Shah Mahmud brought with him a substantial advance payment from the Bacha in gold. After conferring with Nadir Khan, Shah Mahmud joined him and abandoned the Bacha's service, which in any case must have been repugnant to him. See the Secret Memorandum from R. R. Maconachie, Political Agent, Kurram, to the Chief Commissioner, North-West Frontier Province, March 9, 1929, IOL, LPS/10/1288 P53, 1929. Maconachie later became the first British Minister to Kabul under the reign of Nadir Khan.

March 8, 1929, Nadir entered the Afghan tribal area near Khost from Parachinar in the British tribal belt. His brother, Hashem, who had many connections in the Eastern Province, was dispatched to that area to rally the tribes while Nadir and Wali exerted themselves to unite the Mangal, Jaji, Zadran, Ghilzai, and other tribes in the Khost-Gardez area.

Nothing can convey a better picture of the conflict and the nature of tribal society than the difficulties that befell Nadir in his efforts to bring some order and unity to the tribal anarchy which had resulted from the collapse of the authority of the central government. The story is told in harrowing detail in Shah Wali's memoirs. Time and again, with infinite tact, firmness, and patience, Nadir and his brothers would put together what they thought was an effective tribal coalition and time and again, often over the most trivial disagreements (such as the possession of a rifle or which clan was to lead a *lashkar*), tribal fighting would break out and the entire ball of twine would come unwound. Mangal fought Wazir and Zadran fought Jaji and the Ahmedzai Ghilzai fought them all. Again the notorious Ghilzai leader, Ghaus-ud-din, who had betrayed Amanullah, appeared, offering his services to Nadir. Nadir was less insouciant than Amanullah and fully realized that Ghaus-ud-din, whose father Nadir had defeated in battle, could bear no love for Nadir's cause. But necessity drove Nadir to half trust him and again Ghaus-ud-din ran true to form. In April, when Nadir made his first determined attack on Kabul through the Logar Valley, victory was within his grasp when Ghaus-ud-din and his Ghilzai turned on him, causing Nadir to suffer a humiliating and costly defeat.

A number of other important developments occurred in March. In Herat, a key city which had remained loyal to Amanullah, the garrison revolted, killing the governor and the military commander. They were brought under control, however, by the deputy military commander, Mohammad Ghaus.

Herat remained tenuously loyal to Amanullah until May 4, when it fell to Abdul Rahim, one of the Bacha's generals who had marched from Mazar-i-Sharif in the north.

At the end of March, Sher Agha, the brother of the Hazrat of Shor Bazaar, who had been interned in India, demanded from the British the right to participate in his country's internal struggles; in accordance with the self-imposed rule of neutrality adopted by the Government of India, Sher Agha was permitted to enter Afghan tribal territory and began to intrigue with the Suleiman Khel Ghilzai, on whom he exercised great influence. Needless to say, this influence was used against Amanullah. Toward Nadir, his attitude was more neutral at this period. Also at the end of March, Amanullah decided that he must make his move against the Bacha and began his advance to the north from Kandahar. A concerted attack by Nadir from the southeast and Amanullah from the south might have been effective, but the serious disagreements and family quarrels between the two men and the dynamics of tribal politics made collaboration between them very difficult and perhaps even counterproductive. Moreover between the tribes rallying around Amanullah near Kandahar and those opting to help Nadir around Khost lay the bulk of the Ghilzai confederation, not yet openly hostile but surly and obviously biding its time.

In April 1929 the tempo quickened. Hashem Khan in the Eastern Province, after expending much effort, ingenuity, and political credit, had managed to call a great jirgah at which the tribes undertook to observe a six-months truce in order to help Nadir dispose of the hated Tajik in Kabul. By the middle of April Amanullah reached Ghazni. All along the way he was beset with internal squabbles among his own followers and several cases of outright treason among both his civil and military supporters. In early April, too, came encouraging news from the north, which until that time had remained almost completely quiescent and hence in the Bacha's pocket. Ghulam Nabi of the great Charkhi family, who was Amanullah's ambassador in Russia, had convinced the Soviet government to aid Amanullah's cause by permitting him to raise a force in Russia to cross into northern Afghanistan, equipped with Russian arms and materiel.[31] The theory was that such a move would bring about a spontaneous rising in northern Afghanistan in support of Amanullah and the Bacha would be caught between two fires. In other words, the Soviets were reluctantly persuaded to support a Bay of Pigs operation. It was no more successful. Ghulam Nabi found but little support in the non-Pushtun north. Only around Mazar-i-Sharif, where his brother Ghulam Jilani had been governor, did he meet with any success and this only because the Bacha's able general Abdul Rahim had gone south to capture Herat. From Mazar, Ghulam Nabi began to consolidate his position and gather followers who are always willing to join what at the moment seems like a winning team. Amanullah's advance, however, had bogged down near Ghazni because a combination of Ghilzai *Khels* (Andar, Tarak, and Tokhi) began to harass his rear and threaten his line of communications with Kandahar. Still uncommitted was the formidable Suleiman Khel. By the end of April, Nadir's advance through the Logar Valley had succumbed to Ghilzai treachery and he had retired in disarray once again to begin his patient efforts to put together a united tribal fighting force. The only serious threat to the Bacha now came from Ghulam Nabi in the north, who began his advance toward Kabul winning several small victories against such minor forces as the Bacha could spare from his southern and eastern fronts.[32]

In early May the threat to the Bacha from the east evaporated when Hashem Khan's tribal coalition fell apart and fighting again broke out between Khugiani, Surkhrudi, Mohmand, and Shinwari, once again over the right to claim *badraga* fees. In the meantime Amanullah's attack on Ghazni had failed. He had called for help from the Hazaras (who are non-Pushtun, Shiah,

[31] Ali Ahmad, ch. 9.   [32] *Military Report, Afghanistan*, pp. 192 ff.

and traditional enemies of the Ghilzai). This proved a major error because though the Hazaras were courageous and loyal, their entry into the fray roused the hitherto inactive Suleiman Khel Ghilzai, the most formidable fighters of this warlike tribe. On April 19, 1929, some four thousand Suleiman Khel tribesmen rushed Amanullah's position in Ghazni. Though facing stubborn Hazara resistance, they succeeded in inflicting so much damage on Amanullah's forces that a disordered retreat resulted. Now, with the formidable Ghilzai fully committed against Amanullah, his retreat on Kalat-i-Ghilzai became a nightmare. When he reached that city he was caught between the forces of the Bacha's garrison and the Ghilzai in pursuit. Deeming his position hopeless and fearing further treachery from within his own ranks, Amanullah secretly fled with a small party on May 23. He telephoned his family to meet him on the road, cut the telephone wires, and sped on by car directly to Chaman and the Indian border, which he crossed on May 24. Three days later Amanullah, Inayatullah, their two wives (who expected to give birth at any moment), and an intimate party of some thirty relatives and officials reached Bombay in a special train placed at their disposal by the British. On June 22, 1929, Amanullah and most of his party sailed from Bombay for Europe and final exile. Both Queen Soraya and her sister, the wife of Inayatullah, had given birth to baby girls shortly after their arrival in Bombay. Inayatullah sought permission to remain in India. This was denied and he went to Persia.[33]

Ghulam Nabi was poised to descend on the Kohistan area, Bacha-i-Saqao's stronghold, when the news of Amanullah's sudden departure for India reached him. The effect on the morale of Ghulam Nabi's forces was disastrous and they melted away. He quickly retreated to the north and crossed the Oxus into Russia. By the end of May, then, only Nadir, licking his wounds

[33] This account of Amanullah's last days in Afghanistan is drawn from Ali Ahmad and from personal interviews with two informants who were members of Amanullah's party during the escape.

11. The Bacha-i-Saqao, who became Amir Habibullah after the overthrow of Amanullah in 1929.

in the Khost area, remained in the field against the Bacha. On May 31 the Bacha's troops captured Kandahar, taking the hapless Ali Ahmad Jan (who had once again declared himself amir) prisoner and sending him in chains to Kabul and to his death. Just to rub salt into the wounds of the Durrani *sardars*, the Bacha appointed the fierce Abdul Qadir, a Taraki Ghilzai, as governor of Kandahar.

During June, with Ghilzai help, the Bacha's forces made a clean sweep of all pockets of resistance between Kandahar and Kabul; they captured the important stronghold of Gardez on June 26. They also inflicted, on June 28, a second stinging de-

feat on Nadir, who had again collected a tribal *lashkar* that included once again the fickle Ahmedzai Ghilzai. Nadir and his
brothers then withdrew to Hariob in a despondent mood to
await events.[34]

This was doubtless the high point of the Bacha's short reign.
Amanullah had decamped, Ghulam Nabi abandoned the contest,
Hashem Khan was defeated in the east, and Nadir Khan with
his two brothers Shah Wali and Shah Mahmud lay despondent
in the Southern Province unable to consolidate Pushtun tribal
power against the Bacha. Only the Bacha's foreign relations
were unsatisfactory. Russia was almost openly hostile. None of
the powers represented at Amanullah's court had established relations with Amir Habibullah (as the Bacha now styled himself).
Some missions had left skeleton staffs in Kabul but most of them
had followed the British lead shortly after Amanullah's departure from Kabul and evacuated their personnel and as many of
their nationals as they could.[35] *De facto* relations, of course,

[34] *Military Report, Afghanistan*, pp. 198–200.

[35] Great Britain, *Parliamentary Papers*, "Report on the Air Operations
in Afghanistan," cited above. The British evacuation of women and children began in December 1928, even before Amanullah's abdication. It
continued in the first days of Bacha-i-Saqao's reign until all British nationals including the legation staff and the minister, Sir Francis Humphrys, had left. The latter descended from the plane in Peshawar carry-
ing a caged parrot. The British government, urged by Sir Francis, had
put strong pressure on other governments to evacuate their nationals
and diplomatic missions. This was largely done. The wider implications
of this move are considered in Chapter XI. The evacuation itself was accomplished with great panache and gallantry by the RAF, flying Vick-
ers Victorias of World War I vintage in the middle of winter over high
mountains. Under these conditions they moved 586 men, women, and
children of thirteen nationalities from Kabul to British India without a
single casualty except for a hapless German woman who walked into a
propeller and was badly injured. The sole American evacuated was
Carol (Mrs. Allen) Isaacson. She and her husband were on a round-the-
world honeymoon trip in a specially constructed Buick and were caught
in Afghanistan by the revolt. Allen Isaacson refused to leave without his
precious car and eventually managed to drive it out via Kandahar. For a
full description of this spectacular air evacuation, probably the first of

continued, but no country had come forward to recognize *de jure* Habibullah's rule. Now, in July, 1929, he sought to open talks with the British. But officials in India and London were convinced that the proud and aggressive Pushtuns would not long tolerate a Tajik ruler.

The secret correspondence of this period between the British and the various protagonists in the rebellion clarifies a number of controversial issues. All of the principal participants at one point or another earnestly, though secretly, sought British support. To all of them the British replied politely but firmly that their policy of neutrality precluded any help. To none of them did the British reveal that requests for support had been received from the others.[36] But now that the field had narrowed to Habibullah and Nadir, the British found themselves in a quandary. Their official neutrality had worked well enough when many were claiming help, but to fail to choose now would probably mean to let the prize go by default to the Tajik. The British were convinced that this would mean continuing guerrilla warfare by the Pushtun majority, perhaps for many years. Afghanistan would fall into a progressively more chaotic and unstable condition which the Soviets would exploit as a menace to the security of India. In these circumstances the temptation to back Nadir Khan was very powerful, and it must remain to the credit of the British government of that day that they did not entirely succumb to it.

Nadir Khan, in desperate straits and sensing the British dilemma, added to their discomfort. By the summer of 1929, Nadir had concluded that only with the help of tribes from the British side would it be possible to unseat the Bacha. He espe-

---

its kind, see Confidential Report from Sir Francis Humphrys to Mr. A. Henderson, IOL, LPS/10/1289 P53, Part 6, 1929. For a contemporary account of the Isaacson story see article by Roland Wild in the *Daily Mail* for December 29, 1928.

[36] This correspondence is in IOL, LPS/10/1232 P50, 1928–29, and in NAI, Foreign Political Files, 137-F and 40-F, 1929.

cially wanted to recruit among the Mahsud and Wazir, both redoubtable fighters and spoiling to get into the battle. It will be
remembered that in the 1919 Third Afghan War, Nadir had
successfully raised the Wazir and Mahsud against the British.
His credit still ran high among those tribes. He now sent emissaries to call for *lashkars* to come to his support. The British political agents in Waziristan reported these efforts to the Government of India, which in turn raised objections with Nadir. The
British had, of course, insisted from the beginning of the Afghan
rebellion on keeping "their tribes" out of it, fearing that once
stirred up to martial activity these tribes would involve the British in prolonged tribal fighting. Now, however, Nadir replied
that he saw no reason why such tribes as the Mahsud and
Wazir, who had historically been associated with Afghan affairs,
should remain aloof. He pointed to British recruiting among the
Hazara tribes of Afghanistan.[37] He capped his argument by
pointing out that unless he got help from the tribes on the British side, he would have to give up the struggle and leave Afghanistan in a state of chaos.

The correspondence shows that the British were impressed by
Nadir's arguments and did not like the idea of his abandoning
the struggle. Nevertheless their official position remained firm
and they replied to Nadir that tribes from the British side would
not be made available to him.[38] At the same time, the Government of India instructed its political agents in the tribal areas
that individual tribesmen could not be prevented from entering
Afghanistan to participate in the fighting nor should entire *lashkars* be prevented by force from proceeding to Afghanistan
since otherwise the fighting which would ensue would be worse
than the breach of neutrality.[39] Word of this permissive attitude

[37] The British Indian army had traditionally recruited hardy Hazara
tribesmen for sapper and construction units known as Hazara Pioneers.

[38] The correspondence between Nadir Khan and the Government of
India is in IOL, LPS/10/1232 P50, 1928.

[39] For example, instructions to this effect were sent to the Political
Agent in Kurram. This Political Agency included Parachinar and the

spread quickly among the tribesmen, and Mahsud and Waziri *lashkars* entered Afghanistan unmolested to help Nadir Khan. These tribes enabled Nadir to launch his surprise attack in late September and to recapture Kabul on October 12, 1929.

Other factors helped turn the tide in favor of Nadir Khan. Habibullah was running out of money. He had granted generous tax exemptions to anyone who would support him. The tribesmen now realized he was squeezed dry and they began to look for other sources of gain. Habibullah was operating under very difficult conditions. Most of his experienced officials were Pushtuns and could hardly be considered loyal. His administration of Kandahar was unwise to say the least. Setting an embittered Ghilzai to rule over Durrani territory produced the inevitable revolt and the city was besieged by Durrani tribesmen.

His policy in the Eastern Province was no less disastrous. Encouraged by the defeat and flight of Hashem Khan in September, Habibullah, now joined by the Shinwari, recaptured Jalalabad. But he made the fatal error of placing Kohistani (non-Pushtun) governors over them. Mohmand and Shinwari who could agree on nothing else turned on the Bacha and reinvested Jalalabad, drawing away scarce troops from Kabul at the very moment Nadir Khan, with Shah Wali as his spearhead, was making his decisive attack.

Now the Afghan tribes, whose quarrels had prevented Nadir from launching a united attack on the Bacha, realized that, with the entry of the tribes from the British side of the border, Nadir's chances were suddenly greatly improved. They did not want to be left off the bandwagon when there were prospects of looting the capital itself. So now the Mangal, the Jaji, the Khostwal, the Daur, and others belatedly enrolled under Nadir's banner. Perhaps more importantly, Sher Agha, brother of the

Kurram Valley, a principal funnel and gateway for tribesmen seeking to enter Afghanistan to join the fun (Secret Telegram from the Chief Commissioner North-West Frontier Province to Political Agent, Kurram, September 27, 1929, NAI, Foreign Political Files, 40-F, 1929).

Hazrat of Shor Bazaar, who had been lying low among the Suleiman Khel Ghilzai and allegedly nourishing ambitions of his
own to climb the throne, now realized his best hopes lay in
backing Nadir. Accordingly he exercised his influence on the
Ghilzai and won the neutrality and in some cases the active support of important elements of this powerful tribe. It was perhaps the removal of the Ghilzai threat at his back more than any
other single factor which enabled Nadir to launch his bold
stroke under the brilliant tactical leadership of Shah Wali. He
struck directly at Kabul, bypassing the Bacha's strong positions
in Gardez and Ghazni.

With some measure of unity achieved, even if only temporarily, among the Afghan Pushtun tribes, with the backing of
strong Pushtun tribal contingents from British India, and with
the favorable attitude of the Ghilzai assured, the balance shifted
dramatically in favor of Pushtun supremacy and against the Ta-
jik-backed ruler in Kabul. Nadir still suffered some setbacks on
the way. His brother Hashem Khan, still trying vainly to unite
the tribes and threaten the Bacha from the east, made another
valiant attempt on September 13, 1929. His hastily gathered
lashkar of Khugiani and Surkhrudi was decisively defeated by
Saqaoist forces aided again by free-wheeling Ghilzai. Hashem
escaped to India, where he was interned under the neutrality
rules imposed by the British until the rebellion ended.

Fortunately for him the end came suddenly and soon. On
September 27, Shah Wali launched a lightning attack on Kabul
with a large force composed of *lashkars* of Jaji, Wazir, Mahsud,
Daur, Mangal, and Zadran. Taken by surprise, Habibullah's
forces were overrun but rallied around Charasiah, almost on the
outskirts of Kabul, where a decisive battle was fought on October 5 and 6, 1929. The fierce rushes of the Wazir and Mahsud
won the day. By October 10 Kabul was under siege and Shah
Wali's forces were meeting fierce resistance. But with winter
nearly upon them Nadir Khan's forces realized that this was
their last chance to settle the issue. The Bacha, on the other
hand, now faced a threatening *lashkar* from the aroused Eastern

12. Pushtun tribal guerrillas advancing on the Afghan capital during Nadir Shah's campaign against the Bacha-i-Saqao, 1929.

Province as well as Nadir Khan's attack from the Logar. He sought at first to dissuade Nadir by bolting himself and his troops into the nearly impregnable Arg and threatening to kill a number of hostages, among whom were important members of Nadir's family. To make his point, the Bacha disposed of two of Amanullah's half-brothers who were prisoners there. Nadir, however, did not flinch and ordered Shah Wali to bombard the Arg.[40] On the night of October 12, under cover of darkness, the Bacha fled to Jabal-us-Seraj near his own country of Kohistan. On October 16 the Bacha surrendered to Nadir's pursuing

[40] Shah Wali Khan, a principal participant in the history he narrates, dramatically describes this decision in his memoirs. Nadir Khan's relatives had smuggled a letter to him asking him not to spare the Arg even if it meant their destruction.

13. The Bacha-i-Saqao
(formerly Amir Habibullah)
after his capture and
overthrow by Nadir Khan,
1929.

troops under solemn promises of safe conduct. On this same day
Nadir Khan had entered Kabul and had been proclaimed king
by acclamation of the tribal leaders who had fought at his side.
Up to the last moment, Nadir had disclaimed any desire to become king. It was generally supposed that he would put forward the name of his nephew, Asadullah.[41] In the confusion and

[41] Asadullah was a half-brother of Amanullah. It will be recalled that
Amanullah's mother, the Ulya Hazrat or senior queen, disliked the Ulya
Janab, a junior queen, and suspected her of trying to promote the succes-

tribal elation that followed the sudden collapse of the Bacha's government, however, it became fairly evident only Nadir Khan would have the stature and skill to bring the tribes back under control.

Indeed after his victory Nadir Shah (as he was now called) must have felt somewhat like the Sorcerer's Apprentice. The tribes, in the exultation of victory, were almost beyond control. Nadir had no money with which to buy them off so he wisely decided to let them loot Kabul and the surrounding bazaars. Once satiated with loot they were urged to go back to their tribal lands and show off their good fortunes. By stratagems of this kind he managed to avoid fresh disasters and bought some time in which to build a new government. Thus ended the rebellion against King Amanullah and the story of the bandit who dreamed of being a Tajik king in a Pushtun land. To the last the conviction of the Son of the Water Carrier that a Tajik could not expect a fair deal from a Pushtun was amply confirmed. Brought back to Kabul under solemn promises of safe conduct, he was arraigned before King Nadir and a jirgah of tribal leaders. Nadir told him that he personally forgave him as promised but the tribal leaders demanded his death as a traitor to the nation. On November 1, 1929, he and his ten leading supporters and members of his family were hanged.[42]

The end of the rebellion against Amanullah did not immediately bring peace to the country. Afghanistan suffered from a severe hangover for several years, and new tribal uprisings plagued Nadir Shah, but that is part of another era of Afghan political history.

---

sion of her son, Asadullah, who was younger than Amanullah. This dynastic aspect helped to fuel the discord between the Musahiban (Nadir Khan's family) and the Amanullah branch.

[42] Telegram from the Viceroy to the Secretary of State for India, November 4, 1929, IOL, LPS/10/1292 P53, 1929, Part 13.

chapter ix

the rebellion:
a political analysis

A political analysis of the revolt shows that the attitude of the tribes was crucial. The decision to join the rebellion was based on tribal values rather than ideology. British frontier officials in close contact with the tribes at the time were under no illusion that social or religious reforms were behind the revolt. In 1928, prior to the revolt, the political agents of the North-West Frontier Province reported that the tribes were indifferent to the reforms. In spite of the intensive religious and political propaganda to which the tribes were subjected throughout the revolt, their ends at all times remained practical and pragmatic: to enhance the power position of the tribe and get a maximum of material gain for the tribesman. Andrée Viollis, the only foreign correspondent in Kabul at the time it was recaptured by Nadir Khan and his tribal *lashkars*, vividly describes the looting of the city and remarks that "the tribesmen considered Kabul an enemy capital." The only "ideology" of the tribes was that of Pushtun supremacy. Aside from the prospect for loot the one thing that moved them deeply was the sight of a Tajik on the Kabul throne.[1]

The natural result of this lack of ideological orientation was the shifting patterns of loyalty which are so clearly visible in the

[1] Secret Letter from NORWEF to the Government of India, September 3, 1928, IOL, LPS/10/1288 P53, Part 5, 1929; Viollis, p. 68; Secret Telegram from the Chief Commissioner NWFP to the Government of India, no. 79-N, January 23, 1929, IOL, LPS/10/1288 P53, 1929.

course of the revolt. Tribes frequently changed sides and on more than one occasion turned on their allies in the midst of a battle if for any reason they perceived a clear advantage could be gained from such behavior. For example, the Khugiani, after taking solemn oaths to support Ali Ahmad Jan in his bid for the throne, turned on him at Jagdalak after the Bacha's foreign minister, Ata-ul-Haq, had bribed the Khugiani chief, Malik Ahmed Shah.[2]

These shifting tribal loyalties to a large extent influenced the fortunes of the several contestants to the throne during the revolt. An excellent contemporary article in the *Daily Telegraph* traces these ups and downs and the various constellations of tribal power which affected them. In the last act of the tragedy the Pushtun tribes, spurred by tribal pride, found enough common self-interest to turn on the Bacha and drive him from the throne. Even those Pushtun tribes that had become the Bacha's allies, such as the Shinwari and the Khugiani, turned on him when they learned he intended to disarm them and place Kohistani governors over them.[3]

Of crucial importance to the constellation of tribal power which decided the outcome of the revolt was the attitude of the powerful Ghilzai confederation. George MacMunn was fond of quoting an ancient maxim of Afghan politics to the effect that "He who would rule at Kabul must make peace with the Ghilzai and make it to a great extent on their terms."[4] Indeed, it seems clear from the course of the revolt that had the Ghilzai as a whole got into the action earlier, the revolt would have been of much shorter duration. Two things prevented the early commitment of Ghilzai power. One was their traditional policy of remaining aloof from internal Afghan struggles until the value

[2] Telegram from His Britannic Majesty's Minister in Kabul to the Secretary of State for Foreign Affairs, London, no. 189, February 11, 1929, IOL, LPS/10/1288 P53, Part 5, 1929.

[3] *Daily Telegraph* (London), March 26, 1929; the *Times* (London), October 9, 1929.

[4] MacMunn, p. 335.

of their intervention became as high as possible. The other was the fact that the revolt broke out when large sections of the Ghilzai tribes were wintering on the Indian plains.

The British government was well aware that the attitude of the Ghilzai was crucial. J. Patrick, who was in charge of Afghan affairs in the India Office in London, circulated a minute in September 1929 in which he stated the opinion that "no central government is possible in Afghanistan without Ghilzai support." The decision of the Ghilzai to support or at least not to oppose Nadir Khan was influenced by the Hazrat of Shor Bazaar and his brother, Sher Agha, and by growing sentiment within the tribe against the Tajik rule of the Bacha which became even less palatable once Amanullah was *hors de combat*.[5]

The extent of British influence on this decision has remained somewhat nebulous. The documents show that the Ghilzai asked for British advice and guidance as to whom they should support. The British, faithful to their neutral position, refused to endorse anyone. On the other hand, their preference for Nadir Khan over the Bacha was common knowledge on the frontier, and immediately after Nadir captured Kabul the Ghilzai maliks on the British side of the border were urged to refrain from disturbing the new delicate political balance in Kabul.[6] In the end many Ghilzai participated as members of Nadir Khan's *lashkars* in the reconquest of Kabul and those who did not participate directly remained at least neutral, thus assuring Nadir Khan that his back would not be stabbed at the critical moment.

The *Daily Telegraph* describes the situation of tribal conflict in the spring of 1929 in the Eastern Province as follows:

[5] IOL, LPS/10/1292 P53, Part 13, 1929; Telegram from the Viceroy to the Secretary of State for India, no. 1792-S, May 28, 1929, IOL, LPS/10/1290 P53, Part 7, 1929. See also J. Patrick's Minute of May 30, 1929, IOL, LPS/10/1292 P53, Part 13, 1929.

[6] Express Letter from the Chief Commissioner, NWFP, to the Government of India, no. 83 P.S., January 8, 1929, IOL, LPS/10/1288 P53, 1929, and following correspondence.

Today some few miles from Landikhana, in the neighbourhood of Lalpura, very fierce tribal fighting is taking place. In this area directly south of Jalalabad there are three main tribes, the Shinwaris, Khugianis, and Surkhrudis. Immediately following on the abdication of Amanullah the Shinwaris pronounced that Afghanistan was a country unfitted for a central government. Their fathers, they stated, had lived under tribal rule which proved satisfactory, and rather than pay tolls and taxes to a Central Government they would prefer to return to the old regime and govern their own territory.

Both the Khugianis and the Surkhrudis said likewise. Thus in this Eastern Province there are attempts to set up local tribal rule. And the result is heavy fighting and much destruction.[7]

The chief commissioner of the North-West Frontier Province put it this way: "Generally speaking, tribes of this [Eastern] province are more intent on looting than on espousing the cause of any claimant to the throne."[8] The British minister at Kabul had this to say about tribal political attitudes:

Pathan tribesmen generally do not want a king at all. They find exemption from taxes and conscription a pleasant change from the oppression of the old regime and exaction of tolls from passing caravans a lucrative pastime. Moreover they dislike intensely the idea of having to disgorge their stolen rifles and loot.[9]

The political dynamics of the rebellion, then, revolved around tribal attitudes and conflicts. Only when the tribes perceived it in their own best interests to put an end to Tajik rule in Kabul were they willing to overlook their differences temporarily and assume a measure of coherent unity. To a considerable extent this decision was influenced by the perception that a total lack of national authority would result in tribal self-annihi-

---

[7] *Daily Telegraph* (London), May 17, 1929;

[8] Telegram from the Chief Commissioner, NWFP to the Government of India, no. 111–N, February 2, 1929, IOL, LPS/10/1288 P53, 1929.

[9] Telegram from His Britannic Majesty's Minister at Kabul to the Secretary of State for Foreign Affairs, no. 293, April 18, 1929, IOL, LPS/10/1292 P53, 1929.

lation and by the personal stature of leaders such as Nadir Khan, the Hazrat of Shor Bazaar, and his brother, Sher Agha. Tribal perception of British desires for an end to the revolt and preference for Nadir Khan over Bacha-i-Saqao also seem to have played a significant part in jelling tribal political attitudes in favor of restoring a Pushtun-led central government.

In addition to tribal conflicts, another political factor in the rebellion was the poor performance of the army. We have already noted the general dissatisfaction in the army with Amanullah's well-intentioned military reforms. But such dissatisfaction was common enough in most armies of that period and was certainly nothing new in Afghanistan. It cannot wholly explain the almost total abdication by the army of its role as the national keeper of the peace. The basic problem with the army was not that its living and service conditions were unsatisfactory; a much more deep-seated malaise existed because the army was, in Mustapha Chokaiev's words, "an emanation of the tribes." [10] In other words, the lines of loyalty and authority between the government and the army proved tenuous indeed and snapped under the first serious test of wholesale tribal rebellion.

Major F. C. R. Dodd, the British military attaché in Kabul during the revolt, predicted that the army would not only fail to oppose a revolt with any effectiveness but might in fact support such a revolt. "The army is discontented, the mullahs are hostile, the official class apathetic and the treasury is empty," he wrote.[11] With regard to the army, about which the Major was certainly better qualified to speak than on economic matters, his estimate proved only too accurate. On several occasions, such as at Jalalabad and Charikar, the army not only failed to offer the resistance of which it was certainly capable but in fact by its

[10] Musthapha Chokaiev, "The Situation in Afghanistan," *Asiatic Review*, XXVI (April 1930), 321.

[11] This report is contained as an enclosure to Secret Despatch from His Britannic Majesty's Minister at Kabul to the Secretary of State for Foreign Affairs, no. 90, September 22, 1928, IOL, LPS/10/1288, 1929.

prompt capitulation placed valuable arms and supplies in the hands of the rebels who might otherwise have been hard pressed to continue the struggle. In more than one case, too, Amanullah's army units deserted to the enemy, this being particularly true when they were foolishly sent into battle against tribal kinsmen, as at Jagdalak.[12] But on the whole the role of the army in the revolt was a minor one except in the first few days when large-scale defections and surrenders gave the rebels encouragement, loot, and military supplies. Thereafter the course of the rebellion depended almost entirely on tribal warfare.

Another important political factor in the rebellion was the lukewarm loyalty, and in some cases the active disloyalty, of the men who formed Amanullah's government, the very men whose highest duty was to support the government of which they were a part. Except for a few idealists among the Young Afghans, most of Amanullah's officials turned out to be more interested in lining their own pockets with gold and maximizing their personal and family power than in nation-building or modernization of the state.[13] The outstanding example of such disloyalty was Mohammed Wali Khan. He was a man of great ability. As a Tajik, his prospects would normally have been somewhat limited. Yet Amanullah raised him to great heights. He became without doubt the second man in the kingdom, subordinate only to the king himself. When Amanullah went to Europe he named Mohammed Wali as regent, and after Amanullah's return Mohammed Wali was allowed to remain as regent for two months while Amanullah prepared his new reform program.

Mohammed Wali Khan had, in the early part of Amanullah's reign, been selected to head a vital diplomatic mission to obtain

[12] *Military Report, Afghanistan*, pp. 170 ff.

[13] In an interview with the foreign secretary of the Government of India, Sardar Gul Mohammed Khan describes the intrigues and corrupt practices of Amanullah's closest advisers (Confidential Despatch from Government of India to the Secretary of State for India, N.D., 5468-F/29, January 2, 1930, IOL, LPS/10/1292 P53, Part 13, 1929).

international recognition for Afghanistan while the country was locked in battle with Britain in the Third Afghan War. As Amanullah's personal representative he was received in Moscow and later in most of the important capitals of the world, including Washington, bearing the message that Afghanistan intended to throw off the yoke of Britain and thenceforth control her own foreign relations. Yet when the tribes rebelled against Amanullah, grave suspicions arose that Mohammed Wali Khan had been unfaithful to his salt. Certainly his contacts with Bacha-i-Saqao were never satisfactorily explained even though later at his trial he insisted with some credibility that he had acted on behalf of Amanullah.[14] But after the Bacha seized Kabul, Mohammed Wali stayed on, serving the Bacha and at least on one occasion the Bacha publicly thanked Mohammed Wali for helping him gain the throne. Wali also signed a manifesto along with a number of other officials denouncing Amanullah and pledging allegiance to the Bacha.[15]

Closely associated with Mohammed Wali Khan was General Mahmud Sami. This officer, a refugee from Ottoman persecution, had been one of the King's tutors when Amanullah was a young prince. The record of his trial shows consistent duplicity

[14] There is substantial evidence that the Bacha was helped by disloyal members of Amanullah's government. The regent, Mohammed Wali Khan, and General Mahmud Sami, the Mesopotamian Arab, were tried in 1931 by Nadir Shah for alleged complicity in the 1928–29 revolt. They were found guilty but Mohammed Wali insisted that the court question Amanullah, who was in exile. Enough doubt was created so that the court gave Wali only an eight-year sentence. His codefendant, Sami, was executed. Wali was later also executed on a different charge connected with the Charkhi-Musahiban feud. See *Ruyidad-e-Riasat-e-Diwan-e-'Ali-e-Hukmat-e-Shahi-e-Afghanistan* [Record of the Proceedings of the High Court of the Royal Government of Afghanistan] (Kabul: Government Press, 1309 [1930]).

[15] Telegram from His Britannic Majesty's Minister at Kabul to the Secretary of State for Foreign Affairs, no. 221, February 17, 1929, IOL, LPS/10/53, Part 3, 1929; Secret Telegram from His Britannic Majesty's Minister at Kabul to the Secretary of State for Foreign Affairs, London, no. 248, February 17, 1929, IOL, LPS/10/1287 P53, Part 4, 1929.

and disloyalty to Amanullah.[16] An even worse example of disloyalty, because of the close kinship ties which bound him to Amanullah, was the case of Ali Ahmad Jan. He was both cousin and brother-in-law to Amanullah and enjoyed his complete confidence. Yet when Amanullah sent him to the Eastern Province to pacify the tribes with whom Ali Ahmad Jan had great influence, he used this influence to further his own ambitions. He capped his activities by issuing a proclamation in which he declared himself amir.[17] When the officer in charge of Afghan affairs in the India Office learned that Ali Ahmad Jan had been sent by Amanullah to pacify the Eastern Province, he remarked in one of his secret minutes: "Judging from what we know of Ali Ahmad he is quite capable of betraying his master if he thinks it will pay. He made proposals to Mr. Gould [Counsellor of the British Legation in Kabul] last year to this effect." [18] Ali Ahmad was a colorful tribal character with great personality and wit and one can understand his power grab when he saw things falling apart. One can also feel pity for his alcoholism and his having been ruthlessly executed by the Bacha when he was finally captured in Kandahar. But it is more difficult to forgive his ingratitude toward the King who had been his constant benefactor, who had given him his own sister in marriage, and who pinned his hopes on Ali Ahmad's ability to end the rebellion in the east.

These few examples of disloyalty will suffice to depict the political atmosphere of suspicion and intrigue which permeated the central government when the challenge from the tribes came. Such rottenness at the core did not escape the notice of the wily tribesmen who traditionally resisted the extension of national

[16] *Ruyidad-e-Riasat-e-Diwan-e-'Ali-e-Hukmat-e-Shahi-e-Afghanistan.*
[17] Secret Memorandum from the Chief Commissioner, NWFP, to the Government of India, no. 254 P. and S., February 6, 1929, IOL, LPS/10/1288 P53, 1929.
[18] Secret Minute Paper of the Political Department, India Office, London, dated December 7, 1928, IOL, LPS/10/1287 P53, Part 9, 1929. The minute is signed by J. Patrick.

authority and were ever alert for any signs of weakness in the central government.

In evaluating its political weakness we must take into account the special case of Nadir Khan's failure to support Amanullah. It cannot be considered along with those of latent or active disloyalty because of the open manner in which Nadir Khan, a man of great honor and dignity, made his break with Amanullah. When he realized that his personal and official differences with Amanullah had reached a point where his service could not be reconciled with honor, he withdrew, first to take a position as minister to France and later to retire to private life in Grasse in the South of France. There he remained until he heard that the Bacha had seized the throne. Then, although he was seriously ill, he and his brothers, Shah Wali Khan and Hashem Khan, returned post haste to Afghanistan to challenge the Bacha's rule. Nadir felt that he had already severed his connections with Amanullah and therefore owed him no further allegiance. Consequently when Amanullah, then in Kandahar planning his comeback, ordered Nadir to report to him, Nadir ignored the royal command and decided to conduct his own campaign against the Bacha. Whether or not this was technical disloyalty to a sovereign whom he had never openly renounced is open to debate. The facts are that Nadir Khan seems to have been entirely sincere in not wanting the throne for himself up to the moment he finally and unexpectedly entered Kabul as a victor, and the hard political reality was that Amanullah had become a liability among the tribes upon whom Nadir had to rely to displace the Bacha. One report states that as early as April 1929 Nadir Khan was obliged to swear before a tribal jirgah that he was not working for Amanullah's restoration.[19]

It is quite possible—indeed probable—that Nadir Khan's personal inclinations and his differences with Amanullah, which had escalated to the proportions of a tribal *badal*, combined

---

[19] *Military Report, Afghanistan*, p. 188.

14. Nadir Khan (*front center*) and his staff during the campaign against the Bacha-i-Saqao, 1929.

with the political requirements of the moment to separate Nadir Khan and Amanullah irrevocably. This was in many ways a tragic circumstance for Afghanistan, for Amanullah and Nadir Khan needed each other badly. Nadir needed the dynamism and innovative imagination of the young King and Amanullah needed the grave and sober restraints which only the seasoned tribal warrior could contribute. The alienation was, of course, of long standing and took many years to mature. The results were disastrous for Afghanistan, for Amanullah, and for Nadir Khan. The ensuing period of revolt and revival of tribalism could probably have been avoided had Amanullah been able to rely on Nadir Khan's expert knowledge of tribal affairs and his judgment in handling the difficult tribesmen. If the revolt could have been scotched immediately, the modernization program could have moved forward, perhaps with some modifications, and Afghanistan would have gained a half-century of forward motion. Amanullah probably would have retained his throne and Nadir Khan probably would have been spared the assassin's bullet which ended his reign only four years after he mounted the throne.[20]

Thus, in his hour of trial and ordeal, Amanullah looked in vain for the sustaining loyalty of the men around him. Instead he found himself treading on treacherous ground and at every step he found himself facing unknown dangers and latent or active treason from those very men whom he had to trust if he were to preserve his kingdom. Judging from Amanullah's own statements in exile, it was his discovery of disloyalty among those around him, perhaps more than military setbacks, which made him decide to abandon the contest.[21]

No political analysis of the Afghan revolt would be complete without some examination of the propaganda that accompanied the conflict. As might be expected in a nonliterate society, the volume of written propaganda was small. It was largely confined to proclamations issued periodically in poster form by the various contestants. During the first few days Amanullah was able to use the facilities of *Aman-i-Afghan*, but this stopped publication upon his abdication. The Bacha-i-Saqao started a newspaper called *Habib-ul-Islam* as a vehicle for his propaganda. Ali Ahmad Jan decided to publish the *Ghairat-ul-Islam*, which apparently appeared only once. Amanullah seems to have

---

[20] For a brief period after Nadir became king it seemed as though the two men might compose their differences. Elated at the defeat of the Bacha, Amanullah wired Nadir from Italy: "As a patriotic Afghan I congratulate you and your companions on your epoch-making victory" (*Daily Telegraph* [London], October 16, 1929). Nadir Khan replied: "The era of the government of Amanullah will be inscribed in letters of gold in the history of Afghanistan and I will follow the road traced by you" (quoted in Melia, p. 69). But soon thereafter Nadir Khan became suspicious that Amanullah was going to attempt a coup to regain the throne. These suspicions were actively fed by the activities of the Charkhis, Ghulam Nabi and especially Ghulam Siddiq. The result was a complete breach which persisted until Amanullah's death on April 26, 1960. His body was later brought back and buried with all honors next to the tomb of his father, Amir Habibullah, in Jalalabad.

[21] Amanullah's statement in Bombay on May 27, 1929, is quoted in the *Daily Telegraph* (London), May 28, 1929.

made no effort to launch a newspaper during his stay in Kandahar but Nadir Khan founded the paper *Islah* in August of 1929,
in the middle of his campaign, and the journal has continued
publication to this date.[22]

The quality of the propaganda was uniformly low. It consisted largely of outrageous accusations of a personal nature
against opponents, usually couched in religious or quasi-religious
terms. The Bacha, for instance, posed in his proclamations as the
champion of Islam and did not hesitate to accuse Amanullah of
being a drunk, a pork-eater, and a heretic. He also accused
Nadir Khan of having assassinated the Amir Habibullah and of
other, lesser crimes.[23]

The counterproductive quality of much of the written propaganda was noted in the British General Staff Report on the rebellion:

Propaganda on both sides played an important part in deciding the
fate of Amanullah. A number of men left Kabul and the Eastern and
Southern Provinces, ostensibly to show their attachment to Amanullah, but in reality to act as agents for the dissemination of propaganda on behalf of either Habibullah or Nadir Khan. Amanullah's
propaganda was crude and often without even a modicum of truth
in it. After his arrival in Kandahar from Kabul, he frequently gave
out that Habibullah had been killed or taken prisoner. This is a fair
example of the puerile information that was spread in order to discredit his enemies and rally Kandaharis to his cause. Unfortunately
for him the people did not swallow it as easily as he had hoped and
continued to regard even the truth which was given out later as
"Amanullah lies." Amanullah never gained the confidence of the
Kandaharis, and his failure to do so was due largely to his mishan-
dling of the weapon of propaganda. Great reliance was placed on
the vernacular press of India and contributions sent by Amanullah's
agents to the *Zamindar* and other papers were outrageously incor-

[22] The *Times* (London), August 20, 1929, announces the founding of
Islah.
[23] Texts of Bacha-i-Saqao's proclamations may be found in IOL,
LPS/10/1287 P53, Part 4, 1929, and LPS/10/1288 P53, 1929.

rect. Even had Amanullah succeeded in defeating Habibullah at Ghazni, it is very doubtful if he would ever have succeeded in regaining his throne. He had lost the confidence of the nation, whose religious leaders regarded him as an infidel, and who were determined to have no more of him.[24]

The same criticism could certainly be leveled at the propaganda output of other contestants in the rebellion. At no time did political or ideological issues emerge as the subject of intelligent discussion or even of propaganda, probably because such issues did not exist and it seemed quite impossible to justify a straightforward contest between the government and various tribal-ethnic groups except in terms of emotional appeals to religion or personal vituperation.

Far more effective than the written propaganda was the extensive whispering campaign or bazaar rumor. In this kind of word-war the mullahs had the clear advantage of numbers, skill, cunning, and accessibility to the clients. Since the written word was not involved, the most outrageous stories could be coined and circulated and could gain extensive currency before any corrective denials could be made. In any case the spoken word, ephemeral and swift, could always keep ahead of written denials or expostulations. Though some of the stories were so absurd as to gain little credence even among unsophisticated audiences, a great many did manage to take hold and affect political actions. For example, the story that some of the machinery brought from Europe by Amanullah was intended for transforming bodies of dead Muslims into soap, thus depriving them of decent burial, seems to have been widely believed.[25]

In the field of social and religious reforms the oral propaganda

[24] *Military Report, Afghanistan*, p. 197.
[25] Interview with informant in Kabul, 1968. A slightly different version is Amanullah's statement in the *Daily Telegraph* (London), July 15, 1929, where he is quoted as saying that mullahs spread the story that the machinery was to be used for cremating Muslims, a practice contrary to Islamic law.

reached its apogee. Because Amanullah lacked ideologically trained cadres who could communicate with the people, information about the reforms had, by the natural process of oral distortion, resulted in common misapprehensions and misconceptions. In a situation of open warfare these misunderstandings could be skillfully used to distort the truth and convey entirely erroneous notions regarding the modernization program, notions that could justify the inflamed and rebellious condition of the tribal areas. Many stories of this type made the rounds. One such story had it that photographs of Queen Soraya riding naked in an automobile in Europe had been taken or faked by the British and air-dropped in poster form in the tribal areas.[26]

Unfortunately for historians and other scholars, the misleading propaganda was not confined to Afghanistan. Amanullah's flamboyant personality and his attempt to modernize so backward a country, coupled with his recent triumphal tour of Europe, made it inevitable that the foreign press should take an unusual amount of interest in the revolt. Events in Afghanistan were followed closely in the daily press of Britain and to a lesser but still considerable extent in Germany, France, Italy, and Russia. With two notable exceptions (Larry Rue, an American, and Andrée Viollis, a Frenchwoman), there were no foreign correspondents in Afghanistan during this period. The British press had only a few posted in India near the border. Most of the articles in the world press therefore had to be based on fractional information, on word-of-mouth rumor seeping out of Afghanistan, or on poorly informed speculation. This was seasoned with an occasional interview with old Afghan hands, mostly

[26] This story is still widely believed in Afghanistan and I was assured of its veracity by men who were by no means naïve tribesmen. I was never able to obtain a copy of this poster or to learn of anyone who had actually seen it, but the hearsay had done its work so well that it has become firmly established in the common wisdom of most Afghans. A likely explanation is that this story was a distorted exaggeration of the circulation by some mullahs of European newspaper photos of the unveiled Queen.

British officials, whose information was at times biased and often out of date.

The foreign press output on Afghanistan for the period is quite impressive in quantity. Articles appeared almost daily in one or more of the leading British journals. A review of the news files for the period shows coverage of the Afghan situation in the *Daily Telegraph*, the *Daily Mail* (which had the advantage of having Cecil Rice posted in Peshawar), the *Daily News*, the *Morning Post*, the *Scotsman*, the *Daily Express*, the *Observer*, the *Daily Sketch*, and the venerable *Times* and the *Manchester Guardian*. With the exception of the *Times* and the *Manchester Guardian*, whose news coverage was sober as might be expected, the rest of the field went all out in competing on sensationalism and the repetition of unsubstantiated information. The tone for press treatment was set even before the rebellion got under way by the headline in the *Daily Mail* for October 19, 1928, which read: "Fanatics Rise Against Afghan Queen— Islamic Leaders Shot and King's Brother under Arrest." The story following is a distorted version of the arrest of the Hazrat of Shor Bazaar with the false report of Inayatullah's arrest thrown into the bargain.

Another aspect of this external "propaganda" was the assumption by a remarkable portion of the British press and by most of the German, French, Italian, Russian, Turkish, and Indian press that Britain was in some way responsible for engineering the revolt. This aspect will be further explored in a later chapter but we should note at this time that the tone was set by the British Communist press, which openly accused Britain of interfering in Afghan affairs as a step on the way to making war on Russia.[27] The Indian press, under more severe British restraints than the press in England, was nevertheless generally pro-Amanullah in tone and in devious ways managed to spread

[27] Typical articles of this kind, mirroring the Soviet point of view on events in Afghanistan, are in the *Sunday Worker* (London), May 26, 1929, and the *Workers' Life* (London), May 24, 1929.

innuendoes which ascribed to British policy nefarious designs on Afghanistan. An example of this *sub rosa* propaganda is the interview with G. K. Nariman, a Parsi journalist who had talked with Amanullah in September 1928.[28]

A bizarre incident in this welter of propaganda was the sudden appearance of an American journalist, Larry Rue, who arrived by plane in Kandahar to visit Amanullah's headquarters in February 1929. He was the Vienna correspondent of the *Chicago Tribune* and his paper decided the Afghan situation was of sufficient interest to send him to Afghanistan for an on-the-spot review. He went first to Tehran, where he convinced the Persian government to permit him to rent a German plane by offering to take a Persian army observer with him. They stayed in Kandahar for five days. This coincided with the arrival of a Soviet mission to Amanullah. At the same time Michel Clemenceau arrived to continue his survey for the Kabul-Kandahar railroad project. Larry Rue wrote thirteen articles on the situation in Kandahar which appeared in the *Chicago Tribune* between February 25 and March 11, 1929. The articles are sober in tone and constitute a valuable firsthand account, the only one on record by an accredited journalist, of the problems Amanullah faced at this period. Incidentally, Rue states categorically that British intrigue had no part in the revolt.

Objective political analysis of the propaganda is important because it explains how the smoke-screen thrown out by emotional and irrelevant issues obscured the real political factors that underlay the struggle between the central government and the tribes. Misleading propaganda also created foreign and internal complications by disseminating the theme that Russian and British intrigues were behind the rebellion. Finally, both in Afghanistan and abroad, it implanted many erroneous conceptions as to what actually happened and, more importantly, *why* it had happened. Misleading propaganda thus made it much more diffi-

[28] *Bombay Chronicle*, February 2, 1929.

cult for historians and other scholars to separate the cotton from the seed.

Political analysis, then, reveals that the great Afghan rebellion of 1928–29 had all the classical elements of historical tribal conflict. Tribal disunity, reflecting the tenuous character of authority patterns within tribal society, manifested itself in the course of the rebellion by lack of consistent loyalty to any leader or cause. Ethnic tribal conflict came to the surface among Tajiks, Pushtuns, and Hazaras. The revenge motif, classical to Afghan tribal society, also surfaced in many instances; the Mangal, for instance, were able to repay Amanullah for their humiliation after the 1924 Khost revolt. Tribal separatism was greatly aided in the rebellion by disaffection in the tribally rooted army and by the breakdown of the fabric of loyalty among top officials in Amanullah's government. Finally, misleading and mischievous propaganda distorted the perception of the true nature of the conflict both within and outside Afghanistan.

In a sense the rebellion, which destroyed most of what Amanullah had built, was brought officially to an end on November 16, 1929, when the British extended formal recognition to the government of Nadir Shah.[29] In the last analysis, what was at stake in the rebellion was the existence of Afghanistan as a unified nation-state. Afghanistan had become a fully independent nation only in the juridical sense when Amanullah had wrested from the British in 1919 the control of his own foreign relations. The rebellion had proved once again that only a tenuous balance between central government authority and tribal power gave to Afghanistan the outward appearance of a national state. When tribal power had, like an evil genie, burst out of its bottle and overrun the landscape, it became a question whether it could ever be corked up again or whether what was known as Afghanistan was again to be subjected to the periodic process of fission and degenerate into a congeries of tribal peoples living in continuous conflict.

[29] The *Times* (London), November 16, 1929.

15. The Musahiban brothers (*left to right*) Mohammed Aziz Khan, Shah Wali Khan, Mohammed Nadir Khan (Nadir Shah), Shah Mahmud Khan, Mohammed Hashem Khan, about 1930.

To a considerable extent the internal ferments in Afghanistan reflected and interacted with international attitudes and developments with which Afghanistan was closely associated. Having traced and analyzed the course of the rebellion that destroyed a dynasty and nearly destroyed a kingdom, we pass now to an examination of the external relations of Afghanistan and their influence on the political development of the country.

chapter x

external pressures: geopolitics and relations with russia

External pressures on Afghanistan during Amanullah's reign affected the internal political situation. These external pressures arose from a long history of conflict in Central Asia in which Afghanistan had played a prominent part. It is a truism that Afghanistan owes much of its importance to its strategic location; it also owes most of its troubles to this same fact. From the earliest periods of recorded history Afghanistan has been on the principal route of invasion from the great Eurasian heartland to the Middle East and the monsoon lands of South Asia. How many such invasions and migrations took place in prehistoric times it is impossible to say, but in recorded history, starting with the incursion of the Aryans perhaps in the second millennium B.C., we know of at least thirteen major penetrations and perhaps two hundred minor ones.

Of these invaders only the British traveled by sea. The others moved across the land mass of Central Asia seeking vulnerable cracks in the great barriers of mountain massifs and parching deserts which protect the monsoon lands. A few conquerors reversed the current, entering Afghanistan from India, but the great mass of invaders left the Central Eurasian steppes and used Afghanistan as an invasion route or a staging area or both.

The best explanation for the role of Afghanistan as a corridor of power was formulated in geopolitical terms by the great British geographer, Sir Halford Mackinder, and by Captain Alfred

Mahan of the U.S. Navy.[1] Both Mackinder and Mahan wrote about the influence of geography on the political destiny of nations. For Mackinder the central fact was the existence of the "world island," the connected land mass of Africa and Eurasia. The "heartland" of this world island lies in the great land mass of interior grasslands, steppes, and deserts of Central Asia. Protected by geographical isolation from attack, this heartland, operating along internal lines of communication, can exert enormous outward pressure against the "peninsulas" of the world island such as Western Europe, the Middle East, the Indian subcontinent, and Southeast Asia. Population and other pressures originating in the heartland are translated into expansionist forces exerted toward areas with access to warm-water ports. In this way the heartland seeks to dominate the entire world island and eventually the world. Movements from the heartland follow the path of least resistance—that is, through areas where the geographical obstacles are least daunting. This explains the historical expansion of political power from the heartland into such peninsular areas as Eastern Europe, Turkey, and India.

Mahan turned the same propositions around by insisting that the forces bursting forth from the heartland can only be contained by a sea power capable of dominating the approaches to the world island—the narrow seas and straits of the North Sea, the Mediterranean, and the Indian Ocean—and by utilizing powerful land bases along the periphery of the heartland. For example, by controlling India, a "triangle of power" jutting 1,500 miles into the Indian Ocean, a strong land-based navy can be master of the lateral trade routes along the entire Middle East and South and Southeast Asia, making the Indian Ocean in effect a land-locked lake. Moreover such a land-based sea power

[1] The discussion of geopolitical factors is based primarily on Halford Mackinder, *Democratic Ideals and Reality* (New York: Norton, 1962), and Alfred Mahan, *The Problem of Asia* (London: Sampson Low, Marston, 1900).

can control land routes from the heartland and thus contain its expansionist forces.

These geopolitical doctrines apply admirably to the situation of Afghanistan. A study of the topography of the region and of the massive movements of peoples from Central Asia toward India and the Middle East demonstrates that the invaded areas are supremely well protected by natural geographical barriers of mountain, desert, and swamp *except* through the region of Afghanistan, which is a high plateau with a salubrious, exhilarating climate and traversable mountain passes. The denial of Afghanistan to any expansionist power based in the heartland would therefore be an essential policy for any power seeking to retain control of lands in the southern rim of Asia and desirous of containing expansion from Central Asia. Harold G. Josif and many others have pointed out that long before the British gained control of southern Asia, any dominant political power in the Indian subcontinent always moved to control and defend the access routes in the "northwest frontier." [2] This was as true of the Indian empires of the Guptas and the Mauryas as it was of the British who inherited their hegemony. In this contest of strategic equilibrium, however, the British had an overwhelming advantage over the preceding Indian empires in that Britain was not only an Indian land-based power but also a sea power with the capability of replenishing and supplying its strategic needs from bases completely secure from harassment or attack by any land-based Central Asian power.

Historically irruptions and invasions from the Central Asian heartland have been contained only when strong powers were established in the "peninsulas" and controlled the access routes in territory which is now Afghanistan. Such containment usually produced a political and military equilibrium somewhere along a line passing through Afghanistan. If the peninsular power were weakened, pressure from the heartland usually

[2] Josif, pp. 1–6.

broke through, and in nearly every case the breakthrough occurred in Afghanistan. Because of its position in this contentious
zone the area that is now Afghanistan has traditionally been one
of great political instability. The history of Afghanistan thus
tends to support the propositions of the geopoliticians.

The geopolitical theses have been criticized and challenged by
many scholars,[3] but international politics is practiced by statesmen for whom the geopolitical analysis of the Asian problem
carries conviction—witness Lord Auckland's Forward Policy, John Foster Dulles' Northern Tier, and Dean Rusk's Falling Dominoes. In international politics, as in many other arenas,
what people believe is often more important than the facts. The
beliefs of statesmen in one nation lead to actions affecting other
nations. Objective "reality" impinging upon these perceptions
often causes unanticipated results. From this interplay between
perception and fact the stuff of world politics is made and at
times unmade. Nowhere has this been better illustrated than in
the protracted conflict (called by Sir John W. Kaye the "Great
Game") between the Russian and British empires in Central
Asia.

Around the middle of the eighteenth century, Britain became
a land-based sea power entrenched on the southern rim of Asia
with the Indian subcontinent as its principal base. In this same
period Russia began to spill over its European boundaries and
enter Central Asia. The two empires, like inebriated titans,
began to shuffle toward each other, swallowing territory and
subjects on the way and convinced that at some point they
would have to grapple and fight for supremacy. In the meantime the Great Game was played by remote control in one of
the most fascinating periods of Asian history. Each power
sought to ferret out intelligence of the capabilities and intentions

[3] For example, N. J. Spykman, *The Geography of Peace* (New York:
Harcourt, Brace, 1944); H. W. Weigert, "From Mackinder's Heart-
land," *American Scholar*, Winter 1945–46; and Leopold Amery in
Geographic Journal (London), April 1904, p. 441.

of the other and to obtain handholds of influence, no matter how precarious, which could later be exploited. The Great Game was played by real-life adventurers, men like Arthur Conolly, Charles Masson, Alexander Burnes, Vickovich, and many others whose cloak-and-dagger missions, adventures, and hardships far surpass the fictional tribulations of Kim or Mahbub Ali or Robin Savage or James Bond. But to the statesmen in London, St. Petersburg, and Delhi this was serious business, as it was for the hapless Afghans caught in the middle of the intrigue.

The history of the Great Game has been told too many times to bear repetition here. Our field of inquiry is restricted to the pressures that the imperial rivalry between Britain and Russia exerted on Afghanistan and more specifically how they affected internal political developments during King Amanullah's valiant effort to modernize the country.

We can begin this inquiry by noting a strange coincidence of historical and geographic events. In 1757 British and Indian forces defeated the French and their Indian allies at the battle of Plassey, thereby eliminating French opposition to British expansion on the Indian subcontinent. The British progressively abandoned their role of merchants and became more and more rulers and governors of a growing empire in South Asia. At this same period the Russian Empire began to turn its eyes toward the Asiatic part of its dominions. A great military base in the Urals was established at Orenburg and was later followed by a concerted military effort to pacify the fierce nomadic tribes of the Kazakh steppes. Thus the progress of the British Empire up the Gangetic plain toward Central Asia paralleled the push of the Russian Empire across the steppes toward Central Asia. A third important event coincided with these two. In 1747, just a decade before Plassey, Ahmad Shah was elected paramount chief of the Durrani tribe and organized the great tribal confederation in Afghanistan which was eventually to form the nucleus of an Afghan empire. Thus the two contestants and the victim, which was eventually to become the unwilling buffer between them, entered the geopolitical scene in Central Asia almost simultane-

ously. By a geographic coincidence which matched the historical one, the Afghan capital, Kabul, is approximately the mid-
point of a line drawn between Orenburg and Calcutta, the
starting points of the Russian and British advances. The rate of
advance of the two rival empires toward each other during the
eighteenth and nineteenth centuries made it seem increasingly
probable that their eventual clash would occur in Afghanistan.

The pressures on Afghanistan tended to increase as the rival
empires drew closer to each other. On two occasions this resulted in full-scale invasions by Britain (the two Anglo-Afghan
wars of 1838 and 1878) in reaction to fears, real or imagined, of
efforts by Russia to control Afghanistan. This struggle on the
high plateaus of Asia was to a large extent a reflection of rivalry
in Europe, particularly in the Balkans and Turkey, and was aggravated by a long series of misunderstandings as to the intentions and capabilities of both sides.

British and Russian writings of the period amply support the
thesis that British leaders were convinced that Russia was acting
in the historical pattern of previous heartland empires and was
intent on the conquest of the Asian rimlands and on gaining access to the warm seas. Similarly, Russian leaders were convinced
that Britain sought to restrict and frustrate Russia's legitimate
expansion in Asia and at some point would resort to military ag-
gression to insure containment of Russia within limits which the
latter could not accept. Why else all the intrigues of the Great
Game and the frequent probings into Afghanistan? This was a
classical cold-war situation with both sides claiming and to some
extent believing that they were acting in a purely defensive
way while conveying by their actions, and often by the irre-
sponsible talk of their more hawkish leaders, an image of aggressive intentions which the other side felt it could ignore only at
its peril.[4]

[4] A good summary of British and Russian views on the Central Asian
problem is contained in George N. Curzon, *Russia in Central Asia in
1889* (London: Frank Cass, 1967). For a fuller exposition of Anglo-Rus-

By the end of the Second Anglo-Afghan War in 1879, Russian and British leaders had begun to perceive that continued escalation of their rivalry in Asia was becoming counterproductive. Switching belatedly from military to diplomatic means to settle their differences they agreed, in effect, to make Afghanistan a *de facto* buffer between them. Abdur Rahman ascended the throne in 1880 and the British withdrew from Afghanistan, having first obtained a Russian commitment that Afghanistan would remain within the British sphere of influence and a confirmation of the Afghan undertaking to conduct all foreign relations through the British.[5]

Abdur Rahman, ever the political realist, constructed his foreign policy around the triad of national independence, isolationism, and the balance between Russian and British power with Afghanistan as the fulcrum of the see-saw.[6] He too believed in the geopolitical inevitability of the clash of interests in Central Asia but hoped that the conflict might be resolved along peaceful lines (a precursor to the idea of peaceful coexistence) and that both powers could be persuaded to stay out of Afghanistan and use it as a cushion between them. In other words, Afghanistan's independence must be recognized as of paramount interest to Russians, British, and Afghans alike even if the price of such independence entailed postponing modernization of the country. Abdur Rahman therefore resisted the extension of rail-

---

sian rivalry in Asia see: Olaf Caroe, *Soviet Empire* (London: Macmillan, 1954); Edward Allworth, ed., *Central Asia: A Century of Russian Rule* (New York: Columbia University Press, 1966); William P. and Zelda K. Coates, *A History of Anglo-Soviet Relations* (London: Lawrence and Wishart, 1943); William Habberton, *Anglo-Russian Relations Concerning Afghanistan* (Urbana: University of Illinois Press, 1937).

[5] An excellent and detailed explanation of this accommodation may be found in Adamec, pp. 15 ff. The Afghan surrender of the right to conduct its own foreign affairs was first contained in the Treaty of Gandamak (1879). It was confirmed in the correspondence between Sardar (later Amir) Abdur Rahman Khan and Mr. (later Sir) Lepel Grifin during June and July of 1880. See Appendix III in Fraser-Tytler.

[6] Adamec, p. 17.

roads into Afghanistan from either the British or the Russian sides and even went so far as to forbid his subjects to ride on the British railroad on the Indian side which had been pushed into the tribal areas as far as Chaman in the south.[7] Thus geopolitics prevailed over modernization and drove Afghanistan deeper into its isolationist tribal shell.

The partial accommodation between Russia and Britain in Central Asia at the end of the nineteenth century gave Abdur Rahman some breathing space which he utilized effectively to concentrate on his program of "internal imperialism," i.e., subjecting tribal and religious dissidents to the will of the central government. The pressures from the two great powers, however, only relented, they did not cease. In actual practice the Russians continued to interfere in Afghan affairs. In Abdur Rahman's reign there were fairly frequent border clashes and incursions culminating in the Panjdeh crisis of 1885 in which Russian troops occupied a portion of territory traditionally claimed by the Afghans. This almost led to war with Britain and eventually to delimitation of the entire Russo-Afghan border in 1887 by Russian and British negotiators, the latter acting for Afghanistan under their right to conduct Afghanistan's foreign relations.[8]

The British developed an ambivalent policy toward Afghanistan during this period of *détente*. In effect, they wanted Afghanistan to be a unilateral buffer state, that is, a buffer for the British against the Russians but not the other way around. Declaring that they wanted Afghanistan to be fully independent in all internal matters, British leaders nevertheless felt free to push their "forward policy" in the tribal areas although they knew it was bound to have serious political repercussions within Afghanistan. In like manner they pressured Abdur Rahman into accepting a border settlement with British India which split the Pushtun tribes in two and cost Afghanistan several pieces of

---

[7] *Ibid.*, pp. 5 and 22.   [8] *Ibid.*, p. 16.

valuable strategic real estate.[9] In spite of these British pressures, Abdur Rahman on the whole favored the British view of the unilateral buffer state. Although he lamented the fact that Afghanistan was "like a goat between two lions or a grain of wheat between two strong millstones," he also realized that Russia was the more aggressive of his two neighbors and believed that Russia looked upon the Islamic states of Turkey, Persia, and Afghanistan as obstacles to be swallowed up on her march to the sea. For this reason the Islamic states had more of a community of interest with Britain than with Russia and Abdur Rahman believed they should seek British help in maintaining their independence since this coincided with the British desire to contain Russian expansion.[10] This fine balancing of pressures and influences required a masterly manipulation of internal and external affairs which Abdur Rahman executed with great skill and firmness. His son, Habibullah, upon coming to the throne in 1901 essentially continued Abdur Rahman's balancing act.

The geopolitical equilibrium achieved in Central Asia with Afghan cooperation enabled Russia and Britain to move cautiously from a *détente* toward an entente, and this movement was helped along by the changing constellation of power on the world scene. A stinging defeat in the Russo-Japanese War of 1905 made Russia more amenable to a settlement in Central Asia and the rising military and industrial power of Germany materially softened the attitude of the contestants in the Great Game toward each other. All this culminated in the signing of the

[9] The drawing of this "boundary," the so-called Durand Line, has been challenged by the Afghans at various times and has led to the protracted Pushtunistan dispute with Pakistan. For a full treatment of this problem see: D. S. Franck, "Pushtunistan: Disputed Disposition of a Tribal Land," *Middle East Journal*, VI (1952), 49–62; Louis Dupree, "Pushtunistan: The Problem and Its Larger Implications," *American Universities Field Staff Reports*, South Asia series, V, nos. 2, 3, and 4 (1961); Leon B. Poullada, "Some International Legal Aspects of the Pushtunistan Dispute," *Afghanistan* (Kabul), XXI, no. 4 (Winter 1969), pp. 10–36.

[10] Abdur Rahman, II, 280, 259 ff.

Convention of St. Petersburg in 1907 whereby Russia and Britain, with typical European disregard for the wishes of the Asian people involved, agreed on respective spheres of influence in Persia, Afghanistan, and Tibet.[11] Although the Convention was not to become effective until signed by the Afghan amir, Russia and Britain later agreed to recognize its validity despite Amir Habibullah's refusal to sign what he considered a humiliating document.

Thus Russia and Britain moved a step closer to a general settlement in Central Asia and this no doubt facilitated their emergence as allies in the great war of 1914. Had it not been for the early defection of Russia from the war and the drastically different situation which resulted from the seizure of power by the Bolsheviki, it might have been possible for Russia and Britain to have settled their rivalry in Central Asia after the war and thus have permanently relieved Afghanistan of the incubus it had borne for over a century and a half. But this was not to be. On the contrary the substitution of Communist for Czarist power in Russia made the situation in Central Asia more murky than ever and led to a recrudescence of Anglo-Russian rivalry. King Amanullah, who had ascended the throne in 1919, had to bear the full brunt of this revival of the Great Game at the very time when he was trying to concentrate all his energies and those of his nation on an extensive and controversial modernization program.

The Bolshevik Revolution released a number of internal nationalist forces that had been repressed under the Czarist regime. At the very threshold of power the Bolsheviki faced the urgent demands and nationalist aspirations of the Muslims who formed an important part of the former Czarist empire. At the time of

[11] The text of the Convention is given in full in G. P. Gooch and Harold Temperley, *British Documents on the Origin of the War, 1914–1918* (London: H. M. Stationery Office, 1927), IV, 618. Frederick Thienne in his *Die grosse Politik der europaischer Kabinette*, XXV, no. 8357, reported that when the German Kaiser read the convention he wrote in the margin "Yes, taken all around, it is aimed at us."

the 1917 revolution the southern fringe of the Russian empire, from the Crimea to Outer Mongolia, with the exception of Georgia and Armenia, was peopled almost entirely by Muslims numbering about thirty million and constituting about 14 per cent of the population of Russia. The Great Russians who ruled the Russian empire were themselves a minority in the population as a whole.[12] Most of the minorities had been conquered or annexed by the Great Russians and resented their domination in varying degrees. This resentment was especially strong in the Muslim areas, which had been treated virtually as conquered colonies. The demise of the Czarist dynasty with its unifying mystique ("Father of all the Russias") aroused all the separatist and nationalist forces in the Muslim areas and the new Bolshevik leadership headed by Lenin had to face the possible loss of large segments of territory and subjects. It was also threatened by internal opposition from the Mensheviki and the Social Revolutionaries led by Maria Spiridovna. In addition the Bolshevik regime was under attack by the White Russian counterrevolution under Kolchak and Denikin, and by the allied invasions in Murmansk, Vladivostok, and Krasnovodsk as well as the rampaging of the Czech legion.[13]

In these beleaguered circumstances the Bolsheviki were under severe pressure to placate their Muslim subjects. By extension and because of the powerful waves of Pan-Islamic sentiment which were circulating from the Caucasus to the Tien Shan, the Bolsheviki felt the need to win the sympathy of the Muslim countries adjacent to Soviet Russia's Muslim areas. Afghanistan, which adjoined the principal Muslim areas in Soviet Central Asia, figured importantly in Bolshevik plans to pacify their own Muslim minorities. Bolshevik policy was designed to pacify the

[12] G. E. Wheeler, "Soviet Policy towards the Middle East," in J. Penner, ed., *Islam and Communism* (New York: Carnegie International Center, 1960), p. 30. See also Richard Pipes, "Muslims in the Soviet Union," *ibid.*, p. 11.

[13] Alan Moorehead, *The Russian Revolution* (New York: Harper and Row, 1958), pp. 280 ff. See also George F. Kennan, *Russia and the West* (New York: Mentor, 1960), pp. 65–116.

Muslims with promises of autonomy and even independence until the Soviet government had dealt with other threats to its regime, and then to crush Muslim separatism by a combination of force and guile. To achieve this, the Bolsheviki internally adopted a three-pronged policy. They organized a Commissariat for Nationalities headed by no less a personage than Joseph Stalin and gathered leading Muslim liberal intellectuals under this umbrella, promising them that they would be in a position to influence important policy decisions regarding the future of Soviet Muslims. Most of these Muslim leaders were also Communists who had emerged largely from the Islamic reform movement of the Jadists, a movement which sought to modernize the backward Muslim communities in Russia and which saw an alliance with Communism, particularly the Social Revolutionary variety, as compatible with liberal Islamic thought. Among the prominent nationalist Muslim leaders who joined with the Communists in the hope of winning independence for their regions were men like the Tatar Sultan Galiev and the Turkestani Narbutabekev. Galiev was made Stalin's deputy in the peoples' Commissariat of Nationalities and editor of the influential Commissariat organ *Zhizn Nacional'nosti,* and Narbutabekev was one of the leading government spokesmen at the Baku Congress in 1920.[14]

The second Bolshevik policy was to convince Muslims that the Communist regime would grant them autonomy and indeed independence if they wished it. Leaders like Galiev were encouraged to propagate this idea and Lenin himself proclaimed that "the proletarian party insists on the promulgation and immediate realization of complete freedom of secession from Russia for all nations and peoples who were oppressed by tszarism or annexed."[15] This campaign, conducted with the outer trappings of good faith, had a calming effect on many Russian Mus-

[14] A. Benningsen and C. Quelquejay, *Les Mouvements Nationaux chez les Musulmans de Russie* (Paris: Mouton, 1960), pp. 137 ff.

[15] Lenin, "The Agrarian and National Program," in *Selected Works* (Moscow: Foreign Language Publishing House, 1947), II.

lims and a sedative reaction in adjoining Islamic countries such as Afghanistan. Stalin, however, had not become Secretary General of the Communist party in order to preside over the liquidation of the Russian empire. When it came to actual cases such as the establishment of the independent Tataro-Bashkir Republic which Galiev finally succeeded in having approved, Stalin deftly watered down Galiev's project by enlarging the boundaries of the proposed republic so that Muslims were left in the minority and by reserving all important powers to the central government. This and other tactics eventually convinced Galiev of Communist insincerity. His writings became more openly nationalistic and secessionist and he was read out of the party in 1923, imprisoned in 1929, and liquidated in 1940.[16]

The third aim of Communist Muslim policy was the eventual political and cultural absorption or subversion of the Muslim areas. In areas such as Uzbekistan, which from the beginning revolted against Soviet rule, the Bolshevik policy was first to temporize and later to subject by force of arms. By this combination of policies the Communists in the end stifled Muslim nationalism in a manner which, though repellent to Western notions of justice and equity, must be admired for its adroitness and efficacy. Feigned benevolence was followed by gradual Russification, fragmentation of Muslim nationalities, re-education of youth, Latinization and later Cyrillization of the alphabet. Then came deportations, secularization, cultural sterilization, and, where necessary (as in Bokhara), subversion. Half a century later the Communists could feel that they had exorcized

[16] F. Syromolotov, "Lenin i Stalin v. Sozdanii Tataro-Baskirkoj Respubliki," *Revoljucija i Nacional'nosti*, no. 8 (1935). See also Richard Pipes, "The First Experiment in Soviet National Policy: The Bashkir Republic, 1917–1920," *Russian Review*, October 1950. Accounts of Sultan Galiev's career, his efforts on behalf of Muslim nationalism in the USSR, and his disillusionment and downfall may be found in: Walter Z. Laqueur, "Communism and Nationalism in Tropical Africa," *Foreign Affairs*, July 1961, and "Sultan Galiev's Ghost," *New Leader*, February 3, 1958; Benningsen and Quelquejay, pp. 99 ff.

the spectre of Muslim nationalism, reducing it to a wan and harmless ghost.[17] Along with these attacks on the traditional societies of the area, the Soviets launched an extensive program of modernization. Although not very effective at first, over the years this program has substantially achieved many of the same goals pursued by Amanullah in Afghanistan. Women have been liberated, literacy and education have greatly increased, a remarkable measure of industrialization has taken place, and in recent years there has even been a renaissance of indigenous culture, language, and religion. Whether all this has in fact led to closer political integration of the Central Asian Muslims into the fabric of the larger Soviet polity is a much larger question beyond the scope of this study.[18]

Duplicity toward its own Muslim nationalities conditioned Soviet policy toward the Islamic countries on the periphery of the USSR and explains the Byzantine diplomacy, the devious vagaries and apparent inconsistencies of Soviet attitudes toward Afghanistan during Amanullah's reign—a period which largely coincided with the gyrations of Communist manipulation of its internal Muslim problems. In 1919 when Amanullah sought total independence·from Britain and engaged in the Third Afghan War, the Soviets gave him immediate recognition and support. Amanullah's diplomatic initiative in writing to Lenin and sending the Mohammed Wali mission to Moscow

[17] Hélène Carrère d'Encausse, "The National Republics Lose Their Independence," in Edward Allworth, ed., *Central Asia: A Century of Russian Rule* (New York: Columbia University Press, 1967).

[18] On the larger question of Soviet policy toward Muslims in its own and neighboring countries as well as differing assessments of the success of such policy see: J. Stalin, *Marxism and the National and Colonial Question* (London: Lawrence and Wishart, 1942); Caroe, *Soviet Empire;* W. Kolarz, *Russia and Her Colonies* (London: Philip, 1952); Joseph Castagne, "Le Bolchevisme et l'Islam," *Revue du Monde Musulman*, LI, no. 1 (1922), and "Soviet Imperialism in Afghanistan," *Foreign Affairs*, XIII, (July 1935), 698; W. P. and Zelda Coates, *Soviets in Central Asia* (New York: Philosophical Library, 1951); Edward Allworth, *Soviet Nationality Problems* (New York: Columbia University Press, 1971).

was reciprocated by the Soviets with great cordiality. This was the period when the Communists were in desperate need of Muslim allies and were being driven to the wall by counterrevolutionary armies helped by the Allies, principally Britain. By befriending Afghanistan at this critical moment, the Soviets gained merits with their Muslim nationals and at the same time struck back at Britain through Afghanistan. Little wonder then that Lenin replied cordially to Amanullah, personally received Mohammed Wali, and promptly dispatched a Bolshevik representative, K. Bravin, to Kabul with offers of material assistance against the British.[19]

The sudden disappearance of Russian pressure on Afghanistan upon the collapse of the empire of the Czars and the early cordial relations between the new Afghan and Soviet governments left Amanullah free to exploit British postwar weakness in India during and after the Third Afghan War in 1919. This explains in part why Afghanistan was able to turn a military defeat (or at best a stalemate) into a brilliant diplomatic triumph at the peace negotiations in Rawalpindi. In August 1919 the British, though under no overwhelming military pressure, decided to accede to the Afghan demand for complete freedom in the conduct of their foreign relations, thereby reversing a basic British policy of half a century. Amanullah also used the threat of better relations with the USSR very effectively during the negotiations for a permanent treaty with the British, first in Mussoorie in 1920 and again in 1921 with Sir Henry Dobbs in Kabul. This gambit came to a spectacular end when British intelligence cracked the Soviet code and Dobbs was able to reveal to Amanullah that the British knew of Afghan-Soviet talks about concerted military action against Britain. The Afghans then had to settle for less favorable terms in the treaty even though the negotiations still dragged on for several months. The reasons for this Afghan

[19] Adamec, pp. 144–148, details the cordiality of the Soviet embrace in this early period of Amanullah's relations with the Communist regime.

volte-face, which has puzzled historians, are now revealed in Dobbs' secret reports.[20]

The trend toward closer Soviet-Afghan relations was arrested by two major developments. The first was the growing realization by Muslim leaders that Bolshevik policy was designed to suppress rather than to liberate the Soviet Muslims. In Afghanistan this aroused indignation and cooled Amanullah's and Tarzi's early enthusiasm for close relations with the Soviets. The crushing of Muslim nationalism in the USSR and the liquidation of the independent khanate of Bokhara destroyed Amanullah's dreams of being a leader of a Central Asian Pan-Islamic federation. This was a serious drain on Amanullah's internal political capital as a nationalist Islamic leader and this loss of support, especially from the religious community, weakened the political base of his modernization program.

The second major development affecting Soviet-Afghan relations was the course of Anglo-Soviet relations. The reasons for this are obvious. For the Soviets the value of Afghanistan was twofold: it was useful in temporarily pacifying its own Muslim minorities and it was valuable as a base for harassing the British through the potential threat to India. For the British the value of Afghanistan was entirely related to the defense of India and to a lesser extent of the Middle East. When the Bolsheviki first came to power both the Islamic and the British factors in their foreign policy were deemed crucial, hence they were willing to make exaggerated promises and concessions in order to insure Afghan good will. Thus in the negotiations on the Soviet-Afghan treaty of 1921 the Soviets promised to return Afghan territory (the notorious Panjdeh) and to give Afghanistan arms and an economic subsidy of one million gold rubles per year.[21] But even as this treaty was being negotiated the Soviets were slowly

[20] Secret Telegram from Viceroy to the Secretary of State for India, no. X-3061, March 6, 1921 (repeating message from Dobbs in Kabul), IOL, LPS/10/912 P5261, 1920.

[21] Adamec, pp. 157 ff.

strangling the autonomy of the Muslims in the USSR and at the same time seeking an accommodation with Britain by means of a trade agreement which was a prelude to *de jure* recognition.

To the extent that the Soviets were able to accomplish their ends vis-à-vis their own Muslims and Britain, the value of Afghanistan declined in their list of priorities. Eventually they found it convenient to disregard their offer to return Panjdeh; the Soviet arms never did materialize and the subsidy was paid only partially and sporadically. Still, in the absence of a complete entente with Britain, the value of Afghanistan to the Soviets did not decline to zero. As Anglo-Soviet relations blew hot and cold, Soviet-Afghan relations tended to become closer or more distant. Also, Soviet-Afghan relations cooled as the Bolsheviki gained control of their own internal problems and as they crushed the Muslim separatist movements in the USSR.

Soviet-Afghan relations began to cool in 1921 when the Anglo-Soviet Trade Agreement was signed. In 1924 came British *de jure* recognition of the USSR. Soviet interest in Afghanistan declined markedly around this time. Then gradually Anglo-Soviet relations worsened again and Britain withdrew its recognition from the USSR in 1927. This was followed by a gradual process of Anglo-Soviet reconciliation and diplomatic relations were re-established in October 1929.[22]

The dates are highly significant to the political situation in Afghanistan: in 1921 the Anglo-Afghan negotiations over the status of the tribes hung in the balance; in 1924 Afghanistan was in the midst of a major tribal rebellion by the Mangals of Khost; in 1927 Amanullah was on the eve of his trip abroad and about to sign an important aviation agreement with the USSR.[23] In

[22] Xenia Eudin and Robert Slusser, *Soviet Foreign Policy, 1928–1934: Documents and Materials* (University Park: Pennsylvania State University Press, 1966), Document no. 32 (statement of Litvinoff on October 4, 1929).

[23] The Soviet-Afghan Air Agreement was signed on November 28, 1927. The text is given in Royal Institute of International Affairs, *Soviet Documents on Foreign Policy* (London: Oxford University Press, 1952), Vol. II: 1925–1932.

1929 Amanullah was *in extremis* trying to rally his forces in Kandahar for a last attempt to regain his throne.

Consistent and disinterested Soviet assistance and cooperation would have been of great value to Amanullah if for no other reason than to remove his constant concern over Soviet intentions at a time when Afghan energies were so deeply engaged in the modernization program. But it soon became evident to Amanullah and his advisers that Soviet diplomacy was aimed at using Afghanistan as a cat's-paw, first to help pacify the Soviet Muslims and later to apply threats and pressures on Britain whenever Anglo-Soviet relations became strained. Under these circumstances Amanullah could not rely with any assurance on Soviet good will or cooperation. This disillusionment with Soviet policy was fortified by the flight of thousands of Muslim Central Asians who sought and were granted asylum in Afghanistan during this period. Amanullah's relations with the USSR were, therefore, a destabilizing factor and a constant source of concern. During the final tribal rebellion the Soviets were reluctant to give all-out support to Amanullah even though they had encouraged him in his modernization plans and in his anti-British policies. Evidently the Soviets were not prepared to prejudice the Dogalevsky-Henderson negotiations for recognition which were then at a critical stage.

Only when the Soviets erroneously believed that the British had introduced Nadir Khan as their candidate into the civil war did they reluctantly support the Ghulam Nabi expedition from the USSR. This was too little and came too late to save Amanullah. At the end Amanullah apparently felt betrayed by the Soviets. He is reported to have said in Bombay on his way to exile that the Soviets had "instigated him into enmity with the British and then not lifted a finger to help him." [24] This statement merely serves as additional evidence of Amanullah's political naïveté. The USSR can hardly be blamed for acting in what it considered its own best interests and following the traditional

[24] Secret Telegram from Major E. T. R. Wickham to the Government of India, May 28, 1929, NAI, Foreign Political Files, 137-F, 1929.

modes of diplomacy of the great powers of that day. We may ascribe a certain amount of opprobrium to its deliberately deceptive rhetoric about its "benevolent" intentions toward its own Muslims and surrounding Muslim states. But such dissimulation would never have fooled Abdur Rahman and it certainly did not deceive Ataturk or Reza Shah, both of whom were subjected to similar pressures and wiles. Given the long history of Russian tactics toward Afghanistan, an Afghan ruler, of all people, should have been able to see through such Soviet maneuvers and adjust his policies accordingly.

We may conclude, then, that although at first the collapse of Russian power temporarily relieved the traditional geopolitical pressures from the north on Afghanistan, these were soon reapplied by the Soviet regime. This produced, first, an unstabilizing effect on Amanullah's foreign policy, especially on his relations with Britain, and, second, a diminution of his domestic political support for the modernization program. Soviet policy during this period was conditioned not by any sincere regard for the welfare or independence of Afghanistan but by the need to suppress the nationalist aspirations of Soviet Muslims and by the desire to use Afghanistan as a bargaining counter in Anglo-Soviet relations. The effect of these Soviet pressures and vagaries of policy were compounded by Amanullah's innocence in foreign affairs and by the complications of Afghanistan's relations with Britain, to which we now turn.

chapter XI

external pressures: relations with Britain

A detailed diplomatic history of Anglo-Afghan relations during Amanullah's reign is beyond the scope of this book.[1] Instead, this chapter will focus on the changes in British policy which Amanullah forced on Britain, on the conflicts and tensions which these changes generated, and on the role of the British in the rebellion that overthrew Amanullah.

We have already noted that policymakers in England and India looked at Afghanistan through geopolitical spectacles as the point of direct peril in the defense of India. India, "the brightest jewel in the imperial crown," was of central importance to the far-flung, interrelated, and majestic system of imperial power which Great Britain had constructed between the eighteenth and twentieth centuries. Imperial defense was the ruling passion of British statesmen and soldiers and to them it seemed that the most serious threat to Britain's Asian empire was the expanding Russian juggernaut aiming through Afghanistan toward India. Afghanistan itself posed a secondary threat through its capability of stirring up the fierce border Pushtun tribes along the Indian frontier.

Over the years Britain had evolved a complex system of operational policies to accomplish four goals: (a) to apply diplomatic

---

[1] Ludwig Adamec has already provided us with a well-documented diplomatic history of Afghanistan for the first four years of Amanullah's reign. Vartan Gregorian has also covered the history of the Amanullah period in two of his chapters.

and if necessary military counterpressures on Russia through Eastern Europe and the Balkans, (b) to maintain Afghanistan as a buffer against Russian advances, (c) to apply pressures on Afghan rulers to prevent their meddling with the tribes, and (d) to undertake a "forward policy," a long-term program of pacification and penetration of the tribal areas. The emphasis on the various elements of these policies shifted with time and circumstance but on the whole the pattern was kept intact. In a sense the key to their success lay in the degree of harmony between the British and the ruler of Afghanistan. Active cooperation on the part of the Afghan ruler with British policy was not essential; he had only to be a remote but complaisant liege to the British suzerain. To maintain this gentle bondage, the British employed three principal instruments: the conduct of his foreign relations, the payment to him of a generous subsidy, and the control of transit of goods, particularly arms, through India into Afghanistan. As we have seen, Abdur Rahman grumbled and grew restive under this regime, Habibullah accepted it unwillingly and somewhat fatalistically, but Amanullah rejected it *in toto*.

One of Amanullah's first acts after seizing the throne was to write a letter to the viceroy, Lord Chelmsford, declaring Afghanistan to be entirely independent.[2] We have noted in a previous chapter that Amanullah was nurtured in a new atmosphere of Islamic "nationalism" which was strongly anti-imperialist and therefore anti-British. His ascension to the throne presaged a new era in Anglo-Afghan relations and a fundamental challenge to the most hallowed premises of British policy. Documents, now for the first time available, let us look behind the veil of the Amanullah era and examine the *arcana imperii* of British policy concerning Afghanistan. Amanullah's stern resolve to cast off all vestiges of British domination and control at this particular moment in history was especially

[2] Appendix to Document no. 98, NAI, Foreign Political Files, Frontier B., 1919.

menacing to British interests in the area because of three new factors which threatened the security of India: the postwar activism of the Indian independence movement, the threat of Bolshevik subversion of this movement, and the new dimensions of warfare created by the technological development of the military aircraft. Let us look at each of these in turn.

In India the decade of Amanullah's reign was characterized by rising agitation and resistance to British rule. During World War I Britain had managed to keep India fairly quiet by a combination of strict military controls and vague promises of postwar liberal reforms.[3] When it seemed to the Indian nationalists that these promises had been merely a wartime ruse, their fury was aroused. It was fanned to white-hot intensity by the Jalianwala Bagh massacre in Amritsar, which occurred on the very day Amanullah was crowned king.[4] The liberal Montagu-Chelmsford reforms of 1919 did little to pacify this new surge of Indian activism, especially when the reforms were largely nullified in practice by the notorious and repressive Rowlatt Acts.[5] The result of all this was a rising tide of resistance, violence, and sabotage against the British in India during the decade of the

[3] On August 20, 1917, Britain issued a declaration promising India "the gradual development of self-governing institutions with a view to the progressive realization of responsible government in India as an integral part of the British Empire" (Holden Furber, "British Conquest and Empire," in W. Norman Brown, ed., *India, Pakistan, and Ceylon* [Ithaca: Cornell University Press, 1951], p. 167).

[4] The Hunter Commission found that General Dyer had ordered his troops to fire into a packed crowd of 15,000 confined in a stadium, resulting in 379 dead and 200 wounded (*Annual Register*, 1919, p. 272).

[5] In 1919 Montagu and Chelmsford, the Secretary of State for India and the Viceroy, respectively, initiated a series of constitutional reforms giving Indians greater control of local and provincial affairs. During this same period, Lord Rowlatt, Chief Justice of India who was also head of the wartime Committee on Sedition, recommended the continuation in peacetime of wartime emergency "law and order" measures which included preventive detention, accelerated trials, and severe punishments for "seditious" activities. All shades of Indian opinion violently opposed these recommendations, which were nevertheless passed into law.

1920's. This decade saw the rise of the Khilafat movement in protest against British treatment of Turkey after the war and the subsequent exodus of many Muslims from India. It also saw the advocates of total independence take command of the Congress party and the launching of the Non-Cooperation Movement led by Gandhi. Popular Indian Muslim leaders such as the Ali brothers preached a Muslim boycott of the army and were jailed. The Moplahs rebelled in Malabar and were crushed. The Prince of Wales was met by *hartals* (general shutdowns) in most Indian cities during his visit. The Swaraj (self-rule) movement gained momentum, and bitter communal fighting between Hindus and Muslims broke out for the first time. The "No Tax Campaign" was accompanied by a wave of terrorism in which, among other incidents, an attempt was made to blow up the viceroy's train and the governor of the Punjab was assassinated by a student at a university convocation.[6]

Against this background of deteriorating political control in India we must view the British reaction to (or, perhaps, the British obsession about) the "Bolshevik menace." Government of India documents for that period show that contemporary British rulers considered the Indian nationalist movement both subversive and Bolshevik-inspired.[7] In this situation Amanullah's announcement of a new and independent policy in foreign affairs, which included close relations with the new Bolshevik regime, was bound to dismay and alienate the British.

The third new element in Anglo-Afghan relations during the Amanullah period was the technological development of the

[6] This summary of the internal political situation in India during the Amanullah decade is taken from the *Annual Register* for the years 1919 to 1930 and from the *Cambridge Shorter History of India* (Cambridge: The University Press, 1934).

[7] *Bolshevik Activities in India*, a collection of reports, telegrams, and other documents in NAI, Home Political Files, F-18V, 1928, and F-379, 1930. At this period the term "Bolshevik" rather than "Communist" was the preferred usage and carried a more specific meaning as well as a heavier emotional load.

military airplane during World War I and the consequent British concern that Soviet air power, if allowed to secure Afghanistan as a base, could to a large extent circumvent the obstacles of geography and tip the geopolitical equation against Britain. The British were aghast at Amanullah's readiness to develop a Soviet-trained air force. They were even more shocked by his decision to use Soviet planes and instructors in Afghanistan and to develop civil air routes between the USSR and Afghanistan.

These new factors in Anglo-Afghan relations must be coupled with the traditional unstabilizing elements of Anglo-Russian rivalry in Central Asia. In fact, as we have already noted in the preceding chapter, the Amanullah decade was one during which Anglo-Soviet relations ran a very rocky course.[8] If we keep in mind this background of the Indian situation, the "Bolshevik menace," and the air threat, plus the traditional hostility of Britain and Russia in Central Asia and the important role played by Afghanistan in this rivalry, we are in a better position to understand the numerous conflicts that developed between Afghanistan and Britain during Amanullah's reign. Some were based on major policy differences, some on minor and even petty and personal points, but they all added up to a decade of tension during which both Amanullah, who badly needed British help and good will, and the British, who likewise needed Afghan understanding and at least benevolent neutrality, frittered away their diplomatic capital. Britain as a world power could perhaps afford such profligacy but Afghanistan could not. Let us now look briefly at some concrete examples of Anglo-Afghan tensions and conflict.

The first and fundamental conflict, which in a way set the tone for future relations between Amanullah and the British

[8] For an authoritative documented account of Anglo-Soviet relations during this period see the following *Parliamentary Papers* of Great Britain (volumes and titles are given in the Bibliography): Cd. 1869, 1923; Cd. 1874, 1923; Cd. 1890, 1923; Cd. 2822, 1927; Cd. 2874, 1927; Cd. 2895, 1927.

government, was, of course, the Third Anglo-Afghan War of
1919.[9] The military and historical details of this war have been
amply recorded elsewhere, but the undercover political activities which gave rise to British bitterness against Amanullah are
less well known. In essence the British did not resent the fighting itself so much as the timing and manner of the operations.
Amanullah took advantage of the serious internal unrest in
India. India was also in the grip of a major influenza epidemic
which reportedly caused six million deaths. Nearly a half-mil-
lion Indian troops were still in Mesopotamia and those who had
returned were war-weary and physically exhausted.[10] The war
started in May, at the beginning of the hot weather on the Indian plains. Much more serious and reprehensible in British eyes
were (a) the apparently unprovoked nature of the attack, (b)
Amanullah's use of the jihad or holy war against the British, (c)
Amanullah's intrigues with Indian nationalists within India and
with Indian revolutionaries in Afghanistan and the USSR, (d)
Nadir Khan's raising of the Pushtun tribes on the British side of
the frontier, and (e) Amanullah's diplomatic moves to obtain
Bolshevik backing. As we have seen, all of these activities struck
at the very roots of British imperial policy.[11]

Amanullah at first claimed that the British were the aggres-
sors, but the secret telegrams between Amanullah and the viceroy which have now been made public leave little doubt that

[9] A good account of the war may be found in G. N. Molesworth (Lt.
Gen.), *Afghanistan, 1919* (New York: Asia Publishing House, 1962). See
also Government of India, "Official Account of the Third Afghan War,
1919" (Calcutta: General Staff Army Hqrs., 1926). The unseemly haste
in which Amanullah undertook hostilities and the short duration of the
actual fighting are worth noting. Habibullah was assassinated on February 19, 1919; Amanullah was crowned on April 13; hostilities opened
on May 3; and the cease-fire went into effect on June 3, 1919.

[10] *Annual Register*, 1919, Afghan notes by A. Simon.

[11] It also struck deeply into the British purse. According to the *Annual Register*, 1919, the *one-month* Afghan war resulted in an increase
of £14,750,000 in the military budget of the Government of India.

the Afghans initiated the hostilities.[12] The attack was to start as a tribal incursion into a tiny piece of disputed territory in the Khyber Pass and would coincide with an Indian nationalist uprising in Peshawar, the principal British garrison town on the frontier. This uprising was instigated by Ghulam Haider, the Afghan postmaster, in that town.[13] Amanullah believed that the groundwork for a general Indian uprising supporting the Afghan attack had been carefully laid. Tarzi, his foreign commissar, had been instructing the Afghan envoy in India to work with Indian nationalists and to suborn Indian newspapers in preparation for a general rising which would be timed to coincide with Afghan hostilities. These letters were intercepted by the British and the operation was blocked. Amanullah was also receiving glowing reports from exiled Indian revolutionaries in Kabul about the extent of unrest in India. These Indian revolutionaries had taken asylum in Afghanistan during Amir Habibullah's reign and were in close touch with, and to some extent supported by, anti-British Turks and Soviets. They had organized themselves along government lines and amounted to what today would be called a "national liberation front." But in those more innocent and correct times they chose to call themselves "The Provisional Government of India in Exile." Their principal efforts were directed at introducing "subversive" propaganda into India and supplying Indian revolutionaries with bombs and arms.[14] Amir Habibullah had maintained a cool and

[12] See also Great Britain, *Parliamentary Papers*, Vol. XXXVII (*Accounts and Papers*, Vol. 6), "Papers Regarding Hostilities with Afghanistan in 1919," Cd. 324, 1919, p. 1183.

[13] A letter from the Afghan postmaster to Amanullah, assuring him that the Indians would rise as soon as the Afghans attacked, was intercepted by British intelligence. The postmaster was arrested and the conspiracy nipped. See Intercepted Documents, NAI, Foreign Political Files, Frontier B., nos. 1–200, 1919.

[14] Secret Telegram from the Viceroy to the Secretary of State for India, no. 793-S, June 2, 1919, IOL, LPS/10/808, 1919; Sykes, II, 267 ff.; and Ghani, ch. 5. Secret Telegram from the Viceroy to the Sec-

polite relationship with these exiles whom he kept under close surveillance to insure they did not violate the rules of political asylum. Amanullah, on the other hand, had established close contacts with them when, as a prince, he was a member of the War party, and now as amir he continued this relationship and assistance through the head of his Secret Police, Mahmud Yawar. It now seems clear that Amanullah's agents in India and the Indian exiles in Kabul misled Amanullah into believing that his attack on the British would set off a general uprising in India.[15] Moreover, Amanullah's Commander-in-Chief, General Saleh Muhammad, jumped the gun before the Peshawar rising could take place. Amanullah dismissed him, but the damage was done.

British intelligence was well aware of all this skulduggery and British officialdom deeply resented what they considered blatant interference with internal Indian affairs at a moment when they were in a most critical and delicate state. The Afghan attack was accompanied by manifestos and pronouncements declaring a jihad and condemning the Rowlatt Acts and other features of internal British administration of India. The jihad was aimed at arousing the tribes and the Indian Muslims. The general attack on British rule was in effect an open invitation to all Indian subjects to rebel.[16] Nadir Khan's success in raising the Pushtun tribes on the Indian side of the frontier was probably not due so much to the proclamation of jihad (although religious sanction

retary of State for India, no. P377, September 15, 1916, IOL, LPS/10/285, 1929, lists the composition of the Provisional Government of India as follows: President, Mahendra Pratap; Prime Minister, Barakatullah; Minister for India, Obeidullah. See the Secret Reports in NAI, Foreign Political Files, Frontier B., nos. 15–138, 1919.

[15] Interview with informant, Kabul, 1968.

[16] Amanullah's *firman* (decree) of May 3, 1919, castigating the British, is reproduced in the Secret Telegram from the Viceroy to the Secretary of State for India, no. P-2391, May 4, 1919, IOL, LPS/10/808, 1919. The proclamation of jihad is given in full as an enclosure to the Diary of Hafiz Saifullah Khan, the British Resident Agent in Kabul, IOL, LPS/10/809, 1919.

provided a convenient rationalization as it later did for the over-throw of Amanullah) as to the effective tribal diplomacy and charismatic leadership of Nadir Khan and his brothers. His early success in catching the British by surprise produced the usual bandwagon effect among the tribes, and the Wazir and Mahsud soon joined him. At one point the entire frontier threatened to explode in the face of the British Raj and it was fortunate for them that at that particular moment they had as chief commissioner on the frontier the legendary George Roos-Keppel and his able and loyal right-hand man, Sir Abdul Qayum. Their superb handling of the tribal situation, as attested in the documents of the period, saved the day for the British. Nonetheless the situation that developed in the tribal areas was one of the most critical the British had ever faced. The powerful Wazir and Mahsud were in active rebellion. Many of the tribal militia armed by the British revolted and attacked their British officers. The Khyber Rifles, an elite regiment of Afridi, had to be disbanded, and all along the frontier the threat of a general rising hung like a pall during those critical days of May 1919.[17]

From all this it can be readily understood that the circumstances surrounding the Third Anglo-Afghan War created in the minds of British officials a profound distrust of and prejudice against the new amir of Afghanistan. Moreover, although the war lasted only a month and ended in military stalemate, Amanullah managed to bring together such a combination of diplomatic pressures to bear on the British Raj that the Government of India was quite prepared to negotiate a generous peace, one that would recognize the new constellation of forces operating in the area. The viceroy, Lord Chelmsford, and his delegate, Sir H. A. R. Grant, brought this liberal viewpoint to the negotiating table at Rawalpindi in August 1919. But the die-hards in the imperial structure both in India and England wanted to see the upstart young king of Afghanistan, who had dared to challenge

[17] See the series of Secret Telegrams from the Chief Commissioner, NWFP, to the Government of India, IOL, LPS/10/808/1061, 1919.

British power, eat dirt. They objected even to a cease-fire and were outraged at the suggestion that Britain should relinquish control of Afghanistan's foreign affairs.[18]

Thus at the outset of Amanullah's relations with Britain there was, on the British side, a division on the policy to be followed. A few like Lord Chelmsford realized that there was an entirely new game to be played in Asia and that British policy toward Afghanistan would have to change. This new approach was well expressed by Grant in his report on the 1919 treaty negotiations:

The change was bound to come. It accords with the spirit of the age. And perhaps no circumstances more favourable to ourselves than the present could have existed for the initiation of this change. Our policy in the past was dictated by fear of an aggressive Russian Empire, continually intriguing at the gates of India. That Empire has collapsed and in its place we have Bolshevik chaos. . . . The Bolsheviks want to use Afghanistan as a catspaw against Great Britain and the Afghans are perfectly aware of this and have no intention of becoming a catspaw; though they may still try to frighten us with pretended intrigues, in the hope that this will loosen our purse-strings.[19]

But this new approach was not destined to succeed. Imperial, bureaucratic, and geopolitical habits of thought were too deeply ingrained for general attitudes to change to the extent which would have been necessary to make the new policy a success.

[18] The controversy between New Delhi and London on accepting the cease-fire is summarized in the Secret Telegram from the Viceroy to the Secretary of State for India, no. 837-S, June 9, 1919, IOL, LPS/10/808, 1919. Lord Curzon, the secretary of state for foreign affairs, became so indignant over the proposal to grant generous terms to the Afghans that he penned in his own hand a minute stating that he was "completely out of sympathy with the present policy of the Government of India." Because it represents an attitude which strongly affected subsequent relations with Amanullah, it is reproduced in Appendix C.

[19] Report by Sir Hamilton Grant on the Negotiation of the Treaty of Rawalpindi, September 6, 1919, IOL, LPS/10/808, 1919.

Almost at once the policy began to be eroded, and only a few weeks after Grant's report, the viceroy's report to London on the 1919 treaty contained this revealing statement:

Thus, if we have wittingly embarked on an experiment in releasing Afghanistan from our leading strings, it is an experiment to which there is no practical alternative. . . . True, we have relinquished the shadow—the war proved it to be nothing more—of our formal control over Afghanistan's foreign affairs. But Afghanistan's economic and geographical dependence on India justifies the hope that we may exert our control in the substance, provided always that we do nothing to drive her elsewhere for that help of which she stands in need.[20]

Finally, in reply to a telegram drafted by Lord Curzon to the Government of India objecting to the 1919 treaty, the government replied: "While the time has passed for our political control [of Afghanistan] to figure explicitly in a formal treaty, we hope to be able to compass our ends by indirect means." [21] Thus the formal policy to treat Afghanistan as a sovereign, free, and independent nation, although well-intentioned, never became truly operative and the Afghans sensed its administrative insincerity. Deep in the subconscious mind of most British officials dealing with Afghan matters, Afghanistan remained a British dependency and Amanullah something of an upstart king infected with latent but potentially dangerous delusions of grandeur. Amanullah, Tarzi, and the Young Afghans, proud of a new freedom they felt they had wrested from the British by skillful diplomacy and force of arms, deeply resented these patronizing attitudes.

The abrasive character of Anglo-Afghan relations during Amanullah's reign was caused by differences in both policy and

[20] Lord Chelmsford's Secret Report to the Rt. Hon. Edwin Montagu in Despatch no. 73, October 2, 1919, IOL, LPS/10/808, 1919.

[21] Secret Telegram from the Government of India to the Secretary of State for India, no. 1614-S, August 18, 1919, IOL, LPS/10/808 Political and Secret Department Files, 1061, 1919.

style. From the British point of view, Amanullah's activism presented a triple threat to India. But Amanullah believed that Afghanistan, as a fully independent country, was entitled to have close and friendly relations with the neighboring USSR. Moreover, as an Islamic sovereign, he felt an obligation to espouse the cause of millions of Indian Muslims who were still under foreign bondage, and his close relations with the transborder tribes were fully justified by historical, ethnic, and religious ties which were recognized by the British themselves in the 1921 Anglo-Afghan Treaty.[22] Strictly speaking, therefore, Amanullah had some justification for his policies, but his style and manner of executing these policies were characterized by openly expressed anti-British bias. One very knowledgeable informant assured me that Amanullah in fact distrusted and disliked the Bolsheviki yet went out of his way to show them public favor simply to taunt the British. In like manner, Amanullah was not content to maintain his influence and good will among the transborder tribes but engaged in active intrigue to foment anti-British trouble in these areas. Similarly, he could have quietly exerted his influence in favor of Indian independence but instead lost no opportunity to make a public display of his support for the more extreme Indian nationalist leaders and extended active assistance to the exiled Indian leaders in Kabul even though he knew that they were hand-in-glove with the Bolsheviki.[23] On the other hand, British "forward policy" in the tribal areas appeared to Amanullah as menacing probes aimed at Afghanistan. British objections to Afghan support for Indian nationalism seemed to Amanullah

[22] A letter annexed to the 1921 treaty recognized that "the conditions of the frontier tribes of the two governments are of interest to the Government of Afghanistan" (Caroe, p. 465). Fraser-Tytler states that without the letter the treaty would not have been signed by the Afghans and that "for the next twenty-six years the British Government's main objective in frontier policy was to induce the Afghan Government to recognize the illegality of actions which they themselves had by implication sanctioned" (p. 262).

[23] Interview with informant, Kabul, 1967.

and his Young Afghans as confirmation that Britain had no intention of liberalizing its colonial grip on Asian peoples but rather that it sought to expand its hegemony, perhaps even to include Afghanistan.

These conflicting and somewhat distorted perceptions of each other's policies quite naturally provided a fertile spawning ground for misunderstandings and tensions. The importance of this fact from the viewpoint of this study is that the abrasiveness of Anglo-Afghan relations in the Amanullah era was a well-known feature of the Central Asian landscape and inevitably led to the widely held view that the tribal rebellion against Amanullah was instigated and supported by the British.

Let us now briefly examine some specific examples of these Anglo-Afghan tensions:

Both the *Siraj-ul-Akhbar* and later the *Aman-i-Afghan* were consistently anti-British in tone and content. Tarzi, who edited the former journal, made no bones about his anticolonial (which he equated with anti-British) feelings. For example, the *Siraj-ul-Akhbar* was used as a publicity platform by the Niedermeyer Mission, a joint German-Turkish effort to involve Afghanistan in an attack on India during World War I; and it published articles by the Indian "seditionist" Mahendra Pratap who accompanied the mission. Even after the Allies had won the war, the *Aman-i-Afghan* continued to publish articles praising Germany and featuring large pictures of top German military officers as though they were the victors. Eventually the British in India moved to bar both journals from circulation.[24]

Amanullah never lost an occasion to belabor the British for their colonial policies in India. Just before the Third Anglo-Afghan War he wrote to the viceroy demanding repeal of the Rowlatt Acts.[25] On signing the 1921 treaty with Britain, Amanullah read the British plenipotentiary, Sir Henry Dobbs, a lec-

[24] Adamec, pp. 101 ff.; Report by the CID on *Aman-i-Afghan;* NAI, Home and Political Department, Secret Deposit no. 53, 1919.
[25] Adamec, p. 114.

ture on the freedom of India and demanded that this advice be passed on to the British sovereign. Andrée Viollis comments on this speech: "The haughty words of this upstart Asian kinglet must have awakened some redoubtable echoes in the secret labyrinths of the British Foreign Office." [26] Even during his official visit to England, when his British hosts were too polite to disagree openly with him, Amanullah on several essentially social occasions embarrassed both Afghan and British officials by advocating the cause of Indian freedom.[27]

Amanullah also worked closely with "subversive" Indian nationalist leaders. The British intercepted correspondence between Foreign Minister Tarzi and Ghulam Haider, the Afghan postmaster in Peshawar, and between Tarzi and Abdur Rahman, Amanullah's envoy to India; this correspondence revealed Afghan cooperation with Indian agitators. The British also intercepted correspondence between Amanullah and Obeidullah, the *wazir* (minister) of the "Provisional Government of India." One such document was a manifesto by Obeidullah and his aide Zafar Hussain urging all Indians to cooperate with future invading Afghan armies and to kill the British and sabotage railroads, telegraphs, and the like. There was a close linkage between the exiled Indian nationalists and Amanullah's secret agents in India, Hakim Aslam (the "Lawrence of Afghanistan") and Mauli Manzur.[28]

Afghan intrigues in the tribal areas were a constant source of friction. Amanullah's Tribal Affairs Department resorted to extensive subsidies to agitate and propagandize the tribes on the British side. British officials suspected the money was coming from the Soviets who were permitted by the Afghans to infil-

[26] Amanullah's speech is reproduced in *L'Afghanistan Nouveau* (Kabul: n.p., n.d.), pp. 18–23; the comment by Viollis is in *op. cit.*, p. 156.

[27] Interview with informant, Kabul, 1968.

[28] Translation of Intercepted or Captured Documents Relating to Afghan Conspiracy against the Government of India, IOL, LPS/10/808/1061, Parts 3 and following, 1919 (in effect Ghulam Haider operated as a secret agent and liaison with Indian nationalists); Sykes, p. 269; interview with informant, Kabul, 1967.

trate the tribal areas. Amanullah also refused to extradite tribesmen who fled to Afghanistan after committing crimes on the
British side. One case in particular became a *cause célèbre* and
aroused great public indignation in India and England.[29]

British activities in the tribal belt also raised the level of conflict with Afghanistan. Britain adopted a modified "forward" or
"close border" policy which involved gradual, peaceful penetration with extension of roads and railroads up to the Afghan border. Afghans viewed this attempt to eliminate their *cordon sani-
taire* with dismay and alarm.[30] Attempts to negotiate the tribal
problem with the Government of India were coolly ignored.
Curzon, now heading the Foreign Office in London, gave the
Afghan envoy short shrift on the tribal problem. Almost in desperation Amanullah personally appealed to King George during
his visit to England. He was politely referred to Austen Chamberlain, the secretary of state for foreign affairs. The secret record of these conversations reveals the icy politeness with which
Chamberlain refused to give Amanullah any assurances on
British restraint of its tribal forward policy. The conversations
probably only increased the personal antipathies, fears, and
suspicions of both parties.[31]

Britain's failure to treat Afghanistan as a fully sovereign coun-

[29] Interview with informant, Kabul, 1968; Telegrams Indicating Af-
ghan-Bolshevik Connection, IOL, LPS/10/809, 1919; "Soviet Activities
in India," NAI, Home Political Files, F-379, 1930; "Afghan and Russian
Intrigues with British Tribes," NAI, Foreign Political Files, 237-F, 1928,
and 130-F, 1930. One such Soviet agent named Roskolnikov was so
effective in the tribal areas that the British demanded his removal and
the Soviets complied. The *cause célèbre* was the Ellis case. Mollie Ellis,
a young British girl, was kidnaped and her mother was killed by an Afridi band led by one Ajab Khan. Ajab and his band fled to Afghanistan.
Amanullah refused to extradite him and gave him instead some land in
northern Afghanistan where Ajab settled and eventually died peacefully
in 1961. A fuller account of this incident is in Spain, p. 154.

[30] *Spain*, p. 153; *Annual Register*, 1926; Fraser-Tytler, pp. 203–204.

[31] A full account of the Amanullah-Chamberlain conversations is con-
tained in the Secret Despatch from His Majesty's Secretary of State for
Foreign Affairs to His Majesty's Chargé d'Affaires at Kabul, No. 47,
April 4, 1928, IOL, LPS/10/1203 P135, 1927.

try deeply wounded Afghan pride. There are numerous examples. In 1920 an Afghan mission was not permitted to plead the cause of the caliphate in London. Amanullah's attempt to correspond directly with King George met with a cold reply not from the King but from the viceroy of India. The British refused for a number of years to address Amanullah as "Your Majesty." Britain protested to Italy about a projected commercial agreement with Afghanistan on the grounds that Afghanistan lay within the British sphere of influence. The Mohammed Wali mission, which had been well received throughout Europe and the USSR, was snubbed by Lord Curzon, denied an audience with King George, and referred to the India Office. Tarzi was turned back at the Indian border "for lack of proper credentials" when first attending the Mussoorie conference. The viceroy of India developed a convenient illness and would not go to Bombay to greet the Afghan king when Amanullah was en route to Europe. The British continued to impose restrictions on transit of goods through India to Afghanistan. Transit of arms was especially sensitive. When the Mangal revolt was brewing in 1924, the British stopped an arms shipment purchased in France and Germany. Tarzi, then minister in Paris, issued a public protest in an interview in the *Nation* against this "flagrant violation of Afghan sovereignty." [32]

Britian regarded with great suspicion and displeasure the system of interlocking treaties between the USSR, Turkey, Persia, and Afghanistan that had as a common denominator hostil-

[32] NAI, Foreign Secretary Notes, F. no. 356, 1919; Adamec, pp. 136, 141, 163, 164; Castagne, *Les Basmatchis*, p. 13; Secret Telegram from His Majesty's Minister in Kabul to the Foreign Office, London, no. 124, November 3, 1927, IOL, LPS/10/1203 P135, 1927; interview with informant, Kabul, 1967. Tarzi's statement in Paris of December 17, 1923, is quoted in full in Melia, p. 32.

The problem of the British form of address for Amanullah should have been decided on simple principles of protocol, courtesy, and psychology. Instead it became a matter of vigorous controversy within the British government for several years. See the series of secret telegrams on this subject between London and New Delhi in IOL, LPS/10/809, 1919.

ity to Britain. The Turco-Afghan Treaty, for example, was signed in Moscow and provided in Article II that both countries would "oppose with all the means at her disposal any attack made against the other by any imperialistic State in pursuance of the policy of invasion and exploitation of the East." Everyone understood that the "imperialistic State" meant Britain and that the "policy of invasion and exploitation" was part of the standard Bolshevik propaganda line. Pursuant to this treaty the Turks sent to Afghanistan such noted Anglophobes as Jamal Pasha to head the military aid mission and Fakhri Pasha to be Turkish ambassador in Kabul. Jamal Pasha told Chokaiev that the purpose of strengthening the Afghan army was to add to the Soviet threat against India.[33]

Afghan exiles in India were an additional source of friction and suspicion between Amanullah and the British. Longstanding British policy provided pensions for political refugees from Afghanistan in India. They were kept under surveillance and political restraint, but each time there was a rebellion in Afghanistan one of these pensioners would pop up in the tribal area asserting his claim to the throne. Amanullah was convinced the British deliberately unleashed these pretenders or at least kept them for their blackmail value. Secret documents of the period now make it clear that the British did their best to control and restrain the Afghan exiles [34] but Afghans could not believe that the sudden appearance of Abdul Karim (a slave-born son of former Amir Yakub) as a leader in the 1924 Khost revolt was not planned by the British. Similarly during the 1928–29 rebellion Mohammed Umar, a descendant of Sardar Ayub, turned up in Mohmand territory and claimed the Afghan throne.[35]

[33] The Turco-Afghan Treaty is reproduced in full in Adamec's Appendix, pp. 192–193; Mustapha Chokaiev, "The Bolsheviks and Afghanistan," *Asiatic Review* (London), July 1929.

[34] See, for example, the Secret Telegram from the Intelligence Bureau, Quetta, to the Chief of the General Staff, New Delhi, no. 1-Q-9, January 4, 1929, IOL, LPS/10/1203, P135, 1927.

[35] One informant interviewed in Lahore in 1968 assured me that the descendants of Yakub and Ayub had confided to him that they had been

Quite apart from these specific sources of Anglo-Afghan friction, there were serious cultural and psychological communications gaps between Afghan and British officials. These differences in outlook often took the form of personal animus and hostile behavior. Afghan xenophobia, the bitter aftertaste of three Anglo-Afghan wars, was personified by Amanullah, whose Anglophobic reactions drew emotional sustenance from the Ulya Hazrat and intellectual buttressing from Tarzi's anticolonial tutoring. After the 1919 war Amanullah built an impressive monument to independence which featured broken British cannon and British lions in chains; and he delighted in lecturing Dobbs, in taunting the British minister, Sir Francis Humphrys, and in humiliating his British hosts over minor matters of protocol in Bombay during his royal tour.

British officials, for their part, were accustomed to dealing with Indians who tended to cringe before the great white sahibs. They found it difficult to understand the extreme pride and quixotic punctilio of the Pushtun tribal mind. Some of the British frontier officers, of course, understood these things very well indeed, but they were in a minority and their judgments were often overruled by deskbound political officers in Simla or London. For example, Sir Hamilton Grant, who negotiated the 1919 Treaty of Rawalpindi, tried to convey the Afghan mentality to the British bureaucrats in a famous report written to Sir Denys Brays, the foreign secretary of the Government of India. Grant compared the Afghans to the proverbial Scottish Highlander who will cut off his nose to spite his face and stated that the Afghans "will accept the refusal of their most cherished desire, if it is put to them in temperate, friendly words and the reason for the refusal honestly explained. But any attempt to

approached by the British to participate in anti-Amanullah activities. Such soundings by British intelligence are remotely plausible. The Afghan exiles may also have been attempting to build up their own prestige with the British by initiating and circulating such reports. The official documents do not bear them out.

brow-beat them and still more any attempt to trick them, is doomed to instant failure." [36]

Some British officials saw a modernizing Afghanistan as a threat to British rule in India since it offered an example of the kind of progress free Asians could achieve. It was difficult for such officials to keep separate their dislike for Amanullah's policies and for the man himself. This was especially true among the British military. For example, in a minute sent to the Political Committee, General Sir E. Barrows made the point that concessions should not be made to Amanullah because "he may any day be assassinated. Indeed I shall be much surprised if no attempts are made on his life. In that case we need not regret his decease. I am told that he is an ill-conditioned young man who has imbibed strong Anglophobe ideas." [37]

Lack of cultural empathy with Afghanistan, distaste for its nationalist policies, and personal antipathy toward Amanullah were all united in Sir Francis Humphrys, the man chosen to be the first British minister to independent Afghanistan. He arrived in Kabul in 1922, shortly after the signing of the 1921 treaty, and remained until shortly after Amanullah's abdication in 1929. His service thus spanned most of Amanullah's reign. Sir Francis, a former military officer on the frontier, was unquestionably a man of great personal ability, uncorruptible integrity, and fierce British pride. In other circumstances he might have made an excellent envoy but in the entirely novel and fluid conditions that prevailed in Central Asia, he simply could not adapt or bend to the currents of fierce nationalism, independence, and modernization that were sweeping through Kabul during Amanullah's reign. He saw Amanullah essentially as a comic-opera king and a fool who wanted to throw everything of traditional value out

[36] Report by Sir Hamilton Grant to the Government of India, no. 108, September 6, 1919, NAI, Foreign Political Files, Frontier B, nos. 15–138, October 1919.

[37] The document is in IOL, Political and Department Secret Files, LPS/10/808/1061, 1919.

the window. In the actions of the King he saw profound danger to British interests in India and the fact that Amanullah lost no opportunity to tease and taunt him, even over the loss of a cricket match by a British to an Afghan team, caused Sir Francis to conceive a hearty personal dislike for the Afghan monarch.[38]

The documentary record which is now available clearly establishes that Humphrys' total lack of sympathy for Amanullah and his policies had an important effect in the progressive deterioration of Anglo-Afghan relations. So marked was Humphrys' animus against Amanullah and so much did he out-Herod Herod that in several important cases the Government of India and the British government in London had to put their foot down and veto Humphrys' Draconian proposals against Amanullah. The documented instances of Humphrys' bias and anti-Afghan attitudes are so numerous that it is difficult to encompass them in this short review. Yet the following few examples from the latter period of his tenure will establish the point.[39]

---

[38] The incident at the cricket match was related to me in Kabul in 1968 by an informant who was an eyewitness.

[39] The examples cited are taken from documents in the IOL, under these general file headings: LPS/10/1203 P135, 1927; LPS/10/53, Part 3, 1929; LPS/10/1287 P53, Part 4, 1929; LPS/10/1288 P53, Part 5, 1929; LPS/1291 P53, Parts 11 and 12, 1929. The principal documents cited are: (A) Telegrams from Sir Francis Humphrys in the British Legation, Kabul, to the Foreign Office, London: no. 125, November 3, 1927; no. 212, December 14 and 23, 1928; no. 39, January 14, 1929; no. 71, January 20, 1929; no. 117, January 29, 1929; no. 124, January 31, 1929; no. 149, February 4, 1929; no. 159, February 6, 1929; no. 152, February 6, 1929; no. 174, February 10, 1929; no. 191, February 12, 1929. (B) Despatch from Sir Francis Humphrys, British Legation, Kabul, to the Foreign Office, London, no. 106, October 31, 1928. (C) Telegrams from the Government of India in New Delhi to the Secretary of State for India, London: no. 1794, June 29, 1928; no. 549-S, February 5, 1929; no. 672-S, February 11, 1929. (D) Telegram from the Government of India, New Delhi, to the British Legation, Kabul, no. 175-K, February 6, 1929. (E) Minute of the India Office London, prepared by A. Wakeley, no. 1178, February 16, 1929.

Humphrys was unhappy about Amanullah's royal visit to Europe and tried to arrange his passage through India in a way that would put Amanullah in his place. When Amanullah balked at the arrangements, Humphrys recommended petty reprisals that amounted to punishing Amanullah as though he were a spoiled child.

When he learned that the Government of India and London favored the railroad project for Afghanistan sponsored by Clemenceau, Humphrys did his best to discourage it and to arouse British government opposition to it.

When Amanullah returned from England and his foreign minister, Ghulam Siddiq, tried to initiate follow-up conversations on the discussions that had taken place in London concerning British aid, Humphrys coldly rebuffed Siddiq's advances and reported to London that Siddiq was motivated by a desire for personal profit from the aid projects. "The Afghan, both by temperament and habit, possesses a capacity for the unprofitable absorption of gold to an unlimited extent. What he entirely lacks is the aptitude for organization or the honest application of funds," he reported. He also refused even to consider Siddiq's request for negotiation of a new and more friendly treaty.

Humphrys reported to London that Siddiq was Britain's "most implacable enemy" and that he was "confused, ill-balanced and bombastic." Humphrys had no use either for Mahmud Tarzi, Amanullah's other principal foreign adviser. He even strongly recommended that Tarzi be denied a transit visa through India on his way to Afghanistan when the rebellion broke out.

When Kabul was invested by the Saqaoist forces, Humphrys arbitrarily and without consulting the Amanullah government caused British Air Force planes to violate Afghan airspace, fly over Kabul, and distribute pamphlets uncomplimentary to the Amanullah regime. This brought on a bitter exchange of notes between the Afghan Foreign Office and Humphrys in which the latter simply brushed off Afghan complaints by interposing his claim of superior right to maintain communications with his government.

Humphrys kept badgering Amanullah to cancel his reforms and give in to the demands of the mullahs and the most reactionary elements of Afghan society.

Soon after Amanullah's abdication in favor of Inayatullah, which Humphrys characterized as "a hoax and a Cox and Box affair," he decided to withdraw the British mission from Kabul, and he also used this as an instrument for eliminating the influence of other friendly foreign governments. Since he controlled the only means of evacuation (the airlift) to India, he persuaded the British government to put pressure on other governments to evacuate their missions and nationals. They were not allowed to remain in India, however, but had to be evacuated all the way to their homelands. By removing diplomatic representation from the capital, Humphrys made it clear that the race for the throne was open to all claimants. This was an advantage to Nadir Khan, whom Humphrys personally favored.

In his reports to London on the rebellion Humphrys consistently wrote off Amanullah's chances to retain his throne. "Amanullah's cause is dead," he declared and then suggested that Nadir was the best alternative candidate. He recommended that Nadir be given every facility to come to Afghanistan and when the Bacha sent emissaries to persuade Nadir to come back, Humphrys was so pleased that he recommended to the Government of India that the emissaries be given every facility for transiting through India and even that funds be advanced secretly to them for rail and steamship passage. As for Amanullah, Humphrys cabled his government that the "king and his entire family should retire to Switzerland."

To such lengths did Humphrys seek to carry his vendetta that on at least three occasions his superiors in New Delhi and in London found it necessary to overrule his recommendations. In the first case Humphrys suggested that the diplomatic pouch sent by Amanullah's envoy in London should be diverted to the

Bacha's rebel government on the grounds that it was addressed to the "Foreign Office, Kabul." The British government, to its credit, refused to go along with this petty sophistry. In the second instance Humphrys recommended reprisals and deprivation of recognized privileges for Afghan officials in India because they allegedly were engaged in pro-Amanullah propaganda. Both the Government of India and London felt this was going too far and that such measures would simply increase pro-Amanullah agitation in India, where, as we have seen, Amanullah was very popular. In the third case Humphrys recommended that if Amanullah received Soviet representatives in Kandahar, a long list of sanctions should be invoked against him including closing the Indo-Afghan border at Chaman (entry point for Kandahar), withdrawal of the British consul at Kandahar, cancellation of customs exemptions (which were guaranteed by the 1921 treaty), and an arms embargo enforced at Chaman. Both New Delhi and London considered this demand for a virtual blockade beyond reason and likely to result in serious repercussions in both India and the USSR. They overruled Humphrys.

When Amanullah was preparing his comeback from Kandahar and overcame his anti-British bias to the extent of requesting British aid, particularly arms, Humphrys opposed the request with all the vigor at his command, insisting that Amanullah was no longer king in view of his abdication, that Amanullah's retraction of the abdication should not be recognized by the British government, and that in any case to help Amanullah would be to back the wrong horse.

One looks hopefully but in vain among the many hundreds of reports from Humphrys to his government for some words of understanding, sympathy, or encouragement for the valiant experiment and bold effort which Amanullah was making to improve his country. One would have expected from the representative of one of the most enlightened and civilized countries in the world some indication that the Afghan nation and its king should receive some aid or at least moral support from Britain.

Many British officials of that period certainly had such sympathy and understanding for the Afghan nation and its first halting steps on the road to modernity. It was one of Amanullah's misfortunes that the great British Empire did not send as its first envoy to his court a man who had the necessary humility, compassion, and vision. Of all those surrounding Amanullah only his sister, Nur-us-Seraj, seems to have struck a spark of sympathy in Humphrys' heart. Among all his philippics against Amanullah and his officials one warm message shines out like a solitary candle. Nur-us-Seraj, pregnant in Kandahar, wanted to have her baby in India. Humphrys wired the agent to the governor general in Baluchistan: "I suggest every courtesy be shown to her and that she be helped on her way. She is a charming girl." [40]

In spite of many points of conflict and personality clashes, there were periods of relaxation and even friendliness in Anglo-Afghan relations during Amanullah's reign. Amanullah's sojourn in England, for example, was characterized by courtesy, good feelings, and high hopes for future relations. But on the whole relations during the Amanullah period were highly unsatisfactory. It is only natural, then, that when the rebellion broke out in 1928 most observers suspected British instigation. Most Afghans, of course, even highly sophisticated ones, believed and still believe that the British engineered the rebellion. A good portion of the British press and most of the foreign press of the period echoed this belief. The Soviet, French, and German press were particularly accusatory. The leftist press in most countries followed the Soviet line.[41] British ambassadors in Constantino-

[40] Telegram from the British Minister in Kabul to the Agent for the Governor General in Baluchistan, unnumbered, February 15, 1929, IOL, LPS/10/1288 P53, Part 5, 1929.

[41] See, for example, the *Morning Post*, January 31, 1929; the *Bombay Chronicle*, January 19, 1929; the *Indian National Herald*, January 14, 1929; and the *Chicago Daily Tribune*, January 16, 1929. A good summary of the French and German press views is given in the *Times* (London), of January 16, 1929. For an example of the Russian attitude see the *Sunday Worker* of April 21, 1929.

ple, Rome, and Berlin peppered their Foreign Office in London with summaries of press accusations and of private conversations in which British instigation of the Afghan rebellion figured prominently either explicitly or implicitly.[42] Even the American press got into the act with articles hinting at dark British plots.[43] Only a few lonely voices were raised in defense of Britain. The *Morning Post* took indignant exception to insinuations published by the *Daily Mail* and the American reporter Larry Rue wrote in his series of articles for the *Chicago Daily Tribune* that the British had had no part in the rebellion.[44] A good deal of the suspicion of British intrigue focused on the presence in the Indian tribal area of Col. T. E. Lawrence ("Lawrence of Arabia") who at that time was serving under the alias of Aircraftsman Shaw. This naturally caught the imagination of the press and of the romanticizers both of Lawrence and of the Afghan frontier.

Considering Britain's many reasons to be dissatisfied with Amanullah and his policies and all the suspicious circumstances that surrounded the outbreak and progress of the rebellion, it is perhaps anticlimactic to conclude that the British were not secretly behind it, but that is where the documentary evidence, now for the first time available, inevitably leads any impartial and serious scholarly inquiry. This does not mean that British policy and actions did not influence the outbreak and outcome of the rebellion, but there was nothing covert about such policies and actions and they were of a kind which any government might be lawfully entitled to adopt toward a regime with which it was not on especially friendly terms. There can be no doubt, of course, that unsatisfactory Anglo-Afghan relations affected the rebellion in a number of ways. The tribes, for example, were well aware of the bite of British power and would have hesi-

[42] The ambassadors' reports are in IOL, LPS/10/1290 P53, Parts 7, 8, 9, and 10, 1929.

[43] See the *New York World* for February 14, 1929, and the *New York Times* for February 8, 1929.

[44] See the *Morning Post* for January 31, 1929, and the *Chicago Daily Tribune* for February 28, 1929.

tated to attack an Afghan king who might call for and receive assistance from Britain.

There was little risk, however, that Britain would actively help Amanullah. Urged on by unsympathetic reports from Humphrys, the British government assumed what it chose to call a rigorously "neutral" attitude. It did so for a number of reasons. It did not have cordial relations with the Amanullah regime and therefore saw no special reason to go out of its way to support it. Its situation in India was still precarious with regard to the increasingly active independence movement and it probably rightly felt that involvement in the internal quarrels of Afghanistan would further weaken its position in India. Finally it did not want to give the USSR any excuse for interfering in Afghanistan and provoking a confrontation which might undo the patient diplomacy that had been working toward an Anglo-Soviet accommodation. Amanullah unwittingly and unwisely played into the British hand by his precipitate abdication. The British at once seized on this fact to justify their nonsupport for all parties to the internal struggle in Afghanistan. On January 30, 1929, the following exchange took place in the House of Commons:

Mr. Thomas (by Private Notice) asked the Secretary of State for Foreign Affairs whether he has any statement to make regarding the attitude which His Majesty's Government propose to adopt in relation to the present disturbances in Afghanistan?
Sir A. Chamberlain: His Majesty's Government have no intention of interfering in the internal affairs of Afghanistan by supporting or assisting any of the parties at present contending for power in that country. They earnestly desire the establishment of a strong central Government, and they will be prepared, when this Government is established, to show their friendship for the Afghan people by giving it such assistance as they can in the reconstruction and development of the country. King Amanullah has formally announced his abdication to His Majesty's Government, and consequently, until it is clear that in spite of this abdication he is regarded as their King

by the people of Afghanistan generally, His Majesty's Government are unable to regard his Government as the rightful Afghan Government.[45]

This declaration of "neutrality" actually operated unfavorably against Amanullah in a number of ways. First, it told the world that the British had publicly written him off as the legitimate ruler of Afghanistan. This point was not lost on the rebellious tribes. Second, it placed Amanullah on the same basis as any other rebel or pretender such as the Bacha-i-Saqao, Ali Ahmad Jan, Ghaus-ud-din, Muhammad Umar, and Nadir Khan, all of whom were contending for the throne. In other words it reduced Amanullah's legitimacy to the level of that of a pretender and this, as we will recall, was already a weak point in his internal political position. Finally, it deprived him of the advantageous position of a legitimate government to command foreign credits, arms, logistical supplies, and other forms of assistance. For example, when Amanullah, after having rescinded his abdication in Kandahar, was in desperate need of arms and appealed to the British to help him or at least sell him arms, the British coldly replied that they did not recognize the cancellation of his abdication, that in their view Amanullah was just another contender for power in an internal struggle, and that British neutrality prevented helping any of the parties to the rebellion.[46]

It is evident, then, that the British were very influential in the outcome of the rebellion that cost Amanullah his throne. To wield this influence they did not have to be actively against him; all they had to do was proclaim their neutrality and let nature take its course. No doubt Amanullah lived to regret his failure to establish close and cordial relations with the British. Had the British felt toward him as they had felt toward his father, Habi-

[45] Parliamentary Notice, IOL, LPS/10/1289 P53, Part 6, 1929.
[46] Secret Telegram from the Foreign Office, London, to the British Minister, Kabul, no. 36, February 6, 1929, IOL, LPS/10/1288 P53, 1929.

bullah, it is quite likely that they would have taken the risk of extending active help to him in the hour of crisis. This might have swung the balance in his favor. As it was, they felt under no obligation to help a ruler who had consistently posed a threat to British interests in the tribal areas, in Central Asia, and, most importantly, within India itself.[47]

We have seen how the British "hands off" policy worked against Amanullah, but we have not yet answered the question whether the British conducted a secret operation to overthrow him. The extensive secret documents of this period (only recently made public) offer two types of evidence that no such secret British operation ever existed. The first type of documentary evidence is simply the lack of any indication or hint in the secret official papers that any covert operation against Amanullah was ever planned or carried out. Two legitimate objections may be raised against this negative evidence. It could be urged that the anti-Amanullah plot was conceived and carried out by British intelligence at so deep a level as not to appear anywhere in the official archives. It could also be argued that although the documents reflect high official policy, the plot against Amanullah could have been the work of local frontier officers acting on their own initiative to produce a result which they felt would please their superiors.

While neither of these possibilities can be completely ruled out (in the field of intelligence operations one is never on entirely sure ground) they are so unlikely as to shift the burden of proof to those who put them forward. They are unlikely for three reasons: (1) It is extremely difficult, indeed almost impossible, to conduct a covert intelligence operation of the magnitude required to overthrow a reigning monarch in so secret a fashion

[47] It is worth noting that the period of the rebellion coincided with the incumbency of a Conservative government in Britain which was notoriously hard-nosed on imperial matters. Amanullah left Afghanistan for exile in May 1929. In June a Labour government under Ramsay MacDonald took office in London, perhaps a month too late to be of help to Amanullah.

as to exclude completely any reference or hint of its existence from the mass of secret official documents of the period. (2) Even local self-generated intelligence operations among the tribes would involve the cooperation of tribal leaders, instigators, agents, and so on. Eventually people like that talk about their experiences or they become common knowledge among neighbors or tribal companions, yet there is not one authenticated account by a tribal or religious leader asserting that British officials sought or obtained his support for the overthrow of Amanullah. (3) Finally, there is a considerable amount of positive evidence both inherent in British policy itself and explicit in the official documents of the period which makes the allegation of a secret British plot to overthrow Amanullah highly unlikely.

With regard to British policy, the history of Anglo-Afghan relations shows that the British feared nothing so much as chaos in Afghanistan. Their fear of Russian expansion convinced them that nothing was so dangerous as a vacuum of power in Central Asia. Ludwig Adamec has put it very well:

the Indian government itself discouraged such intrigues [to overthrow the Amir]. Britain seemed to fear chaos in Afghanistan more than the unfriendliness of an Afghan ruler, for she preferred to deal with a strong Afghan ruler, who could be induced by subsidies and by British support—in short by self-interest—to refrain from an aggressive policy, rather than rely on the uncertain benefit that might be derived from installing some other aspirant on the Afghan throne.[48]

From the standpoint of general British policy, therefore, it seems most improbable that they would have launched a major secret operation to overthrow Amanullah merely because they disliked him and his policies. This type of operation appears even less likely during the Amanullah era than in former times because of the new kinds of threats posed by the Bolshevik regime in the USSR and the unknown opportunities which Af-

[48] Adamec, p. 4.

ghanistan in the melting pot might offer Soviet agents who, as we have seen, were already active there.

Apart from considerations of general policy, however, the most convincing evidence against a secret British plot is to be found in the internal communications of British officials in the archives of the period. This positive evidence is of two kinds: (1) explanations or denials of specific incidents which have been used to give verisimilitude to the charge of British involvement, and (2) general denials of secret British actions against Amanullah. The probative value of this type of evidence lies in the fact that these are not statements made for public consumption, which one might reasonably expect would deny secret involvement even if in fact it existed. Rather there are denial statements, usually in secret documents, from one British official to another or contained in nonpublic internal memoranda or minutes of British government agencies in India and London. These officials when communicating confidentially with each other would hardly play the charade of denying the existence of an operation. This is simply not the way governments operate. If the operation were one involving the deepest "cover" it might conceivably be possible to exclude all reference to it from official correspondence, but to mention it negatively would hardly conform to the dictates of security or good sense. Yet such negative references are precisely what we find interspersed throughout the documents of the period.

A few examples of these types of documentary evidence will make the argument clearer:

During the Bacha's first attack on Kabul in December 1928 it was alleged that he had been wounded, taken into the British Legation, and treated there. This was supposed to show complicity between the Bacha and the British. We now have available for examination the official secret diaries of L. W. H. D. Best, the British military attaché in the Legation, which detail almost on an hourly basis what occurred during this attack. No mention whatever is made of any refuge or treatment given to the Bacha, surely a remarkable omission from a secret internal record.[49]

It was widely believed that the British had reproduced photographs of Queen Soraya immodestly dressed (some said naked) and distributed them in the tribal areas to arouse the tribes against Amanullah. Quite to the contrary we find in the documents secret messages between British political agents in the tribal areas and their headquarters reporting and denying these rumors and explaining that some Afghan opponents of Amanullah, including, alas! some of his own officials, had distributed clippings of European journals showing the Queen in low-cut evening dress.[50]

Best known of all were the allegations that Col. T. E. Lawrence had been sent secretly to the frontier to stir up the tribes against Amanullah. Quite apart from the fact that nothing supporting this allegation is to be found in the extensive general literature on Lawrence's life and that his service in India under the alias of Shaw has been amply examined and explained without recourse to any sinister motives, the internal documents show that the British government was considerably embarrassed by the coincidence of Lawrence's presence in the frontier with the Afghan rebellion and that they withdrew him from India as soon as they realized that suspicion would be raised by his presence there. This internal and secret correspondence makes it clear that the highest British officials most intimately concerned acted on the clear assumption that Lawrence was in no way involved in any tribal intrigues against Amanullah. In addition to this internal correspondence, the British, of course, issued public denials both in the press and the House of Commons of Lawrence's complicity in the rebellion, but these denials are of a

[49] Annex to Secret Despatch from the British Legation in Kabul to the Foreign Office, London, no. 4, January 5, 1929, IOL, LPS/10/1290, 1929.

[50] Secret Telegram from the Government of India to the Chief Commissioner, NWFP, no. 862-S, April 28, 1928, and Secret Telegram from Chief Commissioner, NWFP, to the Government of India, no. 259-P, April 30, 1928, IOL, LPS/10/1203 P135, 1927.

lower probative value since governments have been known to deny publicly what they condone privately.[51] Another canard which made the rounds was that Lawrence had been seen and photographed wandering in the tribal areas disguised as a faqir. A man answering the description in the photographs was actually arrested near Matun and it turned out to be a German named Sparling who had escaped from Kabul to avoid paying his creditors.[52] It is from such gossamer material as this that legends are spun into history.

As for more general denials of British participation in a plot to overthrow Amanullah, a few examples will suffice to establish the point. An internal India Office memorandum dealing with evacuation of the British mission from Kabul refers to various rumors of British involvement in the origin of the rebellion, and does so in terms that clearly label such reports untrue.[53] In an internal minute of the Foreign Office, regarding the belief among some editors in Fleet Street that the British had engineered the rebellion, E. M. B. Ingraham comments that the British government can, with a clean conscience, assure these journalists that its skirts are clean.[54] A final example is a confidential despatch from Sir Richard Maconachie to the Marquess of Reading written in 1931 after the rebellion was over and a new

[51] The following secret telegrams form the significant part of this correspondence: from the British Minister in Kabul to the Government of India, no. 211, December 13, 1928; from the Government of India to the British Minister in Kabul, no. 458-K, December 14, 1928; from the British Minister in Kabul to the Government of India, no. 6-A.T., January 3, 1929. These telegrams are in IOL, LPS/10/1203 P135, 1927. Denials in the press and in the House of Commons are reported in the *Times* (London), July 1, 1929, and July 29, 1929.

[52] Secret Telegram from the British Legation in Kabul to the Government of India, no. 95, January 24, 1929, IOL, LPS/10/1203 P135, 1927.

[53] India Office Minute of February 14, 1929, on the Coordination of Evacuation of the British Mission in Kabul, IOL, LPS/10/1288 P53, Parts 3 and 4, 1929.

[54] Foreign Office Minute from E. M. B. Ingraham to Sir A. Willert, January 23, 1929, IOL, LPS/10/1290 P53, Parts 7, 8, 9, and 10, 1929.

period of improved Anglo-Afghan relations had begun. Maconachie had been both an intelligence officer and a political officer
on the frontier, including service in the critical Kurram Agency
during the 1929 revolt. He had therefore been intimately involved in Afghan affairs during the rebellion. He was appointed
British minister in Kabul when Nadir Khan ascended the
throne. If there had indeed been a secret British plot against
Amanullah, Maconachie would almost certainly have known
about it. Yet we find him commenting to Lord Reading that he
is completely mystified how reports of British involvement per-
sist "in spite of the absence of any evidence to support them." [55]
This type of internal evidence is very persuasive because although the British are quite capable of deceiving others when
their national interests are involved, their national character and
their system of government make it extraordinarily difficult for
them to deceive each other for any length of time.

The only conclusion, therefore, which coincides with the political, historical, and documentary evidence is that there was no
British plot to overthrow Amanullah. British policy favored a
stable status quo in Afghanistan; immediately before the rebellion Amanullah's relations with Britain had greatly improved
and the British were preparing offers of extensive aid to
Afghanistan; [56] and the secret British documents not only fail to
mention such a plot but contain numerous pieces of evidence to
the contrary. It is true, of course, that the British were involved
in extensive intelligence-gathering operations in Afghanistan.
They also used subventions to win sympathy for Britain from

[55] Confidential Despatch from the British Minister in Kabul to the
Secretary of State for Foreign Affairs, no. 113, September 2, 1931, IOL,
LPS/10/285, 1929.

[56] A Joint Political and Military Subcommittee of the Committee on
Imperial Defence had recommended an extensive program of military
and economic aid to Amanullah shortly before the rebellion broke out.
The secret memorandum prepared by this subcommittee and signed by
Lord Birkenhead is dated November 9, 1928, IOL, LPS/10/1232 P50,
1928.

tribal and religious leaders. Such activities by men like Sheikh Mahboob Ali, the so-called Oriental Secretary attached to the British Legation in Kabul, are well known.[57] But these general intelligence activities are recorded in the documentation and are of an entirely different order from an operation designed to overthrow a regime.

We must conclude that Amanullah's relations with Britain were less than satisfactory when taken in their over-all context. They were still heavily influenced by old geopolitical shibboleths that generated many points of conflict and tension. These frictions were exacerbated by serious differences in style and especially by cultural, psychological, and personal incompatibilities. Anglo-Afghan tensions undoubtedly hampered the full development of the modernization program and contributed to the onset and the outcome of the rebellion in a number of ways unfavorable to Amanullah. They did not, however, lead to secret British intervention in the overthrow of Amanullah. The principal onus for the fall of King Amanullah must still be placed on the conflict between tribal power and centralized authority.

[57] See, for example, NAI, Foreign Political Files, 212-F, 1930, which shows that Sheikh Mahboob Ali was to receive 6,000 rupees per month (a very large sum in those days) to finance his intelligence activities.

chapter XII

Lessons and Reflections

It is dangerous and scholastically shoddy to construct a vast edifice of generalizations on inadequate empirical foundations. Nevertheless, it seems appropriate to draw some cautious conclusions from the Amanullah case history. Many so-called new nations in the world today are facing problems of modernization within the context of societies that are more or less tribal in outlook. Can the Amanullah experiment give us some indications of the special problems they are likely to face? If so, then a contribution will have been made by this book, not only to modernization theory, but to public policy as well.

The first and perhaps most obvious lesson to be learned from the Amanullah experience is that a tribal society tends to be extraordinarily resistant and indeed hostile to the unifying political discipline required for nation-building. If the long history of Pushtun tribal intractability could leave any room for doubt on this score, the experiment of the Amanullah era would surely suffice to banish it. A corollary to this would seem to be that a tribal society, such as the Pushtun, is more resistant to national integration to the extent that it is fractured by geography, hardened by climate, and constrained to a rapacious way of life by the barrenness and indigence of its economic base.

It also seems fair to hypothesize that resistance to absorption into the national political body is enhanced to the extent that a given tribal society emphasizes inward-looking values, kinship, a loose authority structure, and xenophobia. This linkage between tribal cultural characteristics and resistance to political integration is to some extent confirmed by groups around the world (such as the Tajik, the Ewe, and the Hopi) whose kinship ties are fairly loose and who are organized into guilds or some other similar division rather than along strict tribal lines. Such groups have, on the whole, accepted more readily an active or passive role in the surrounding political life.

Some lessons can also be learned from the Amanullah case about the interrelationship between tribal politics and an entrenched religious establishment. The Afghan situation highlights the reinforcement between the traditional separatism of the tribes and the resistance of the mullahs to political control. This resistance was based on perceptions of threats to the entrenched political and economic power of the religious leaders and was expressed for propaganda purposes in religious terminology. Amanullah did not understand the political nature of this resistance and somewhat naïvely believed that the mullahs were simply ignorant of the blessings that would follow the adoption of a reformed version of Islam and the surrender of their secular privileges. His efforts to win over the clergy took place for the most part in the early stages of his modernization program, several years, in fact, before either Ataturk or Reza Shah had to deal with similar problems. In that early period Amanullah was still strongly influenced by Tarzi's theories, as enunciated in the *Siraj-ul-Akhbar*, that reform in Islamic countries would be spearheaded by a combination of intelligentsia and enlightened religious leaders. With the passing years Amanullah's hopes of converting the mullahs faded. In the final stages, influenced perhaps by Ataturk's decision to break the power of the religious establishment, Amanullah opted also for a direct confrontation. The mullahs in Afghanistan, however, had an option which was not open to those in Turkey—namely, to join forces with powerful, armed, and warlike tribes in overt rebellion against the central government. From this experience it seems fair to anticipate that in similar situations one could expect to find a conservative religious establishment allied to, and providing religious justification for, tribal resistance to national integration.

What conclusions can we reasonably draw about the relationship between the modernization program and the rebellion? I believe this study has shown that there was no direct cause-and-effect relationship between the two. There were, of course, a number of linkages. Indeed, as I have pointed out, the modernization program was, to a large extent, the victim of the rebellion rather than its cause. Another linkage was the perception of the tribal and religious leaders that certain elements of political centralization in the modernization program represented a threat to them. A subtle but important distinction must be made on this point. Any central government seeking to assert its political influence throughout a given territory is almost certain to engage in activities that encroach on the local power structure. This is equally true whether the central government is controlled by a tyrant whose intention is to impose his will by force or by an enlightened ruler whose intention is to integrate the local power structure peacefully into the broader national polity. In such a situation the *perception* of the local leaders is all-important. If because of characteristics inherent in a tribal society they cannot readily distinguish between attempts to dominate and efforts to integrate, they will resist with equal vigor the encroachments of the reactionary tyrant and the benevolent advances of the modernizing ruler. In both cases the outward symbols of political control—systematization of taxes, registration of citizens, curbing of private graft and corruption, equalization of the burdens of conscription, extension of roads and communications, and the like—may be strikingly similar; only the intentions are different. Tribal societies find it difficult to make this distinction. To the Afghan tribes, Amanullah's benevolent measures seemed as threatening as Abdur Rahman's iron-handed controls and they reacted with violent resistance to both. The difference was that Abdur Rahman had the skill and power to enforce his policies of internal imperialism while Amanullah lacked both the knowledge of tribal politics and the political adroitness to persuade the tribes to accept peacefully his policies of national integration and reconciliation. The lesson to be drawn from this is that tribal societies tend to give a high priority to autonomy and will resist with equal vigor both political domination and political modernization since both lead to the same result: loss of tribal sovereignty.

The Amanullah experiment also teaches the lesson that formal-legal instruments of reform, such as constitutions and legal codes, are not very effective means of bringing about political change unless the political culture is predisposed in their favor. The essentially informal structures of political power which characterize tribal societies are not so predisposed. In such a situation short-term results of formal-legal institutions are almost certain to be disappointing. Disenchantment with parliaments is a common theme with most political reformers. A fairly good case can be made, however, that for longer-term results, the ideals, social goals, and standards implicit in most formal-legal systems tend, over the years, to give a society a direction and orientation toward the rule of law which it might not otherwise spontaneously develop. This seems to have been the experience in Afghanistan where the formal-legal system pioneered by Amanullah was a failure during his time but over the next forty years moved the country gradually but steadily in the direction of congruence between the informal power structure of the tribal society and the formal framework of constitutional government.

Another important lesson of the Amanullah experiment is that, in a society where tribal elements represent a significant alternative center or centers of power to that of the central government, there will tend to develop a dynamic equilibrium characterized by periodic fusion and fission of political authority. During periods of government strength it will probe and challenge tribal power to the full limit of its own resources, at which point a balance favorable to central authority will be struck. This will be the high point of the process of fusion. As strong leadership declines in the central government, the flow will be reversed and fission of authority will follow with consequent strengthening of the alternative centers of tribal power. These periods will be characterized by tribal probes and challenges, at first to the peripheral areas of central power; if these are successful, they will be directed more and more at the complete elimination of central authority. Matters rarely reach that stage before a new balance is struck. In the Amanullah case, however, tribal power did succeed in bringing about total collapse of the central authority. In such cases a chaotic scramble for power usually follows until some strong leader succeeds in re-establishing a measure of centralized control. Ironically, the tribes themselves will eventually tend to bring about this result because they need a "devil" against whom their power and independence can be tested but even more because in a situation of chaos intertribal and intratribal animosities flourish to the point where the danger of mutual annihilation looms large.

While it is tempting to read into the Afghan case a confirmation of the theory of political homeostasis advanced by some social scientists (in all societies there is a built-in tendency to respond to sudden change with compensatory moves to restore equilibrium), historical evidence in Asia, Africa, and elsewhere casts considerable doubt on such a conclusion. It is true that the Afghan tribes during the Amanullah rebellion pulled back from the abyss at the last moment, but this has not been the case in other eras. During such periods a central government simply did not exist, the country was fractionalized into inimical and competitive tribal groups, and often the result was to make conquest from outside relatively easy. The break-up of great African empires into warring tribal factions similarly provided a fertile field for European colonial invasions.

It is difficult to delve into the dramatic incidents of the Amanullah period without reflecting on what might have been.

The alternatives to history are, of course, hidden from human eyes but it is tempting and perhaps useful to speculate whether Amanullah's brave experiment could have succeeded if he had done things differently, if he had been a different kind of man. With the benefit of hindsight and knowing what we now know about the processes of modernization (which is little enough), could we devise a strategy by which Amanullah could have succeeded? There are two angles to this question which merit exploration: the quality of the man himself and the possibility of developing a strong institutional framework to carry out his plans.

We have already noted that in a situation of delicate balance between central government and tribal power, the personal authority, skill, and personality of the ruler are critical. Tribal societies tend to bestow legitimacy on their leaders on the basis of personal epitomization of tribal ideals and values rather than by the sanctions of custom or religion or the mystique attached to an office *per se*. We have noted that Amanullah's dynamism, boldness, and imagination were diminished by his pompousness, his pseudo-egalitarianism, his mercurial instability, his susceptibility to flattery, and his almost total lack of political sense, particularly his ignorance of the realities of tribal power in his own country. Even if we admire this early champion of Afghan modernization, we must, by any objective standards, conclude that the personal qualities he brought to his task were simply inadequate. What then would it have taken?

Certainly a total reorganization of his priorities, methods, and institutional framework would have materially increased his chances of success. First of all, the herculean task Amanullah set for himself required a realistic assessment of the extent to which the pacification of the tribes started by Abdur Rahman had proceeded. Such an assessment would certainly have shown to any acute political observer that it was still highly dangerous for the central government to extend its political power into the tribal areas. Amanullah's first priority, therefore, should have been to complete the task of pacification so that the independent centers of tribal power were broken or weakened. For this he needed at least two things: a strong, loyal army and the cooperation of the British government to control the tribes on the Indian side of the frontier. A strong army did not necessarily mean a modernized army. Abdur Rahman had developed a force capable of challenging the tribes on their own ground by relying primarily on traditional methods of organization and warfare and by careful selection of able and loyal officers aided by a very few technical foreign advisers. Amanullah, instead, tried to transform the army from top to bottom with foreigners (Turks) virtually in charge. Moreover he tried to do that at the same time that he was trying to effect profound changes throughout the rest of Afghan society. He should not have tried to accomplish both at the same time. Nadir Khan advised working on the army first, as Prince Daud did thirty years later; modernization of other segments of the society could better be undertaken after having established an adequate military base.

Amanullah might have met with more success if his methods for handling his relations with Britain had been substantially different. He ought to have made a choice: either to take a strong anticolonialist stance against the British or to concentrate on the transformation of Afghan society. He simply could not handle both problems at the same time. As we have seen, his entire background and emotional makeup rebelled at the thought of achieving an accommodation with Britain on British terms. His anti-British bias also made him an easy prey for the deceptive maneuverings of Soviet policy.

Amanullah's chances of success could also have been materially enhanced if he had played down the social and religious reforms, which offended the sensibilities of traditional Afghans and gave his opponents such good propaganda material. These reforms could have been delayed while committing the bulk of the government's energies and resources to the economic and political reordering of the society. Prince Daud's successful pro-

gram in the 1950's utilized this strategy. Had Amanullah moved
with the discretion and caution demonstrated by Daud on such
reforms as the status of women he could have avoided waving
this red flag before the eyes of a predominantly male-oriented
society. Similarly, the privileges and emoluments of the tribal
aristocracy, which provided the essential power and political
linkages with the tribes, should not have been attacked until he
had provided himself with alternative power-brokers. The best
surrogate would have been a political party of young, energetic
workers imbued with nationalist ideology and dispersed
throughout the country to influence the centers of local political
power. Amanullah moved too slowly in this direction. Only in
1928, shortly before the rebellion, did he begin to talk about
founding a political party. His almost total lack of political sense
is reflected in his belief that his progressive ideas would sell
themselves on their own merits. Accordingly he never established a government propaganda or "information" department
even though he often expressed exasperation and even despair
when his actions and ideas were misunderstood or deliberately
distorted by his opponents.

In order to achieve his goals, Amanullah also needed a solid
institutional framework within his government to plan, coordi-
nate, and execute the modernizing ideas which flowed from his
fertile brain. Such governmental institutions would have required staffs of dedicated top- and middle-level officials. The
production of such officials is slow work since they usually have
to be extruded from the normal process of the educational system. To some extent foreign technical assistance could have
helped bridge the gap, but in any case a serious start on institu-
tion-building was needed and Amanullah never quite grasped
this concept. He preferred to rely on brilliant *ad hoc* perfor-
mances rather than on the slower but more reliable processes of
a competent bureaucracy. No doubt he was hampered by the
limited sources of talent and manpower available to him. He
could not concentrate his efforts on producing an urban mod-

ernizing elite and disregard the rural, tribal areas, as the Turks did, because in Afghanistan the only elite available to him was the tribal elite or its scions. This group was not a basically different social class from the tribesmen, whereas in Turkey the elite group could be drawn from a social class entirely different from the peasants. In a predominantly tribal society, recruiting a modernizing elite must almost by definition be done by the conversion or assimilation of the younger tribal aristocrats.

It is, of course, impossible to say that modernization would have succeeded in Afghanistan during the Amanullah era if the ruler's personality, priorities, methods, and organizational structures had been different. All we can reasonably do is reflect that without the necessary political insights, and without adequate priorities and methods, Amanullah was almost certain to fail in his attempt to modernize a tribal society.

A final reflection is warranted on the effect of pressures by major powers on a brittle polity (characteristic of most nations with tribal power centers) engaged in the deadly serious business of modernization. Judging from the Amanullah case, such pressures may not be a determinant factor on modernization, but they can certainly play a substantial role. The taming of a tribal society into habits of domestic tranquillity and national unity are difficult tasks in themselves, but they become doubly so when complicated by intervention or threat of intervention by major powers for geopolitical, strategic, or economic reasons. Therefore, it seems reasonably safe to state as a testable generalization that the difficulties of modernizing tribal societies tend to become increasingly intractable to the extent that the major powers intervene or become involved in the internal political processes of the modernizing country. This would be true whether the country in question is Afghanistan, Morocco, the Congo, or Vietnam.

appendix a

the constitution of afghanistan

(*Nizamnamah-ye-Asasi-e-Daulat-e-'Aliyah-e-Afghanistan*)

April 9, 1923   (20 Hamal 1302)

From the Persian Text, which is a Translation
from the Original Pushtu

*Translated by M. A. Ansari under the Supervision of Leon B.
Poullada with Corrections and Verifications by Faruq Farhang*

Article 1

Afghanistan is completely free and independent in the administration of its domestic and foreign affairs. All parts and areas of the country are under the authority of His Majesty the King and are to be treated as a single unit without discrimination between different parts of the country.

Article 2

The religion of Afghanistan is the sacred religion of Islam. Followers of other religions such as Jews and Hindus residing in Afghanistan are entitled to the full protection of the state provided they do not disturb the public peace [see Appendix B].

Article 3

Kabul is the capital of Afghanistan but all the people of Afghanistan are entitled to receive equal treatment from the government and the people of Kabul are not entitled to any special privileges not extended to the people of other cities and villages of the country.

Article 4

In view of the extraordinary services rendered to the cause of progress and independence of the Afghan nation by His Majesty the King, the noble nation of Afghanistan pledges itself to the royal succession of his line on the principle of male inheritance through selection to be made by His Majesty and by the people of Afghanistan. His Majesty the King on ascending the throne will pledge to the nobles and to the people that he will rule in accordance with the principles enunciated in the Shari'a and in this Constitution and that he will protect the independence of the country and remain faithful to his nation.

Article 5

His Majesty the King is the servant and the protector of the true religion of Islam and he is the ruler and King of all the subjects of Afghanistan.

Article 6

The affairs of the country are administered by the Ministers of the government who are selected and appointed by the King. Each Minister is responsible for his Ministry; therefore the King is not responsible.

Article 7

Mention of the King's name in the *Khutba* [Friday prayers]; minting of coins in the King's name; determination of the rank of officials in accordance with appropriate laws; awarding of medals and decorations; selection and appointment, dismissal and transfer of the Prime Minister and other Ministers; ratification of public laws, promulgation and protection of public laws and of the Shari'a; being commander-in-chief of all the armed forces of Afghanistan; promulgation and protection of military rules and regulations; declaring war, making peace and other treaties; granting amnesty, pardoning and commuting legal punishments; are among the rights of His Majesty the King.

General Rights of the Subjects of Afghanistan

Article 8

All persons residing in the Kingdom of Afghanistan, without respect to religious or sectarian differences, are considered to be subjects of Afghanistan. Afghan citizenship may be obtained or lost in accordance with the provisions of the appropriate law.

Article 9

All subjects of Afghanistan are endowed with personal liberty and are prohibited from encroaching on the liberty of others [see Appendix B].

Article 10

Personal freedom is immune from all forms of violation or encroachment. No person may be arrested or punished other than pursuant to an order issued by a Shari'a court or in accordance with the provisions of appropriate laws. The principle of slavery is completely abolished. No man or woman can employ others as slaves.

Article 11

The press and the publication of domestic newspapers is free in accordance with the appropriate press law. The right to publish newspapers is reserved to the government and to citizens of Afghanistan. Foreign publication may be regulated or restricted by the government.

Article 12

Subjects of Afghanistan shall have the right to organize private companies for purposes of commerce, industry, and agriculture, in accordance with the provisions of the respective laws.

Article 13

Subjects of Afghanistan shall have the right to submit individual or collective petitions to government officials for the redress of acts committed by officials or others against the Shari'a or other laws of the country. In appropriate cases if such petitions are not heeded citizens may appeal successively to higher authorities and in case they still feel aggrieved they may appeal directly to the King.

Article 14

Every subject of Afghanistan has the right to an education at no cost and in accordance with the approved curriculum. Foreigners are not permitted to operate schools in Afghanistan but are not barred from being employed as teachers.

Article 15

All schools in Afghanistan are under the control, supervision, and inspection of the government which is charged with developing the scientific and national education of all citizens on the basis of unity and discipline but the methods and teaching of the beliefs and religions of protected and refugee subjects [Hindus and Jews] shall not be interfered with.

Article 16

All subjects of Afghanistan have equal rights and duties to the country in accordance with Shari'a and the laws of the State.

Article 17

All subjects of Afghanistan shall be eligible for employment in the civil service in accordance with their qualifications and abilities and with the needs of the government.

Article 18

All determined forms of taxation are to be collected in accordance with appropriate laws and in proportion to the wealth and power of the citizen.

Article 19

In Afghanistan everyone's real and personal property in his possession is protected. If real property is required by the government for a public purpose then in accordance with the provisions of a special law, first the price of the property shall be paid and then it may be expropriated.

Article 20

The dwellings and homes of all Afghan subjects are sacrosanct and neither government officials nor others may violate a subject's home without his permission or due process of law.

Article 21

In the courts of justice all disputes and cases will be decided in accordance with the principles of Shari'a and of general civil and criminal laws.

Article 22

Confiscation and forced labor is absolutely prohibited except that during time of war, labor services may be required in accordance with the provisions of appropriate laws.

Article 23

Except as provided in the laws of the State [Nizamnamah] nothing will be requisitioned from anyone.

Article 24

All types of torture are hereby prohibited. No punishment may be imposed upon any person except as provided in the General Penal Code and the Military Penal Code [see Appendix B].

Ministers

Article 25

The responsibility for the administration of the government is vested in the Council of Ministers and Independent Departments [Idarah-ye-Mustaqel]. The Chairman of the Council of Ministers is His Majesty the King. In his absence the acting chairman will be the Prime Minister or in his absence the Minister heading the ranking Ministry [see Appendix B].

Article 26

When an Acting Minister is appointed in the absence of a Minister, the Acting Minister will have all the authority and rights of the Minister.

Article 27

A special High Assembly [Darbar-e-'Ali] will be convened each year before the independence celebrations on a day to be determined by His Majesty the King. This Assembly will be under the chairmanship of His Majesty the King and will be composed of the high officials of the government, the elders of the people, the nobles and others selected specially by the King. In this Assembly every Minister and the Heads of Independent Departments will report in open session on the achievements and services rendered during the past year.

Article 28

His Majesty the King will select and appoint the Prime Minister and other Ministers.

Article 29

The Council of Ministers will formulate the foreign and domestic policies of the government. Decisions of the Council of Ministers, treaties, agreements and other matters that may require ratification by His Majesty the King will become effective only after such ratification.

Article 30

Every Minister will execute the duties appropriate to his ministry to the full extent of his authority. Matters appropriate for decision by the King will be referred to him and matters governed by the regulations of the Council of Ministers will be referred to it. The Council of Ministers will discuss the matters referred to it in accordance with its special law and sign the decision and views expressed by the Council.

Article 31

All Ministers are responsible to His Majesty the King both regarding the general policy of the government as a whole and the individual responsibilities of the Minister himself.

Article 32

Oral communications and commands from His Majesty the King to Ministers should be reduced to writing and signed by the King.

Article 33

Trials for official misconduct of Ministers will take place before the High Court [Diwan-e-'Ali] in accordance with the special law on this matter. Trials for personal misconduct outside the purview of their official duties will take place in the courts of justice as for ordinary citizens.

Article 34

A Minister who is accused before the High Court will be suspended from his official duties pending the outcome of his trial.

Article 35

The size and organization of the various ministries and their offices and duties are prescribed in the law entitled Basic Organization of the Government of Afghanistan [Nizamnamah-ye-Tashkilat-e-Asasiyah-e-Afghanistan].

Government Officials

Article 36

Officials will be appointed on the basis of competence and in accordance with the appropriate laws. No official can be dismissed unless he resigns or for misconduct or for the best interest of the government. Officials who maintain good performance records will be considered worthy of promotion and eventual pension.

Article 37

Duties of officials have been described in appropriate legislation. Every official will be responsible for the performance of his duties in accordance with such legislation.

Article 38

All officials are required to obey the lawful orders of their superiors. If an order is deemed by an official to be without sanction of law it is his duty to refer the matter to the central authorities of his ministry. If he executes such an illegal order without first having referred it to the central authority of his ministry, he will be considered to be equally responsible with the official who gave the order.

Provincial Councils and the State Council

Article 39

There is hereby established a State Council in the capital of the kingdom and local Councils in the provincial and district centers, these councils to act as advisory bodies. [*Translator's Note:* District centers consisted of five different levels less important than a province. These were (1) *Huqumat-e-'Ala* or High Governorship which was equivalent to a province but smaller or less important; (2) *Huqumati* of 1st, 2nd, and 3rd degrees which depended from the Provincial or *Huqumati-e-'Ala* governments; and (3) *Alaqadari* or Districts which depended from the *Huqumati*.]

Article 40

Membership in the State and Local Advisory Councils consists of both appointed and elected members.

Article 41

Appointed members of the advisory councils are those officials enumerated in the Law on the Basic Organization of the Government of Afghanistan. The appointed members of the State Council are directly selected and appointed by the King. The number of appointed members will be equal to the number of elected members. The elected members will be selected and appointed by the people. Separate articles in the Law on the Basic Organization of the Government of Afghanistan prescribe the election procedures for these members.

Article 42

The State and Local Councils in addition to those duties prescribed in the Basic Organization Law will:

a. Make suggestions to the government for the improvement of industry, commerce, agriculture, and education.

b. Petition the government regarding any irregularities in matters of taxation or general government administration with a view to demanding remedial action [see Appendix B].

c. Complain to the government regarding any violations of the basic rights conferred upon the people by this Constitution.

Article 43

Suggestions, petitions, or complaints by the Advisory Councils will be presented in the first instance to the Governor or executive official of the district pertaining to the Council. Such Governor or other local official will take appropriate measures within the scope of his authority. If such measures would go beyond the scope of his authority he will forward the matter to the appropriate ministry which in turn will take the necessary action or in appropriate cases will proceed in accordance with Article 30 hereof or if the matter be one of legal nature then in accordance with Article 46 hereof.

Article 44

If within a month after presenting a petition, suggestion, or complaint to the Governor or other local official, the Advisory Council has not received a reply, it may on its own initiative forward the matter directly to the State Council.

Article 45

The State Council will thereupon prepare an opinion on the case and forward it to the appropriate ministry. If the ministry delays action of the case the State Council may forward it directly to His Majesty the King.

Article 46

Legislation prepared and proposed by the government will be scrutinized by the State Council and then passed to the Council of Ministers for further examination. If approved in both bodies they may then forward it to His Majesty the King for ratification, after which such legislation becomes the law of the land.

Article 47

In addition to the permanent appointed members of the State Council, certain top-ranking civil servants and military officials above the rank of district and provincial governors and governors-general and from the military rank of *lewa mishr* [brigadier-general] respectively, may be appointed as temporary members of the State Council until their appointment to a new post, provided they have not been relieved from duty awaiting trial.

Article 48

The State Council will review the yearly budget prepared by the Ministry of Finance in the manner prescribed in the General Law of the Budget [Nizamnamah-ye-Bujet].

Article 49

The State Council will review all contracts and treaties and agreements made between the government and foreigners.

The Courts

Article 50

All trials in courts of justice will be public provided that for certain special matters enumerated in the General Law on Courts [Nizamnamah-ye-Mohakam], the judge may prescribe a closed trial.

Article 51

Every citizen or person appearing before a court of justice may use any legitimate means to insure protection of his rights.

Article 52

Courts of Justice will not delay the hearing and settling of cases which it is their duty to hear.

Article 53

All courts of justice are free from all types of interference and intervention.

Article 54

The various types and hierarchy of courts are set forth in the Law on the Basic Organization of the Government of Afghanistan.

Article 55

No special court to hear and adjudicate a special case or issue may be established outside the framework of the regular judiciary.

The High Court

Article 56

A High Court will be established on a temporary basis from time to time for the special purpose of trials of Ministers. After completing its task it will be dissolved.

Article 57

The organization and procedures of the High Court will be prescribed in a special law.

Financial Affairs

Article 58

Collection of all State taxes will be in accordance with general laws on taxation.

Article 59

A yearly budget detailing the income and expenditures of the government will be prepared and all revenues and expenditures of the government will be in accordance with the budget.

Article 60

At the end of each year a financial report will be prepared relating actual revenues and expenditures of the previous year to those detailed in the budget.

Article 61

In accordance with a special law passed for this purpose, an auditing office will be established. The principal function of the auditing office will be to inquire and report whether the revenues and expenditures of the government have actually coincided with those prescribed in the budget.

Article 62

The organization and implementation of the financial report and of the budget is prescribed in a special law passed for this purpose.

The Administration of Provinces

Article 63

Provincial administration is based on three basic principles: (1) Decentralization of authority; (2) Clear delineation of duties; (3) Clear determination of responsibilities. All the duties of provincial officials have been determined on the basis of the above principles and in accordance with the pertinent laws. The authority of these officials is likewise limited by these principles and laws and every official is responsible to his superior on the same basis.

Article 64

Branch offices of the ministries are established in the provinces, and citizens, depending on the subject matter, should initially have recourse to these branch offices for help in solving their problems.

Article 65

If the solution of the problems of the citizens cannot be found by the officials of these ministry branches, or if these officials do not dispose of the case in accordance with the laws, the aggrieved citizen may have recourse to the superior officials of the ministry branches or if necessary to the District and Provincial governors or governors-general.

Article 66

The organization, functions, and duties of municipalities have been set forth in the special Law on Municipalities [Nizamnamah-ye-Baladiyah].

Article 67

Military government and military administration may be proclaimed by the government in any part of the country in which signs of disobedience and rebellion are such as to disturb the public security.

Miscellaneous Articles

Article 68

Elementary education is compulsory for all citizens of Afghanistan. The various curricula and branches of knowledge are detailed in a special law and they will be implemented.

Article 69

None of the articles of this Constitution may be cancelled or suspended for whatever reason or cause.

Article 70

This Constitution may be amended in case of necessity upon proposal of two-thirds of the members of the State Council followed by approval of the Council of Ministers and ratification by His Majesty the King.

Article 71

If necessary any clarification or interpretation of any article of this Constitution or other laws of the State must be referred to the Council of State and following correction and explanation by the Council of State and approval by the Council of Ministers it will be printed and published.

Article 72

In the process of legislation the actual living conditions of the people, the exigencies of the time and particularly the requirements of the laws of Shari'a will be given careful consideration.

Article 73

Security of personal correspondence is one of the rights of all citizens and all communications handled by the post office will be secure from search and inspection and will be delivered to the addressee in the same condition they were received unless a court order has been issued permitting inspection.

The articles of this Constitution have been approved unanimously by the Ministers of the Government and by all the representatives of the nation gathered in a Grand Council [Loya Jirgah] in the Eastern Province [Mashriqi] and 872 members of that Grand Council have signed and sealed this document for the successful foundation of the exalted state of Afghanistan. It is our will and command that this Constitution be included among the other laws of the Government and that all its articles be implemented.

[Seal of King Amanullah]

appendix B

annotated amendments of
January 28, 1925 [8 dalw 1303]

The Constitution of 20 Hamal 1302 (April 9, 1923) was amended by the Loya Jirgah which met in Paghman in 1924. The amended text became effective on 8 Dalw 1303 (January 28, 1925).

The amendments were a direct result of the rebellion of the Mangal tribe in 1924. This rebellion was given a religious flavor by certain religious leaders who sided with the rebels. King Amanullah in order to expose this offered to send a delegation of religious scholars from Kabul to discuss the objections of the Mangal mullahs and promised to make any changes agreed upon. The discussion took place but no agreement was reached it becoming evident that the tribal mullahs simply wanted pretexts to justify the rebellion. Nevertheless Amanullah's delegates on returning to Kabul recommended that certain provisions of the Constitution and of some laws be changed so as to remove all pretext for opposition. The King then summoned a Loya Jirgah which met in Paghman at the end of 1924 and recommended certain amendments and changes. The amended Constitution was then reissued with the following imprimatur by the King:

> The Articles of this Constitution which were approved unanimously by the Ministers of the Government and the representatives of the Grand Council which met in the Eastern Province for the foundation of the exalted state of Afghanistan, have also been presented to the Grand Council of Paghman and in accordance with the votes of the Ministers of the Government and all the representatives of the nation including scholars, *sadats* and other religious leaders, these articles have been approved. Dalw 8, 1303.

> [Seal of King Amanullah]

Following are the substantive differences between the original and the amended versions of the Constitution.

Article 2 was amended by adding to the provision that the "religion of Afghanistan is the sacred religion of Islam" the following: *"and its official religious rite is the sublime Hanafite rite."* Also added at the end of the article is the provision that *"Hindus and Jews must pay the special tax and wear distinctive clothing."*

Article 9 was amended by adding the following: *"Afghan subjects are bound by the religious rite and political institutions of Afghanistan."* The intent of the original version was clearly to eliminate invidious discrimination on the basis of religion or other similar distinctions. The amendment in effect places a religious limit on the freedom of the citizen. Moreover it is ambiguous, since it could be interpreted to mean that all citizens must be Muslims of the Hanafite rite. This apparently was not intended, the only meaning, judging from subsequent practice, being that all citizens of whatever creed must respect the fact that the state religion was Hanafite and Sunni.

Article 24 was amended by adding at the end of the article the following: *"except those punishments which are in accordance with the rules of the Shari'a and which are in accord with other public laws which are themselves codified according to the rules of Shari'a."*

Article 25 was amended by removing the word "acting" before the word "chairman" when referring to the Prime Minister in this capacity in the absence of the King. The reason for this amendment is obscure and seems to be based on considerations of personal relations between the King and the Prime Minister at the time.

Article 42 (b) was amended by adding the word "State" before the word "taxation." According to some sources, the purpose was to spare the central government from complaints about local taxes. According to other sources the purpose was to clarify the position that the taxing power was vested only in the state and was not to be used by officials or local chiefs.

appendix c

Lord Curzon's minute of December 14, 1919

A transcription of the handwritten document in the Archives of the India Office Library, London (LPS/10/809, 1919)

I remember Torkham very well. I understand that it is now proposed to concede the full claim of the Afghans which we have successfully contested for 30 years.

This is described as a pure act of grace.

Simultaneously with this telegram comes another from the Viceroy suggesting two more acts of grace, viz:

(1) recognition of Amir's title of His Majesty:

(2) acceptance of Afghan representative in London.

Where on earth are we to stop? I am not aware of a single quid pro quo that we are to obtain from Afghanistan for all these pure acts of grace. If the present Government of India lasts long enough, the next gracious act will be the acceptance of the Indus as a frontier.

As I am wholly out of sympathy with the present policy of the Government of India, I would prefer, while thanking the Secretary of State for his courtesy, not to express an opinion on this telegram.

C. [Curzon]

14/12

appendix d

principal localities in afghanistan in the 1920's

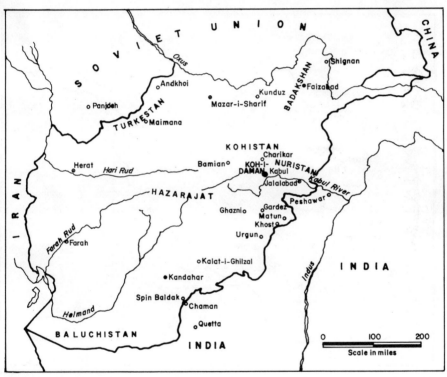

Map 1

appendix e

general location of principal tribes in afghanistan

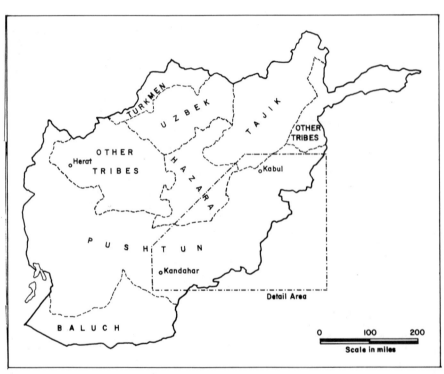

Map 2

appendix f

location of principal
pushtun tribes

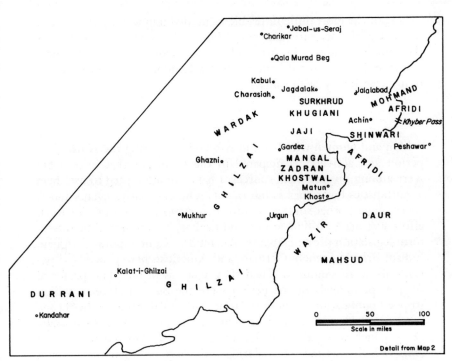

Map 3

295

bIBlIOGRaphIC essay

One of the most difficult problems involved in writing the present work was the scarcity and unreliability of research materials. For the benefit of those who may follow in my footsteps a brief resumé of the sources, materials, and problems I encountered in the course of my search may be of value.

Sources

Men and women who lived in Afghanistan during the Amanullah period and actively participated in the events of that critical era were among my principal sources. I have not attempted to use them as authorities but rather as informants who can clarify events and at times suggest other sources of information, written or oral. A special effort was made to find, study, and analyze for the first time the reform legislation promulgated by Amanullah. Contemporary Afghan, Indian, British, French, German, and American newspapers and periodicals were examined when they were available. The principal Afghan periodicals of the period were the *Siraj-ul-Akhbar*, which stopped publication at about the time Amanullah came to the throne but had deeply influenced him while still a prince, the *Aman-i-Afghan*, which was published during most of the Amanullah era, and *Anis*, which was published during only part of Amanullah's reign but was very useful in filling in blanks.

Archival material and documents were among the most valuable primary sources examined. Both in the National Archives of India in New Delhi and in the India Office Library in London there exist vast, and by no means duplicate, collections of official documents, minutes, correspondence, telegrams, position papers, memoranda, and the like, which cover events in Afghanistan during the period studied; most are classified "confidential" or "secret" but have now become available under the liberalized thirty-year rule.

Secondary sources for the Amanullah period have always been notoriously inadequate. Nevertheless, a conscientious effort was made to examine the entire corpus of books and articles written on the Amanullah reign, the only notable exception being some of the articles which may have appeared in Russian journals which were not available to me. It is my hope that some other scholar who can obtain access to the Russian materials and who is better equipped with the necessary language competence will be inspired to fill in these lacunae. I was fortunate to find a few secondary sources which to my knowledge have only seldom been studied or referred to in the literature of this period. Among the old *kitab furushi* (book vendors) in the Kabul bazaar I was able to find now and again a book like the pseudonymous one by C. Morrish, *Afghanistan in the Melting Pot*, which provides contemporary flavor and detail to the involved politics of the period. This applies also to the manuscript by Ali Ahmad, "The Fall of Amanullah." This contemporary narrative by one of Amanullah's private secretaries provides illuminating detail to the events of the crucial 1928–29 revolution. I have cited these and other similar secondary sources wherever I felt they contributed authoritative information and in some instances as examples of the distortion and mendacity which characterize most of the literature of that period.

Problems of Research

The subject and the era selected for study presented many research problems. The foremost was the inadequacy of sources. Very few books, other than travelogues and books on art or ancient history, are written about Afghanistan. Of these, even fewer deal with specific periods in any depth and they tend to steer clear of the controversial and poorly understood problems surrounding the reign of Amanullah. The residue tend to be propaganda tracts or frankly sensational accounts written to capitalize on the human-interest aspects of Amanullah's tragic end which captivated and titillated the world audience of that era. These are usually based on ignorance or on deliberate efforts to mislead and misrepresent.

They fall into two principal categories. First there is the type of book or article that took its information at second hand from sensational press reporting, much of which was also based on rumor, hearsay, or propaganda and which stressed superficial and dramatic events at the expense of accuracy. Roland Wild's *Amanullah, Ex-King of Afghanistan* is such a book. The second type of work is traceable, either directly or indirectly, to the unfortunate controversy between the present ruling dynasty of Afghanistan and the Amanullah branch of the family. One of the effects of this falling-out was that, rightly or wrongly, anyone writing after the exile of Amanullah seemed to feel that any praise or indeed any favorable mention of Amanullah would be looked upon with disfavor by the present rulers of Afghanistan. This naturally tended to discourage objective scholarly inquiry by most Afghans. A good example of this type of book is Ikbal Ali Shah's *The Tragedy of Amanullah*. The result has been an almost complete blackout in Afghanistan of information about the Amanullah experiment. His name almost disappeared from texts used in Afghan schools and an entire generation of Afghans grew up with distorted versions of, or with no knowledge at all about, one of the most important decades of Afghan history. Even Amanullah's progressive constitution and his comprehensive legal codes fell into oblivion. Although several of my informants mentioned these sources to me I could find no trace of them in any Afghan library or government ministry and finally stumbled across them in the hands of an old retired Hindu merchant who had saved copies as souvenirs of his youth. When the Ministry of Justice learned of my find they asked for permission to make copies for their library.

Another example of this disappearance of Afghan sources was my inability to find anywhere in Kabul a complete file of the newspapers published during Amanullah's reign. The Central Library in Kabul had only four years of issues of the important *Aman-i-Afghan* and the Historical Society had only two other years. A few private citizens had odd copies, mostly duplicates of those to be found in libraries. After an entire year of constant search in old bookshops, private collections, and the like, I had to concede defeat and was unable to consult news files for four crucial years of Amanullah's reign.

Apart from those writers who either wittingly or unwittingly distorted the record of the Amanullah period, there were a few Western authors, principally British, who for the most part relied on hearsay or news accounts or highly colored personal narratives. A few who had personal knowledge of events tended to be biased against Amanullah for reasons which appear in the course of this study.

A number of research problems were connected with utilizing the primary sources. In Kabul the government archives are not in usable condition. Only recently have they begun to be indexed and, while it is almost certain that valuable items repose there, it will be some years before serious researchers can utilize these sources. The archives in New Delhi and London presented other problems, principally that of overabundance. Several hundred volumes in each library contain documents which have only recently been opened to the public and which I found to be germane to this study. Imbedded in this mass of material was much trivia as well as gems of the first magnitude. The simple physical problem of examining, sorting, rejecting, and absorbing these voluminious materials was daunting. Their value may be judged from the many sources cited in this study.

The problems surrounding the interview program were many and fascinating. Structured interviews were abandoned after a few attempts to obtain responses to a prepared questionnaire. Informants simply would not confine themselves to the questions and tended to become unresponsive and even uncooperative if I insisted. I soon found it much more rewarding to keep the questionnaire in my head and use it as a guide to direct the conversation into productive channels. Of course there was a great deal of repetition and duplication among informants. Surprisingly, however, there was much less disagreement than I had expected even over quite controversial questions such as the reforms involving the status of women. Legal practice has shown me the vagaries and the low reliability of oral testimony and I therefore ran a control experiment by asking all informants a short set of identical questions about which I felt certain they would have some knowledge and on which they were likely to disagree. I was at first agreeably surprised at the degree of similarity in the responses until I reminded myself that I was working in what still remains largely an oral culture, one in which memory and narration still play a very important part. This was of course especially true of the age group I was interviewing (sixty to eighty). These reflections and tests gave me a good deal more confidence in the reliability factor of the information received even though the small number of informants ruled out the possibility of conducting any of the standard statistical reliability checks.

Although I talked to nearly a hundred people who had some personal knowledge of events during Amanullah's reign I found that most of the information was repetitive and that about twenty "solid" informants could provide the bulk of the data I wanted without the problem of diminishing returns. I therefore concentrated on the most knowledgeable and reliable group. Most informants, however, were reluctant to discuss frankly or speak openly about politically sensitive subjects. In most cases it took many hours and the intervention of mutual friends before an atmosphere of rapport and confidence could be established. Even then, all but three informants insisted that they not be quoted or identified as sources of information. In fact, after a few false starts, I soon discovered during the early interviews that I was getting very little more than polite clichés. I then began to volunteer at the start of each interview the assurance that all information obtained would be for scholarly research and in case of publication would not be attributed by name to any informant. For this reason citations to informants' interviews are identified only by place and date. The identities are, of course, available to interested scholars or others with a legitimate need to know but only on condition that they respect the confidential nature of the source.

Several excellent bibliographies on Afghanistan are already in print, notably those by Donald Wilber, Vartan Gregorian, and Mohammed Akram. Accordingly I have included in my bibliography only those sources which are cited in the text.

BIBLIOGRAphy

Documents

Several thousand documents were examined in the course of the research for this study. The lists below of materials in the Archives of the India Office Library in London and of the National Archives of India in New Delhi are not individual documents but rather the principal files or volumes in which the documents cited in the text may be found. The dates on these files or volumes are not necessarily indicative of the dates of specific documents since some files or volumes contain documents dated earlier or later than the file or volume itself.

Archives of the India Office Library, London

LPS/10/808, 1919
LPS/10/809, 1919
LPS/10/808, Political and Secret Department Files, 1061, 1919
LPS/10/912, 1920
LPS/10/1112, 1924
LPS/10/1203, 1927
LPS/10/1232, 1927
LPS/10/1232, 1928
LPS/10/Afghan Series, 1928
LPS/10/53, 1929
LPS/10/285, 1929
LPS/10/295, 1929
LPS/10/1232, 1929
LPS/10/1285, 1929
LPS/10/1287, 1929
LPS/10/1288, 1929
LPS/10/1289, 1929

LPS/10/1290, 1929
LPS/10/1291, 1929
LPS/10/1292, 1929

National Archives of India, New Delhi

Home and Political Department, Secret Deposit nos. 21, 31, 53, July, October, and November, 1919
Foreign Secretary Notes, no. 245, 1916; no. 356, 1919
Foreign Political Files, Frontier B. nos. 1–200, 1919
Home Political Files, F-18V, 1928
Foreign Political Files, 237-F, 1928
Foreign Political Files, 51-F, 1928
Foreign Political Files, 40-F, 1929
Foreign Political Files, 137-F, 1929
Foreign Political Files, 182-F, 1929
Foreign Political Files, 130-F, 1930
Foreign Political Files, 212-F, 1930
Home Political Files, F-379, 1930

Parliamentary Papers, Great Britain

Vol. XXXVII (*Accounts and Papers*, vol. 6), "Papers Regarding Hostilities with Afghanistan in 1919," Cd. 324, 1919, p. 1183.
Vol. XXV (*Accounts and Papers*, vol. 13), "Correspondence between His Majesty's Government and the Government of the USSR Respecting the Relations between the Two Governments" (Russia No. 2), Cd. 1869, 1923, p. 497.
Vol. XXV (*Accounts and Papers*, vol. 13), "Reply of the Soviet Government Respecting Relations Existing between the Two Governments" (Russia No. 3), Cd. 1874, 1923, p. 511.
Vol. XXV (*Accounts and Papers*, vol. 13), "Further Correspondence between His Majesty's Government and the Government of the USSR Respecting the Relations between the Two Governments" (Russia No. 4), Cd. 1890, 1923, p. 519.
Vol. XXVI (*Accounts and Papers*, vol. 14), "Note from His Majesty's Government to the Government of the USSR Respecting Relations Existing between the Two Governments and Note in Reply" (Russia No. 1), Cd. 2822, 1927, p. 301.
Vol. XXVI (*Accounts and Papers*, vol. 14), "Documents Illustrating Hostile Activities of the Soviet Government and Third International against Great Britain," Cd. 2874, 1927, p. 327.

Vol. XXVI (*Accounts and Papers*, vol. 14), "A Selection of Papers Dealing with Relations between His Majesty's Government and the Soviet Government, 1921 to 1927" (Russia No. 3), Cd. 2895, 1927, p. 359.

Vol. XXIII (*Accounts and Papers*, vol. 6), "Report on the Air Operations in Afghanistan, December 12, 1928, to February 25, 1929," Cd. 3400, 1929–30, p. 813.

Other Documents

Royal Government of Afghanistan, Ministry of Planning. "Pilot Scheme for Collection of Employment Market Information in Kabul." Mimeographed, Kabul, February 1960.

Ali Ahmad. "The Fall of Amanullah." Manuscript in the Archives of the India Office Library, London, 1929

Cornelius Van H. Engert. "A Report on Afghanistan." U.S. Department of State, Division of Publications, Series C., no. 53, Afghanistan, no. 1, 1924.

Government of India, General Staff. "Summary of Events in Afghanistan." Simla: n.p., 1920–22.

Government of India. "Official Account of the Third Afghan War, 1919." Calcutta: General Staff Army Hqrs., 1926.

Government of India. "Military Report, Afghanistan." Simla: Government of India Press, 1941.

"Report from Chief British Representative, Indo-Afghan Conference, to the Foreign Secretary to the Government of India." Public Records Office, London, F.O. 371/5381.

"Who's Who in Afghanistan." Enclosure to despatch no. 22, 28 February 1931, from British Legation, Kabul, to Foreign Office, London. Archives of the India Office Library, London.

Books

Adamec, Ludwig W. *Afghanistan, 1900–1923: A Diplomatic History*. Berkeley: University of California Press, 1967.

Afghanistan dar Pinja Sal-e-Akhir. Kabul: Book Printers Assn., 1968.

L'Afghanistan Nouveau. Kabul: n.p., n.d.

Aibak, Zafar Hasan. *Ap Beti*. Lahore: Mansur Book House, 1967.

Ali, Mohammed. *Afghanistan: The War of Independence, 1919*. Kabul: n.p., 1960.

Allworth, Edward, ed. *Central Asia: A Century of Russian Rule.* New York: Columbia University Press, 1967.

———. *Soviet Nationality Problems.* New York: Columbia University Press, 1971.

Anis, Mohiyudin. *Bohran Wa Nijat.* Kabul: Anis Press, n.d.

The Annual Register. London: Longmans, Green & Company. Annually. New Series, 1919–1930.

Babur, Zahiruddin Mohammed. *Babur Nama.* Translated by Annette S. Beveridge. 4 vols. London: Luzac and Co., 1922.

Bacon, Elizabeth E. *Obok.* New York: Wenner-Gren Foundation, 1958.

Barth, Fredrik. *Political Leadership among the Swat Pathans.* Monograph of Social Anthropology, no. 19. London: London School of Economics, 1959.

Barton, William. *India's Northwest Frontier.* London: John Murray, 1939.

Bell, Marjorie Jewett. *An American Engineer in Afghanistan.* Minneapolis: University of Minnesota Press, 1948.

Bellew, Henry W. *Afghanistan and the Afghans.* London: Sampson Low, 1879.

———. *The Races of Afghanistan.* London: W. Thacker, 1880.

Bennigsen, A., and C. Quelquejay. *Les Mouvements Nationaux chez les Musulmans de Russie.* Paris: Mouton, 1960.

Bolton, H. N. *Summary of the Tribal Customs of the Dera Ismail Khan District.* Peshawar: North-West Frontier Province Government Press, 1907.

Brown, W. Norman, ed. *India, Pakistan and Ceylon.* Ithaca: Cornell University Press, 1951.

Cambridge Shorter History of India. Cambridge: The University Press, 1934.

Caroe, Olaf. *Soviet Empire.* London: Macmillan, 1954.

———. *The Pathans: 550 B.C.–A.D. 1957.* London: St. Martins Press, 1958.

Caspani, E., and E. Cagnacci. *Afghanistan: Crocevia dell' Asia.* Milan: Antonio Vallardi, 1951.

Castagne, Joseph. *Les Basmatchis.* Paris: E. Leroux, 1925.

Coates, William P. and Zelda K. *A History of Anglo-Soviet Relations.* London: Lawrence and Wishart, 1943.

———. *The Soviets in Central Asia.* New York: Philosophical Library, 1951.

Coon, Carleton. *Caravan: The Story of the Middle East.* New York: Holt, 1951.

Curzon, George N. *Russia in Central Asia in 1889.* London: Frank Cass, 1967.

Darmesteter, James. *Chants Populaires des Afghans.* Paris: Imprimerie Nationale, E. Leroux, 1888–90.

Davies, C. Colin. *The Problem of the North-West Frontier, 1890–1908.* Cambridge: The University Press, 1932.

Dupree, Louis. *Afghanistan.* Princeton: Princeton University Press, 1973.

Elphinstone, Mountstuart. *An Account of the Kingdom of Caubul and Its Dependencies in Persia, Tartary and India.* London: Longman and J. Murray, 1815.

Eudin, Xenia, and Robert M. Slusser. *Soviet Foreign Policy, 1928–1934: Documents and Materials.* University Park: Pennsylvania State University Press, 1966.

Fletcher, Arnold. *Afghanistan: Highway of Conquest.* Ithaca: Cornell University Press, 1965.

Fouchet, Maurice. *Notes sur L'Afghanistan.* Paris: Maisonneuve Frères, 1931.

Fraser-Tytler, W. K. *Afghanistan: A Study of Political Developments in Central and Southern Asia.* 3rd ed., rev. London: Oxford University Press, 1967.

Ghani, Abdul. *A Review of the Political Situation in Central Asia.* Lahore: n.p. 1921.

Ghobar, Mir Ghulam Mohammed. *Afghanistan dar Masir-e-Tarikh.* Kabul: Government Press, 1967.

Gooch, G. P., and Harold Temperley. *British Documents on the War, 1914–1918.* London: H. M. Stationery Office, 1927.

Grassmuck, George, and Ludwig Adamec, eds. *Afghanistan: Some New Approaches.* Ann Arbor: University of Michigan Press, 1969.

Gregorian, Vartan. *The Emergence of Modern Afghanistan.* Palo Alto: Stanford University Press, 1969.

Griffiths, John C. *Afghanistan.* London: Pall Mall Press, 1967.

Habberton, William. *Anglo-Russian Relations Concerning Afghanistan, 1837–1907.* Urbana: University of Illinois Press, 1937.

Habibullah. *My Life from Brigand to King.* London: Sampson Low, Marston, n.d.

Halpern, Manfred. *The Politics of Social Change in the Middle East and North Africa.* Princeton: Princeton University Press, 1963.

Humlum, J. *La Geographie de L'Afghanistan.* Copenhagen: Gyldenal, 1959.

Kakar, M. H. *Afghanistan, A Study in Internal Political Developments: 1880–1896.* Lahore: Punjab Educational Press, 1971.

Katrak, Sorab K. H. *Through Amanullah's Afghanistan.* Karachi: D. N. Patel, 1929.

Kennan, George F. *Russia and the West.* New York: Mentor, 1960.

Khan, Said Alim, (S. H. l'Emir de Boukharie). *La Voix de la Boukharie Oprimée.* Paris: Maisonneuve Frères, 1929.

Klass, Rosanne. *Land of the High Flags.* New York: Random House, 1964.

Klimburg, Max. *Afghanistan, Das Land im historichen Spannungsfeld Mittelasians.* Vienna: Osterreichischer Bundesverlag, 1966.

Kolarz, W. *Russia and Her Colonies.* London: Philip, 1952.

Kohzad, Ali Ahmad. *Men and Events through Eighteenth and Nineteenth Century Afghanistan.* Kabul: Historical Society of Afghanistan, n.d.

Kuhn, Delia and Ferdinand. *Borderlands.* New York: Knopf, 1962.

Kushkaki, Burhanudin. *Nadir-i-Afghan.* Kabul: Government Press, 1931.

Lockhart, Laurence. *Nadir Shah.* London: Luzac, 1938.

Mackinder, Halford. *Nations of the Modern World.* London: George Philip & Sons, 1911.

——. *Democratic Ideals and Reality.* New York: Henry Holt & Co., 1942.

McLuhan, Marshall. *Understanding Media: The Extension of Man.* New York: McGraw-Hill, 1964.

MacMunn, George. *Afghanistan from Darius to Amanullah.* London: G. Bell & Son, 1929.

Macrory, Patrick A. *The Fierce Pawns.* New York: Lippincott, 1966.

Magnus, Julius. *Die hochsten Gerichte der Welt.* Leipzig: W. Moeser, 1929.

Mahan, A. T. *The Problem of Asia: Its Effect upon International Policies.* London: Sampson Low, Marston, 1900.

Melia, Jean. *Visages Royaux d'Orient.* Paris: Bibliothèque Charpentier, 1930.

Molesworth, G. N. *Afghanistan, 1919.* New York: Asia Publishing House, 1962.

Moorehead, Allan. *The Russian Revolution.* New York: Harper and Row, 1958.

Morrish, C. (pseud.). *Afghanistan in the Melting Pot.* Peshawar and Lahore: Civil and Military Gazette Press, 1930.

Pennell, T. L. *Among the Wild Tribes of the Afghan Frontier.* London: Seeley, 1927.

Penner, J., ed. *Islam and Communism.* New York: Carnegie International Center, 1960.

Pernot, Maurice. *En Asie Musulmane.* Paris: Hachette, 1927.

Rahman, Abdur. *The Life of Abdur Rahman.* Edited by Mir Munshi. London: John Murray, 1900.

Rawlinson, Henry. *England and Russia in the East.* London: John Murray, 1875.

Rishtya, Syed Qasim. *A History of Afghanistan in the 19th Century.* Kabul: Education Press, 1949.

Robertson, George S. *The Kafirs of the Hindu-Kush.* London: Lawrence & Bullen, 1896.

Royal Institute of International Affairs. *Soviet Documents on Foreign Policy.* London: Oxford University Press, 1952.

Ruyidad-e-Riasat-e-Diwan-e-'Ali-e-Hukmat-e-Shahi-e-Afghanistan. Kabul: Government Press, 1930.

Schlegelberger, Franz. *Rechsvergleichendes Handwortbuch für das Zivil und Handelsrecht des in- und auslandes.* Berlin: F. Wahlen, 1927.

Schurmann, Herbert Franz. *The Mongols of Afghanistan.* The Hague: Mouton, 1962.

Schwager, Joseph. *Die Entwicklung Afghanistans als Staat und seine zwischenstaatliche Beziehungen.* Leipzig: Noske, 1932.

Scott, George B. *Afghan and Pathan.* London: Mitre Press, 1929.

Shah, Ikbal Ali. *The Tragedy of Amanullah.* London: Alexander Ousely, 1933.

Silvert, K. H., ed. *Expectant Peoples: Nationalism and Development.* New York: American Universities Field Staff, 1963.

——, ed. *Churches and State: The Religious Institution and Modernization.* New York: American Universities Field Staff, 1967.

Singh, Ganda. *Ahmad Shah Durrani: Father of Modern Afghanistan.* Bombay: Asia Publishing House, 1959.

Spain, James W. *The Pathan Borderland.* The Hague: Mouton, 1963.

Spykman, N. J. *The Geography of Peace.* New York: Harcourt, Brace, 1944.

Stalin, J. *Marxism and the National and Colonial Question.* London: Lawrence and Wishart, 1942.

Stenz, Edward. *The Climate of Afghanistan.* New York: Polish Institute of Arts and Sciences in America, 1946.

Stewart, Rhea Talley. *Fire in Afghanistan, 1914–1929.* New York: Doubleday, 1973.

Sykes, Percy. *A History of Afghanistan.* 2 vols. London: Macmillan, 1940.

Thomas, Lowell. *Beyond Khyber Pass.* New York: Century, 1925.

Toynbee, Arnold. *Survey of International Affairs.* London: Oxford University Press, n.d.

Viollis, Andrée. *Tourmente sur L'Afghanistan.* Paris: Librairie Valois, 1930.

Wali Khan, Shah. *Yaddashtha-i-man.* Kabul: Government Press, n.d.

Wilber, Donald. *Afghanistan: Its People, Its Society, Its Culture.* New Haven: Human Relations Area Files Press, 1962.

Wild, Roland. *Amanullah, Ex-King of Afghanistan.* London: Hurst and Blackett, 1932.

Yunus, Mohammad. *The Frontier Speaks.* Bombay: Hind Kitabs, 1947.

Zalmai, Mohammad Wali. *Mujahid-i-Afghan.* Kabul: Government Press, 1967.

Articles

"L'Afghanistan." In *Corpus Constitutionnel*, Vol. I. Leiden: E. J. Brill, 1968.

Aslanov, M. G., E. G. Gafferberg, N. A. Kisliakov, K. L. Zadykhina, and G. P. Vasilyeva. "Peoples of Afghanistan." Translated by M. and G. Slobin. In George Grassmuck and Ludwig W. Adamec, eds., *Afghanistan: Some New Approaches.* Ann Arbor: University of Michigan Press, 1969.

Bacon, Elizabeth E. "An Inquiry into the History of the Hazara Mongols of Afghanistan," *Southwestern Journal of Anthropology*, VII (1951), 230–247.

Batuta, John. "Islam and Communism." In J. Penner, ed. *Islam and Communism.* New York: Carnegie International Center, 1960.

Carrère d'Encausse, Hélène. "The National Republics Lose Their Independence." In Edward Allworth, ed., *Central Asia: A Century of Russian Rule.* New York: Columbia University Press, 1967.

Castagne, Joseph. "Notes sur la Politique Extérieure de L'Afghanistan depuis 1919," *Revue du Monde Musulman*, December 1921.

——. "Le Bolchevisme et l'Islam," *Revue du Monde Musulman,* January 1922.

——. "Soviet Imperialism in Afghanistan," *Foreign Affairs,* XIII (July 1935), 698.

Cervin, Vladimir. "Problems in the Integration of the Afghan Nation," *Middle East Journal,* VI (1952), 408.

Chokaiev, Mustapha. "The Basmaji Movement in Turkestan," *Asiatic Review,* XXIV (1928), 284–285.

——. "The Bolsheviks and Afghanistan," *Asiatic Review,* XXV (1929), 322–331.

——. "The Situation in Afghanistan," *Asiatic Review,* XXVI (April 1930).

Dane, Richard. "Some Features of the Afghan Problem," *Asiatic Review,* XXV (July 1929).

Dupree, Louis. "Pushtunistan: The Problem and Its Larger Implications," *American Universities Field Staff Reports,* South Asia series, V, nos. 2, 3, and 4 (1961).

——. "Tribalism, Regionalism and National Oligarchy." In K. H. Silvert, ed., *Expectant Peoples: Nationalism and Development.* New York: American Universities Field Staff, 1963.

——. "Mahmud Tarzi: Forgotten Nationalist," *American Universities Field Staff Reports,* South Asia series, VIII, no. 1 (January 1964).

——. "Constitutional Development and Cultural Change—The 1964 Afghan Constitution," *American Universities Field Staff Reports,* South Asia series, IX, nos. 1–4 (1964).

——. "Tribal Traditions and Modern Nationhood," *Asia,* I (1964), 1–12.

——. "Political Uses of Religion: Afghanistan." In K. H. Silvert, ed., *Churches and State: The Religious Institution and Modernization.* New York: American Universities Field Staff, 1967.

Eberhard, Wolfram. "Afghanistan's Young Elite." In *Settlement and Social Change in Asia.* Hong Kong: Hong Kong Press, 1967.

——. "Labour Sources for Industrialization: The Case of Afghanistan." In *Settlement and Social Change in Asia.* Hong Kong: Hong Kong Press, 1967.

Ferdinand, Klaus. "Preliminary Notes on Hazara Culture." In *Notes of the Danish Scientific Mission to Afghanistan of 1953–55.* Copenhagen: n.p., 1959.

Foucher, Alfred. *Bulletin de la Chambre de Commerce Franco-Asiatique,* Special Number, January 1928.

Franck, Dorothea S. "Pashtunistan: Disputed Disposition of a Tribal Land," *Middle East Journal*, VI (1952), 49–62.

Furber, Holden. "British Conquest and Empire." In W. Norman Brown, ed., *India, Pakistan and Ceylon*. Ithaca: Cornell University Press, 1951.

Gregorian, Vartan. "Mahmud Tarzi and Saraj-ol-Akhbar," *Middle East Journal*, XXI (1967), 345–368.

Guha, Amalendu. "The Economy of Afghanistan during Amanullah's Reign, 1919–1929," *International Studies* (New Delhi), IX, no. 2 (October 1967), 167–182.

Josif, Harold G. "Political Stability on the Northwest Frontier of South Asia." Mimeographed. Washington, D.C.: Department of State, Foreign Service Institute, August 1951.

Kohzad, Ali Ahmad. "Two Coronations," *Afghanistan* (Kabul), V, no. 3 (1952), 38–40.

Laqueur, Walter Z. "Sultan Galiev's Ghost," *New Leader*, February 3, 1958.

——. "Communism and Nationalism in Tropical Africa," *Foreign Affairs*, July 1961.

Lenin, Vladmir Il'ich. "The Agrarian and National Program." In *Selected Works*. Moscow: Foreign Language Publishing House, 1947.

MacMunn, George. "Afghanistan and the Outer World," *Nineteenth Century* (London), CIII, no. 613 (March 1928), 344 ff.

Najibullah Khan. "Afghanistan in Historical Perspective." In *Current Problems in Afghanistan*. Princeton: Princeton University Conference, 1961. Pp. 1–14.

Pipes, Richard. "The First Experiment in Soviet National Policy: The Bashkir Republic," *Russian Review*, October 1950.

——. "Muslims in the Soviet Union." In J. Penner, ed., *Islam and Communism*. New York: Carnegie International Center, 1960.

Poullada, Leon B. "Problems of Social Development in Afghanistan," *Journal of the Royal Central Asian Society*, XLIX, Part 1 (January 1962), 28–36.

——. "Some International Legal Aspects of the Pushtunistan Dispute," *Afghanistan* (Kabul), XXI, no. 4 (Winter 1969), 32–49.

——. "Political Modernization in Afghanistan: The Amanullah Reforms." In George Grassmuck, ed., *Afghanistan: Some New Approaches*. Ann Arbor: University of Michigan Press, 1969.

Schinasi, May. "Sir Âdj Al-Akhbâr: L'Opinion Afghane et la

Russie," *Cahiers du Monde Russe et Soviétique*, XII (1971), 467–479.

[Spencer, Richard]. "A Demographic Study of the Village of Baghrami, Province of Kabul." Mimeographed. Kabul: USOM Afghanistan Public Administration Service in Cooperation with Columbia University, July 1959.

Syromolotov, F. "Lenin i Stalin v. Sozdanii Tataro-Baskirkoj Respubliki," *Revoljucija i Nacional'nosti*, no. 8 (1935).

Taillardat, F. "Le Voyage du Roi Amanullah," *L'Asie Française*, February 1928.

——. "Le Roi Amanullah en Angleterre," *L'Asie Française*, May 1928.

——. "La Fin du Voyage du Roi Amanullah," *L'Asie Française*, September/October 1928.

Tuden, Arthur. "Leadership and the Decision-Making Process among the Ila and the Swat Pathans." In Marc J. Swartz, ed., *Political Anthropology*. Chicago: Aldine, 1966.

Waleh, A. H. "Five Books and the Old Curriculum," *Kabul Times*, June 1, 1968.

Weigert, H. W. "From Mackinder's Heartland," *American Scholar*, Winter 1945–46.

Wheeler, G. E. "Soviet Policy towards the Middle East." In J. Penner, ed., *Islam and Communism*. New York: Carnegie International Center, 1960.

Yapp, M. E. "Disturbances in Eastern Afghanistan, 1839–42," *Bulletin of the School of Oriental and African Studies*, XXV (1962), 499.

——. "Disturbances in Western Afghanistan, 1839–41," *Bulletin of the School of Oriental and African Studies*, XXVI (1963), Part 2, 288.

——. "The Revolution of 1841–42 in Afghanistan," *Bulletin of the School of Oriental and African Studies*, XXVI (1964), Part 2, 333.

Newspapers (1911–1930)

Afghan: *Aman-i-Afghan, Anis, Ghairat-ul-Islam, Habib-ul-Islam, Haqiqat, Islah, Kabul Times* (1967–68), *Seraj-ul-Akhbar*.

American: *Chicago Daily Tribune, New York Times, New York World, Saturday Review*.

British: *Birmingham Post, Britannia, Christian, Daily Express, Daily Mail, Daily Mirror, Daily News, Daily Sketch, Daily Telegraph, Evening News, Irish Telegraph, Manchester Guardian, Morning Post, Nottingham Journal & Express, Observer, The Referee, Scotsman, Sunday Times, Sunday Worker, Sunderland Echo, Times, Workers' Life.*

French: *Journal des Debats, Le Temps, Universe.*

German: *Kreuz Zeitung, Localanzeiger.*

Indian: *Bombay Chronicle, Civil and Military Gazette, Indian National Herald, Zamindar.*

index

*Reform and Rebellion
in Afghanistan, 1919–1929*

Designed by R. E. Rosenbaum.
Composed by Vail-Ballou Press, Inc.,
in 11 point linofilm Janson, 3 points leaded,
with display lines in Libra.
Printed offset by Vail-Ballou Press.
Bound by Vail-Ballou Press
in Columbia book cloth
and stamped in All Purpose foil.

Library of Congress Cataloging in Publication Data
(For library cataloging purposes only.)

Poullada, Leon B   date.
    Reform and rebellion in Afghanistan, 1919–1929.

    Bibliography: p.
    1. Afghanistan—Politics and government.
2. Amanullah Khan, Amir of Afghanistan, 1892–1960.
I. Title.
DS369.P68   1973   958.1'04   72-12291
ISBN 0-8014-0772-9